Everyone Is NOT Doing It

Everyone Is NOT Doing It

Abstinence and Personal Identity

JAMIE L. MULLANEY

The University of Chicago Press
Chicago and London

Jamie L. Mullaney is assistant professor of sociology at Goucher College.

The University of Chicago Press, Chicago 60637
The University of Chicago Press, Ltd., London
© 2006 by The University of Chicago
All rights reserved. Published 2006
Printed in the United States of America

15 14 13 12 11 10 09 08 07 06   1 2 3 4 5

ISBN: 0-226-54756-6 (cloth)
ISBN: 0-226-54757-4 (paper)

Library of Congress Cataloging-in-Publication Data

Mullaney, Jamie L.
    Everyone is NOT doing it : abstinence and personal identity / Jamie L.
Mullaney.
        p. cm.
    Includes bibliographical references and index.
    ISBN: 0-226-54756-6 (cloth: alk. paper) — ISBN: 0-226-54757-4 (pbk. : alk.
paper)
    1. Identity (Psychology)—Social aspects.   2. Self-denial—Social aspects.
3. Taboo.   4. Temptation.   5. Temperance.   6. Sexual abstinence.
7. Vegetarianism.   I. Title.
    HM1051.M85 2006
    155.2'5—dc22
                                                            2005016384

*To Nan (1911–2003), whose absence never leaves me,
and to Luca, whose presence brings me joy*

CONTENTS

ACKNOWLEDGMENTS

In thinking about the many individuals who made this book possible, I must first thank the men and women who allowed me entrance into their lives—if only for a day—to talk about their individual forms of abstinence. I recognize that they were in many ways taking a great chance in participating in this project, trusting me to compare their experiences to ones that, at first glance, seem worlds away from their own. I am immensely grateful for their time, candor, flexibility, referrals to other potential interviewees, and fascinating perspectives.

The ideas for this book have several origins, all of which stem back to my time as a graduate student at Rutgers University. For their guidance through courses, qualifying papers, and the dissertation, I am especially grateful to Richard Williams and Ben Zablocki. Richard's identity class sparked my interest in the topic, and Ben, as he has heard too many times, must be credited for the idea of the book as a whole. His comment regarding his mother's pride at having never eaten pork got the wheels turning, so to speak. Thanks to both of them and also to Robert Zussman, my outside dissertation committee member, for their wonderful insights.

As my dissertation advisor, Eviatar Zerubavel did more than I would ever have expected in his nurturing of both the project and myself. I have told him before that everyone should have an Eviatar, and it is difficult to express adequately the gratitude I feel toward him for always treating me as a scholar while also being there to share joys and offer support during difficult times. Eviatar referred to this project as "the book" before I had written a word, and it is this type of mentorship that enabled me to write that first word and navigate through a sometimes overwhelming process with confidence.

A fellowship at the Center for the Critical Analysis of Contemporary Culture (CCACC) at Rutgers provided financial support for the project, and the

2001–2002 seminar there, led by Carolyn Williams, introduced me to a fabulous group of scholars in other fields at Rutgers. Thanks to Carolyn for her leadership and to the other fellows at the CCACC for their ideas regarding this work.

Goucher College also provided a small summer research grant during the early stages of writing. My department has been incredibly generous in its intellectual and moral support. Special thanks to my colleague and close friend Janet Shope for reading parts of the manuscript with a careful eye and offering pep talks when needed. My students at Goucher, particularly those in my Deviance and Social Control class, offered great suggestions along the way. They inspired me to rethink things just as I thought I had considered all possible angles.

One of my former students, Brian Buta, worked as an assistant for me while I was researching some of the later chapters. In addition to reading through the entire manuscript, Brian spent many hours retrieving sources that were not available on our campus, freeing up a lot of needed writing time for me. His dependability is unparalleled. In the early stages of the research, Shayna Alt transcribed many of the interviews. I appreciate her care and accuracy with such an important yet at times regrettably tedious task. At the final stages, Miriam Stewart and Ryan Mathus provided invaluable editorial assistance.

Thanks to Dan Ryan for encouraging me to share my work during what is becoming a tradition at the annual meeting of the American Sociological Association: the culture section's informal "soon-to-be-author-meets-noncritics" session. The quality of the company more than made up for the poor acoustics of the hotel bar. I am particularly grateful for the thoughts shared that night and in outside conversations with Rachel Askew, Wayne Brekhus, Dan Chambliss, Julie McLaughlin, Dan Ryan (and some of his students, as well), Tom DeGloma, and Robin Wagner-Pacifici. Wayne and Julie in particular have been continual sources of support, feedback, and friendship since our time together at Rutgers.

At the University of Chicago Press, Doug Mitchell has provided extraordinary support and enthusiasm at all stages of this process. I appreciate the time and patience he and Tim McGovern have extended to me while guiding me through what was "virgin territory" (pun intended) on my part. I am also grateful for the critical comments of two anonymous reviewers; their ideas pushed the manuscript in exciting new directions. Many thanks also to those individuals at Chicago who were so instrumental in the making of this final product: Christine Schwab, Susan Olin, David O'Connor, Vin Dang, and Peter Cavagnaro.

While this book resulted in part from various sources of intellectual support, it depended at least as much (and sometimes more) on different forms of personal support. I wrote much of this book as a single mother of a small child. My parents and my daughter's grandparents—Gail and Ed Mathus, Ken and Getta Mullaney, and Rose and Ron McCracken—provided hours of care too numerous to count. They allowed me to rest assured that Luca was in the good hands of her doting grandparents.

I also need to thank my partner, Adam Bowman, for having the courage and patience necessary to start our relationship during a very intense period of writing. His superb culinary abilities, reminders to breathe, and our long walks together nourished me along the way.

I dedicate this book in part to my late great-grandmother, neighbor, and dear friend, Mildred McMahon ("Nan"), who always wanted to know why I worked so much; she passed away just a week before I learned of my contract with Chicago. I also share it with my daughter, Luca Green. Here is to the remarkable women I see in them, past and future.

There is an old joke about a rescuer who stumbles across a Jewish Robinson Crusoe on a desert island. After a tour of Crusoe's hut and vegetable garden, the rescuer asks him to explain the need for two synagogues on an island inhabited by no one else. Pointing to the first synagogue, Crusoe says, "You see that synagogue? That's where I pray. The other one? *I wouldn't set foot in that one!*"

The joke's humor lies in its lighthearted exaggeration of the lengths to which certain Jews will go in order to distinguish themselves from those practicing other forms of Judaism. Not only does our Jewish Robinson Crusoe build a synagogue that meets his spiritual needs, he erects a second one that serves no purpose other than to highlight what he does *not* practice. In other words, Crusoe's need to identify himself both by what he does *and by what he refuses to do* is so powerful that he makes both visible on the island where he is the sole inhabitant.

In his spiritual journals, the monk Thomas Merton once wrote, "In a way each one judges himself merely by what he does" (1999, 183), and, to a large degree, he was right. When we think about our identities, what makes us "who we are," we are likely to conjure up the things we actively do: parent our children, work at our careers, practice religion, contribute to causes we support, participate in a hobby or sport. We believe doings tell us a lot and, as a result, spend a fair amount of time displaying our own and trying to discern those of others. In situations ranging from cocktail parties to first dates to random conversations with strangers on an airplane, we find ourselves continually asking others what they do, what they enjoy doing, what they wish they had more time to do—as if the answers to identity lie at the heart of actual and desired doings. Merton, it seems, was on to something.

But what about the things we do not do? Each of us, of course, has a host of acts we do not perform. Yet, the behaviors in which we do not engage pass through our social filters with varying degrees of success. Some escape our attention entirely, as we believe they carry little significance in influencing identity. For example, we might never notice that someone does not wear green shoes (and would not care much if the fact were brought to our attention). We fail to notice them, then, because they are *expected not doings*, becoming visible to us only upon their breaching. (Consider how habitually remaining silent in the library, at a play, or in the symphony hall escapes our attention until someone yells, coughs, or crackles a candy wrapper.)

On the other hand, we believe some things a person may choose not to do send powerful and explicit messages about who that person "is." We notice them precisely because they are breaches of *expected doings*. So while not wearing shoes of a particular color may fail to command our attention, we would probably take more interest in a person's deliberate refusal to engage in sexual intercourse. Unlike the above examples, where not doing becomes visible only subsequent to its violation, this alternative form itself attracts attention precisely because it violates an unwritten—but widely accepted—code of social behavior.

It is this latter form of behavior that we identify as *abstinence*. Abstinence is not mere avoidance; instead, it entails a voluntary refusal to perform acts one can and is expected to do. We do not "abstain" from things that we cannot do or that we are prevented from doing. As a result, we do not talk about avoiding foods that make us ill as "abstinence," nor do we categorize infertile, childless individuals as "abstainers." Similarly, others cannot make the decision to abstain for us. While the Catholic Church might demand a priest's celibacy, it is only he that can declare sexual abstinence.[1] In a way different from those things over which we have no control, we may use our conscious and intentional decisions to abstain as important organizational pieces of our personal identities.

In this book, I examine abstinence as a constituent and generic quality of identity. Rather than overemphasizing the idiosyncratic workings of one form of abstinence (e.g., virgins or recovering alcoholics),[2] I explore the commonalities among those who do not participate in expected doings and seek to explain how the acts in which we deliberately do not engage influence our identity. By focusing on *breadth across many forms* of abstinence rather than *depth within one type*, I consider abstinence as what Prus terms a "generic social process." Situating this work in the logic that "one can learn something about any group by examining similar processes in any other setting," my goal is to "enable persons to tie together and benefit from materials that might otherwise seem highly diverse" (Prus 1987, 264).

To achieve such breadth, I rely on in-depth interviews with thirty-eight individuals who abstain from a variety of expected social behaviors.[3] It is important to note, then, that the book relies on *narrated accounts*—rather than observations—of abstinence. Certainly, many may abstain and never verbalize it, but it is my position that abstinence often must be made visible (typically through language) in order to have some degree of social meaning. Through such firsthand accounts, a picture emerges of abstinence as an active performance, shaped by how one defines abstinence, when one abstains, for whom one performs, and the existence (or nonexistence) of words to capture these performances. While I recognize differences across various forms of abstinence, my larger goal is to bring to the fore this taken-for-granted yet instrumental piece in our understanding of the self and our everyday interactions in the social world.

Doings, Not Doings, Not-Doings, and Identity

Since at least Aristotle, social thinkers have pondered what makes us "who we are." Frequently, these discussions of the self have relied on notions of *essence*, the belief in underlying qualities or characteristics that are in some way innate. Unlike potentially transient parts that are not necessary in defining one's identity (which Aristotle labeled "accidental"), essences persist over time and remain fundamentally unchanged. In short, those who adopt an essentialist approach to the self focus on "the invariable and fixed properties that define the 'whatness' of a given entity" and suggest that such essences are "transhistorical, eternal, [and] immutable" (Fuss 1989, xi). Under such an approach, behaviors do not create the self; instead, they are clues to what lies beneath, signifiers of "genetic, biological, or physiological mechanisms" at work (Vance 1989, 14).

As a counter to essentialism, social constructionists reverse the arrow of causality by maintaining that the social produces the "natural" (Fuss 1989, 3). In the place of doings indicative of "beings," social constructionists insist that doings are not beings but are subject to various interpretations based on situational context. Rather than lumping similar acts in a rigid manner (Zerubavel 1991), constructionists "adopt the view that physically identical acts may have varying significance and subjective meaning depending on how they are defined and understood in different cultures and historical periods" (Vance 1989, 18). Rejecting an essentialist interpretation of the self, constructionists suggest (in a Nietzschean fashion) that "there is no 'being' behind doing" and that "'the doer' is merely a fiction added to the deed—the deed is everything" (Butler 1990, 25).

Nevertheless, not all deeds are everything, and it would be shortsighted to assume that all doings carry equal weight in the presentation and attribution of identity. Behaviors may vary in the degree to which they count. The literature offered by those interested in the sociology of attention remind us that, amid the vast waters of acts, some get caught by our cognitive nets while others float away to sea, remaining imperceptible. We may literally and physically see such acts, but our social lens does not allow us to process such acts, as they do not "count" (Mullaney 1999). Though we experience such physical stimuli as individuals, the process of differentiating objects and behaviors according to the dichotomies of relevant/irrelevant, worthy/unworthy, meaningful/meaningless has powerful social origins, as our "mental horizons" are the result of diverse forms of socialization based on our participation in varying "optical communities" (Zerubavel 1997, 33).

Frequently, our ability to perceive things revolves around their marked qualities. An idea first introduced in linguistics by Jakobson and Trubetzkoy (Trubetzkoy 1975), "marked" and "unmarked" describe the unequal relationship within phoneme pairs. While one half of the pair gets "marked" or highlighted, the other half gains its meaning exclusively by the *absence* of such a quality. This linguistic distinction carries over to everyday life, as well, as social actors must frequently learn to "perceive one side of a contrast while ignoring the other side."[4] Such a black-and-white distinction, however, oversimplifies matters in that, even within marked and unmarked categories, entities and behaviors may count to different degrees. That is, while many acts may appear significant to identity, they do not carry the same social weight (Mullaney 1999). Records of our marked doings (both positive and negative) illustrate this point. In a positive way, résumés and curricula vitae serve as accounts of our marked doings within our careers. Yet, in determining one's worthiness for tenure as an academic, completing a joint-authored article typically counts as a less marked "doing" than a sole-authored article, which amounts to less than a book. Criminal records testify to another set of our doings, albeit in a different but no less marked way.[5] Legal distinctions in the classification of crimes (misdemeanor vs. felony) and the varying penalties within these categories mandate that certain crimes (e.g., killing a police officer) count more than others (e.g., committing petty theft). There appear to be shades of gray among marked doings, then, as all do not fare equally in their ability to shape identity.

Even as we acknowledge degrees in markedness, we must be careful not to assume that the categories of marked and unmarked are fixed in any way. Using sexuality as his case, Brekhus shows how unmarked categories may become marked under certain conditions. Quantity, for example, can alter our perceptions, as what we perceive as too much or too little leads to very different sexual labels.[6] Consider a nonsexual example of scratching an "innocuous" body part, such as one's arm. Under normal conditions, most people will not notice my engagement in this act; yet, my *repeated* doings may mark this act and raise questions about the state of my skin (Do I have a disease?), my habits (Am I on drugs?), or even my psychological state (Am I mentally ill?).

When an act occurs in regard to one's behavioral biography may also affect its significance. More so than subsequent performances, *first* acts often appear to count greatly toward one's identity. Certainly, individuals may not execute complete agency in the selection of which firsts will bear meaning; firsts must in some way be "referenced in cultural norms" (Robinson 1992, 232) in order to transform the self. At times, linguistic designations accompany and highlight the perceived change between not doing and doing.[7] For example, while I lose the ability to convincingly present myself as a "virgin" following the first time I engage in intercourse, no terms of identity mark the shift between the eighth and the ninth times I have sex.[8]

Taken together, the above examples demonstrate that some doings count in identity presentations and attributions, some escape unnoticed, and still others are thought to be critical identity indicators. Among those that do count, there is variation as to the significance and consequences of such acts. Finally, even those acts that initially "don't count" may become marked under the right conditions.

Accepting the premise that *doings* constitute the self, a seemingly logical extension of this argument would be to assume that the things we do not do make up an unmarked, inactive, and unnoticeable ground behind this figure of doings. In fact, we often define entities in a negative fashion, that is, by distinguishing them from their grounds, consequently delineating what they are not. The structuralist tradition in linguistics, with its interest in how signs obtain meaning through negative definitions, serves as a case in point. Referring specifically to words, Saussure notes how they acquire meaning through no intrinsic value of their own but instead "by their relations with the other terms of the system, [as their] most precise characteristic is in being what the others are not" (1959, 117).

This process of defining things negatively appears in areas beyond linguistics as well. In researching their well-known study on gender, for example,

Kessler and McKenna presented their subjects with figures of individuals having male cues, female cues, or a combination of the two. While male cues led unambiguously to designations of "maleness," the only consistent quality of "femaleness" appeared to be the *lack* of male attributes, not the possession of female ones. Specifically, the lack of a penis predictably led to female gender attributions. Not only did the penis count more in gender attributions; femaleness was determined by default, that is, by the *absence* of "male" characteristics rather than by the *presence* of female characteristics (Kessler and McKenna 1978, 150–53). This finding, of course, has the ring of Freud's psychoanalytic theory of gender development, arguably the classic example of definition by lack. Freud claims that little girls realize they lack a penis, blame mother for the lack, and subsequently embark along the path of "normal" female development, replete with "penis envy," a desire to fill the void (1966, 588).

The relative ease and frequency with which we define things by their absence coupled with our efforts to consider the performative element of identity make it almost commonsensical or natural to dismiss all "not do-ings" as lack or absence. In other words, if doings constitute the self, not doings *must be* the noninfluential, unmarked, default category. Yet, it would be erroneous to regard all acts in which we do not engage as unmarked absences or lacks. It is important, then, to distinguish unmarked *not doings* from the marked *not-doings* of abstinence, that is, those based on intention and careful action to avoid doing. To abstain, then, is to actively engage in a *not-doing*. Of course, not-doings may also vary in the degree to which they affect identity. What distinguishes them as a category, however, is that they are about neither lack nor inactivity. Throughout this book, I will refer to abstinences as "not-doings" in order to highlight their active quality and to distinguish them from the unmarked "not doings" that simply fail to enter our consciousness.

The question remains as to why we have neglected to consider the gen-eral category of not-doings in our theorizing about identity. Perhaps doings have largely been the sexier candidates in the thinking surrounding how identities operate in that they may appear more observable and capable of being performed than are the things we choose not to do, but not-doings also involve performance in that they require a degree of agency and choice. It is necessary, then, to make a momentary gestalt shift in our thinking about what counts in identity and to consider more seriously the implications of abstinence. Not unlike the concepts of marked and unmarked, figure and ground may appear to constitute a set relationship. Yet, Koffka demonstrates the flexibility of the figure and ground in his discussion of the meaning of "stillness" (typically ground) for city dwellers. He says, "In favor of the claim that stillness is not, or need not be, simply nothing, but will frequently serve as ground I shall only adduce the fact that stillness may become figure, as when we leave the city and spend our first nights in the lonely mountains" (1935, 201). Similarly, playing with and troubling the figure and ground of identity will also avoid relegating them to essential and unchanging categories and overlooking critical components of how individuals understand themselves and others.

To say that we must force this gestalt shift on our thinking, of course, needs qualification. On the one hand, thinking about not-doings as serious candidates for understanding the workings of identity "run[s] against our strongest mental habit,"[9] as we are used to equating who we are with what we do. With that said, however, the established, voluminous literature on taboo reminds us that what individuals do not do has formed the basis for personal and social identities as far as our collective memory will serve us. Furthermore, contemporary discussions of abstinence inundate us, coming in many forms, sometimes testing our patience and exhausting us. As I write this chapter, Americans are in the midst of an anticarbohydrate diet craze and under the leadership of a president who will only support abstinence-only sexual education in schools. Taken together, our recognition of taboo coupled with the recent touting of the benefits of abstinence—whether it be from carbohydrates or sex—seem to suggest that we *are* tuned in to not-doing and have been for some time. Yet, both the society-wide proscriptions of taboo and the popular approaches to abstinence fail to complete our understanding of not-doing as a generic organizational piece of identity.

Traditional Understandings of Not(-)Doing

The anthropological and sociological work on taboo, through its consideration of the ways in which identity may rely on the active and intentional avoidance of certain behaviors, offers an initial glimpse into how one might avoid a case-by-case treatment of not-doing. Linguistically, the word *taboo* (or, alternatively, *tabu* or *tapu*) highlights the significance of the act of avoidance, the origin deriving from *ta* ("to mark") and *pu* (an adverb of intensity) in the languages of the Pacific Islands (Webster 1942, 2). Though commonly known among the people to whom they apply, taboos instruct individuals to avoid something, generally with little or no explanation of why (Thody 1997, 309). As a system of prohibition, taboo centers around that which is assumed to be dangerous, though the true degree of danger is rarely apparent to the one avoiding (Webster 1942, 13). While taboo may involve any of the senses, we most associate taboo with restrictions on touch. Perception of the dangers that surround touching a forbidden object runs so strong that "there is just simple dread of the consequences of disobedience, and since the consequences are often left indeterminate the dread is all the more impressive" (14). Taboo, then, involves action and not simply prescriptions for action (Lambek 1992, 246). In this sense, the observance of taboo may do "more than express the self: it [may] constitute the self" (Gell 1979, 137). Those concerned with taboo recognize this constructed part of the self that hinges not on lack but on a *performance* of that which one does not do.

Taboo, like abstinence, can affect how one experiences the self. Nevertheless, taboo differs from abstinence freely chosen in that the former originates from ideas about what a dominant group feels is acceptable and a desire to influence the behavior of others (Thody 1997, 310). The goal of taboo, then, is expression of power through the use of separation. Through their acts of separation, taboos offer us a glimpse into the possibility of defining a person or group by what is not done. Over time, however, academics have increasingly come to scorn the concept of taboo, arguing that it is no more than another tool of power (312) that intensifies during times of crisis or insecurity and that holds back society and impedes social progress (Browne 1984, 2, 4).

For these reasons among others, taboo is what linguistic philosophers would refer to as a "boo word," one that comes with an almost immediate sense of disapproval (Thody 1997, 4). Part of this scorn undoubtedly stems from the association between the separations of taboo and a group's claim to moral superiority. Yet, separation need not always imply superiority or inferiority. Using the category of holiness as her example, Mary Douglas argues that instances exist in which we "require that different classes of things shall not be confused." Through the cases of incest and adultery, Douglas demonstrates how such acts "are against holiness, in the simple sense of right order," but not necessarily in the sense of morality. Though "morality does not conflict with holiness" in these instances, the latter remains "more a matter of separating that which should be separated than of protecting the rights of husbands and brothers" (Douglas 1966, 54–55).

Like taboo, abstinence, too, has become a bit of a "boo word" in its own sense, wrapped up in issues of morality, right versus wrong, good versus evil.[10] Despite my insistence that the moral dimension was a small and insignificant piece of the abstinence story presented by the individuals in my project, many around me remained unconvinced, and I needed to consider why that might be the case. One experience in particular revealed to me that it was I who had to come to terms with the moral component of abstinence

and to acknowledge what many view as the inseparable package of abstinence and morality.

In the early stages of my research, I was invited to give a presentation
on my work to high school educators at a one-day seminar with the theme
"The Performance of Culture." The question-and-answer session was lively
and engaging: the participants seemed genuinely interested in hearing more
about some of the interviewees and their respective abstinences, their
decision-making processes, and their overall experiences. Just as the session
was winding down, one woman asked me, in a very frank manner, what
I planned to do with the moral aspect of the research. My initial reaction
was a combination of confusion and frustration, as I felt she had missed the
main focus of my project, that is, exploring the behavioral and performative
aspects of abstinence. I reiterated to her that I wanted to see the similarities in the ways in which people "do abstinence" and incorporate it into
understandings of the self across a variety of types of abstinence. I told her
that, while I did ask about the motivations behind individuals' decisions
to abstain, they occupied a more tangential space in the research. Still not
quite sure where she was headed with this question, I decided to address
the moral issue from the angle of religion. In the course of conversations
with others regarding the project, I found that many people immediately
assumed or inquired whether the informants were "religious fanatics." As in
these earlier conversations, I was sure to clarify that, while some abstinences
seemed connected to religion, the majority in the study did not.

These responses did not satisfy my listener, and I continued to talk in
circles with her about the "moral question" while still not having a clear
sense of what she was asking. A few of the other audience members inter-
vened, including the session's organizer, but she could not be persuaded by
anything we had to say. Exasperated, she looked at me and said, "I guess
I am just wondering how it is you could stand to interview these people."
Completely at a loss for words at this point, my silence was not noticed by
her, as she proceeded to tell me that abstainers not only flaunt their abstinence, but they continually place themselves on a moral high ground and
look down on those who do not abstain. She repeatedly used the example
of what she considered to be the prototypical abstainer: a fanatical animal
rights activist who throws orange paint on fur coats (her language).

I cannot recall how the conversation ended: perhaps we ran out of time,
energy, or both. I left the conference that day feeling completely unsatisfied
with our unresolved conflict and cheated by her unwillingness to hear the
voices of the abstainers I had tried to share with her. This exchange, however, continued to haunt me. I have returned to that encounter repeatedly,

wondering what I could have added or changed. In more judgmental moments, I have written her off as "just not getting it." Certainly, she had reduced all the individuals in my project to one type, vegetarians, and to a portrait that fit none: the orange-paint-throwing animal rights activist.[11]

In another sense, though, her response made perfect sense. Thinking further about some contemporary promoters of abstinence, it soon became clear why this woman reacted in the tired and impatient way that she did: the messages we receive regarding abstinence are almost exclusively framed in moral terms. We are unable to deny the overwhelming presence of what Edgley and Brissett call "meddlers by profession" (or, as a friend of mine shrewdly dubbed them, "abstinence entrepreneurs"),[12] that is, those individuals who make their living by informing others what not to do.[13] Unlike times past when individuals could tell others to "mind their own business," the current spirit is one of total immersion into the lives of others. The consequence, Edgley and Brissett lament, is that "we meddle with just about everything people do as long as it happens to be something we ourselves do not do" (1999, 3). We need not look hard to see the presence of such "anti-themes" (10), the ubiquitous urging of others to "just say no." Anti-drug campaigns are couched in highly moralistic terms. Dieting ads tell us how to be "good" when our temptations and cravings urge us to do otherwise. Everywhere we turn, there seems to be some message implying that, when it comes to certain things, abstinence is *right*. As mentioned earlier, even the current president of the country has taken a stand on abstinence. A small paragraph in the February 11, 2002, edition of *Newsweek*, for example, commands attention with the sexy headline: "Values Trumps Data." The statement (made by one of President George W. Bush's top advisers on welfare) attempts to resolve the contradiction between the stated goal of the "No Child Left Behind" education bill—to provide federal funds only to programs backed by "scientifically proven" findings—and Bush's clear refusal to accept the best available data on sex education programs. Ignoring research by the National Campaign to Prevent Teen Pregnancy (a non-partisan campaign) that suggests the most effective sex education programs are those including information on both abstinence *and* contraceptive measures, Bush decided to back abstinence-only programs with $135 million of federal funds.[14] Despite scathing criticism and efforts to discredit the president's unscientific approach to the data, he ultimately got the final word (at least financially) on abstinence, and the word is that abstinence is "right."[15]

Research often hinges on this moral dimension, if not in support of or defense of abstinence, in reaction to the moral question in some way. Rather than considering what different forms of abstinence share in common (or how they deviate from one another), we continue to treat them on a case-by-case basis, looking at one type of abstinence at a time, frequently through a moral lens. For example, in response to the most popular abstinence topic—sex education in schools—scores of studies address the success and practicality of a variety of programs, ranging from abstinence-only programs to ones denoted "abstinence plus" (which provide information on contraception while keeping abstinence as the focus) to more comprehensive forms of instruction and information. Though changing in form, the issue of sexual abstinence maintains continual momentum throughout time and space. Contemporary concern with sexual abstinence spans the globe, rekindling old debates in both new and familiar forms. Not surprisingly, virginity appears to trump all other forms of sexual abstinence despite variations on the theme. Such research explores, troubles, and at times validates issues such as the instrumental and social utility of presenting a "virgin" self, whether it be symbolically (through demonstrated appearances of virginity)[16] or physically (through practices such as hymen reconstruction);[17] the effectiveness of virginity "pledging" or vowing not to engage in sex until marriage;[18] or the possibility of reclaiming virginity subsequent to its loss.[19] Recent books and articles[20] offer guidance (aimed mostly at women) as to how to participate in the "new non-sexual revolution" by claiming a "new virginity" (Foston 2004, 122) subsequent to sexual experience.

Alcohol, drugs, and food appear to be the other long-standing "hot topics" of abstinence. Though changing in content, emphasis, and recommendations, both scholarly research and popular literature abound with recommendations for the best way to lose weight, go vegetarian, purify the body through temporary fasts, or quit smoking, drinking, or using drugs.[21] Coming from very different angles in their research, sociologists, psychologists, dietitians, substance abuse counselors, neurologists, and the like seem to have a continuing, vested interest in touting the benefits of abstinence from certain foods and substances. The predominance of food, sex, and substances in the literature likely stems from traditional definitions of abstinence, which focus almost exclusively on these areas.[22] Furthermore, these things all affect the body directly, and many believe the body serves as the home of one's self. When certain substances come to bear negative associations, controlling one's appetites for such "indulgences" becomes one way in which individuals can make positive statements about who they are.

Though the substantive areas of research inquiries into abstinence differ, collectively they promote two dominant approaches to studying abstinence: investigations into *why individuals abstain* (or why they should) and *how to get them to abstain*. Approaches of the first kind—those that attempt to explain why individuals abstain—vary in that some consider why an individual might abstain with reference to his or her personal biography while others also consider the historical contingencies that foster abstinence. Through such accounts, we know that individuals abstain as an instrument to achieve a particular end, such as self-purification or social reform. We also learn that, in addition to these instrumental uses, abstaining may perform symbolic functions as well. In his analysis of the American Temperance movement, for example, Joseph Gusfield delineates how abstinence from alcohol could distinguish "the industrious from the ne'er-do-well," as the abstainer embodied nineteenth-century Protestant values of self-control, productivity, and impulse renunciation (1963, 5, 4). Gusfield's analysis, while limited to the substantive area of alcohol, also offers a critical insight into any study of abstinence, as it illustrates the changing meanings attached to doings and not-doings over time. Depending on factors such as the social climate, political agenda, persons abstaining, and so on, a given abstinence can be regarded with admiration, scorn, or a combination of the two.[23]

In addition to exploring the "why" of abstinence, another (although less common) thread present in the literature involves the "how-to" of abstinence. This theme, too, taps into issues of morality, an underlying assumption of such literature being that abstinence is a *good* thing, and therefore, we must determine what allows individuals to succeed at abstaining at least temporarily, if not permanently. The "how-to" literature of abstinence also enjoys a long history, dating back as far as the fourth-century monk Cassian, who outlines a clearly delineated system for achieving chastity (Foucault 1985; Paden 1988). Believing that the eight vices form a causal chain, Cassian claimed it impossible to conquer vices later in the chain before those that precede them. Although greed occupies the status of the first vice and fornication the second, Cassian argued that the latter should receive the most attention. Fornication has the potential to be the most damaging vice, as it embodies the most disgrace and causes the most spiritual turmoil. The six-step (and somewhat impossible) mission to achieve chastity, then, begins with controlling first carnal impulses, then voluptuous thoughts, and finally sexual responses and images even during the unconscious state of sleep, that is, nocturnal emissions and sexual dreams (Foucault 1985).

Contemporary recovery programs for addiction resonate with Cassian's tiered model for achieving abstinence in their use of "steps." Traditionally associated with Alcoholics Anonymous, other "anonymous" groups have since adopted the twelve-step program regardless of the "addiction" at hand: overeating, gambling,[24] and so on. As in Cassian's system, one may make progress toward but never truly reach the final goal, as one is always recover*ing* and never recover*ed*. Despite the impossible aim, these models clearly delineate the "how-to" for the would-be abstainer.[25] While unarguably serving a purpose for many, the literature on the topic of quitting promises that abstinence (or moderation at a minimum) will save us from both ourselves and the addictions lurking around the corner.[26]

What This Book Does and (of Course) Does NOT Do

Quite in line with the way abstinence has been presented to us, when I told people that I was writing a book on abstinence, they often made two assumptions: (1) that I was interested in the moral dimension of abstinence and/or (2) that I was focusing on a particular form of abstinence (usually, sexual abstinence or, to a lesser degree, abstinence from drugs and alcohol). My response has been that I am "abstaining" from both.

In a sense, groups as diverse as academics, health professionals, and politicians have fleshed out the specific sites of abstinence (e.g., virginity, recovery from addiction, vegetarianism), the motivations behind abstaining, issues of morality, and what leads to "successful" abstainers. The question remains, then, whether there is any uncharted territory. One possibility, of course, would involve a consideration of an unexplored or inadequately explored form of abstinence. While it is important to continue to examine abstinence on a type-by-type basis, our understanding of how abstinence operates as a generic process of identity will remain somewhat piecemeal and incomplete until we begin to make comparisons *across* types. The absence of simultaneous explorations of various forms of abstinence perhaps implies that there is only *difference* to be seen between types and that such studies would be exercises in comparing apples and oranges. Yet, in order to see if abstinence does, in fact, operate not only as a personal marker of identity but as a social, behavioral, and cognitive process as well, we need to explore the *commonalities* across types, especially since social identity "is the systematic establishment and signification between individuals, between collectivities, of relationships of similarity and difference" (Jenkins 1996, 4). Again, if we are to understand the place of abstinence in identity theory, it is not enough to explore issues of sameness and difference *within* a particular type of abstinence; this examination must transcend the boundaries of type as well.

In addition to moving beyond a case analysis of one form of abstinence, the book takes the "hows" of abstinence rather than the "whys" or the "how-tos" as the center of its analysis. For sure, my decision to avoid the more psychological question of "why" will frustrate some readers since many widely known psychological disorders, especially phobias, find their roots in avoidance of doing certain things. Yet attempting to trace the roots of abstinence with psychology runs the risk of simply dismissing any form of abstinence as a fear response. Just as fear gets systematized in taboo (Webster 1942, 14), so might a purely psychological understanding of avoidance. Having said that this book is not psychological in its perspective or scope, it may nonetheless inform our ability to think through what we perceive as "normal" amounts of both doing and not-doing something and to recognize at what point the violations of these unspoken but understood parameters constitute disorders of "not enough" doing (phobias) or those of "too much" doing (obsessive compulsiveness).

This book, then, does not take on the issue of the rightness of abstinence, nor does it attempt to evaluate the efforts of abstinence entrepreneurs who try to sway others into believing in their cause. Instead, the book explores the lives of what I call "everyday abstainers," those who actively incorporate not-doing into their sense of self. Rather than musing about the psychological impetuses behind their decisions, the book focuses on the ways in which the contemporary conditions and historical changes in our understandings of abstinence can dramatically impact not only the ways in which we, as a collective, perceive not-doing, but also the very personal, day-to-day practices of those who choose abstinence as an organizational component of identity.

The Structure of the Book

Part 1 of the book focuses on the social shape of abstinence. Chapter 1 explores the challenge of seeing something that others do not do. It asks the specific question as to what, beyond the level of individual discretion, allows unmarked not doings to transform into significant markers of identity, into not-doings. The elements of time, place, and language serve as the brief answer to this question. Time, of course, can apply from the scope of personal biography to larger historical eras. Regardless of which level of time we consider, abstinence becomes meaningful and visible to us if it seems somehow off track with what one "should" be doing given one's place in the life course or in terms of what others are doing. Place, too, can increase our ability (or inability) to see abstinence. Certainly, large geographic moves bring varying expectations regarding behavior, but the differences may also appear among more subtle locations, such as those associated with social groups and personal networks. Finally, though we constantly create new terms for referring to certain types of abstinence, these terms remain largely inadequate. In addition to simply not having terms to identify a given form of abstinence, the available terms come with built-in assumptions as to directionality (e.g., can one move freely between abstinence and doing or must one qualify such moves, as in the case of "born-again" virgins?) and ideas about "acceptable" ways to not-do (e.g., vegetarians *always* eat no meat).

Chapter 2 takes a temporary step back from the informants in order to more thoroughly flesh out the issues of time and place in the larger history of abstinence. By tracing some of the ways in which abstinence has been framed over time (e.g., religious salvation, social protest, and entertainment), it becomes clear that the current zeitgeist and ways of thinking about the self inform what abstinence means to the individual practicing it and the larger society around him or her. Dominant frames also influence the assumptions others make regarding the motivation of individuals to abstain. Chapter 3 picks up the framing theme of chapter 2 by considering contemporary abstainers and the frames they invoke when describing their abstinence. Though the reasons behind their decisions to abstain vary, it becomes clear that abstinence is a low-cost, high-control identity option in a world of an unprecedented and sometimes overwhelming degree of choice (for many, not all, of course). Abstainers describe their not-doing as an active factor (rather than a lack), qualitatively different from the expected not doings at other points in their lives.

Chapter 4 explores the critical issue of how abstainers come to abstain in the first place. More so than the type of abstinence one practices, the factors of whether one has participated in the act in the past and whether one intends to do so in the future strongly shape how one tells one's personal story of abstinence. Identifying as a "waiter," "never," "time-outer," or "quitter" influences how one views the past, present, and future, as well as which narrative tools (e.g., turning points, defining moments) one uses to describe the journey to abstinence. The chapter also explores the importance of contingent abstinence (not-doing as a prerequisite to joining a group or organization) and conjoint abstinence (the decision to abstain in conjunction with others) in one's decisions.

Part 2 of the book moves to the more narrow focus of *how* abstainers not-do in a day-to-day sense. Chapter 5 details the two main ways abstainers tend to conceptualize abstinence: as a point or as a zone. Whereas those who believe abstinence to be a set point see it as an "absolute zero" of sorts, those who approach abstinence as a zone perceive abstinence to lie somewhere in the space between the integers of 0 and 1. What one decides counts as abstinence influences the ways in which one will abstain, and it is this topic to which I turn in chapters 6 and 7. Chapter 6 explores the strategy of what I call "fire walking," a performance strategy that hinges on the "abstinence as zone" counting scheme. When fire walking, individuals willfully play with "fire" in order to test their commitment to not-doing, reaffirm their abstinence, and see how they fare in the face of temptation. Alternatively, as chapter 7 shows, many not only avoid the fire, but they also desire to remove themselves one degree farther away from it. When fence building, one erects a protective "fence" around one's abstinence as an extra insurance policy that one will not violate one's abstinence. Interestingly, this ultraprotective identity stance becomes difficult to maintain, and strategies of negotiation are often needed to restore the purity of one's abstinence. Chapter 8 reiterates the point that fire walking and fence building are not fixed identity types but are instead ways of *performing* abstinence contingent on factors such as time spent abstaining, the presence of multiple abstinences, beliefs about one's personality, and the audience for whom one is performing.

While it is important to recognize the differences among the ways abstainers not-do, it is equally important to keep in mind that the fact that one engages in not-doings does not necessarily mean that others will know of these decisions. For sure, not-doings carry strong implications for our personal identities, but their salience intensifies as others become aware of and react to them. Chapter 9 takes a closer look at the verbal performances of abstinence, ranging from initial disclosures of abstinence to repeat performances in response to others' "forgetting" one's decision to not-do. The chapter considers the uses of such verbalization, not only for those who abstain but for the audiences to abstinence as well. In it, the informants briefly become audiences to the abstinences of others, and their somewhat surprising reactions highlight the difficulty of not-doing in a context of expected doing.

I conclude the book by returning to the issue of personal choice in the decision of abstinence, as well as to some ideas regarding how the study of not-doing might inform our understandings of identities based on doings and identity theory in general.

PART I

The Social Shape of Abstinence

CHAPTER ONE

Seeing Not-Doing:
Time, Place, and Language

How do we "see" the things that others do not do? At first glance, the question may appear to be the great riddle of abstinence. After all, if individuals choose not to do something, we might view the quest to recognize abstinence as a daunting (and perhaps impossible) task, believing that we must rely entirely on announcements by abstainers themselves. Though I am making the case for distinguishing between unmarked not doings and the not-doings of abstinence, for sure, one characteristic they share lies in the potential difficulty of perceiving them. The field of cognitive sociology in general and the sociology of perception in particular together offer us the tools with which we can begin to take on a question that seems unanswerable and unsolvable.

If our sociomental lenses (Zerubavel 1997, 34) mediate our perception in everyday life, we should expect their influence on our perception of abstinence too. These lenses, shaped by our personal backgrounds, experiences, group affiliations, and physical and social locations, ensure that no observations are "pure" or even consistent from one person to the next (24–34). With that said, certain conditions more readily allow us to see abstinence in ways independent of disclosure by individuals engaged in not-doing. The social climate, for one, may influence our ability to literally see abstinence in certain times and places. For not-doings to attract our attention, they often need to occur in a context where an expectation of doing exists. Of course, settings in which doing a given act is the default—the unmarked category—fluctuate. Abstinence, too, may change in its degree of salience under certain conditions. Designations of "marked" and "unmarked" do not stem from inherent qualities; instead, the unmarked may suddenly appear marked (or the marked suddenly unmarked) and an already-marked quality may intensify under the right circumstances.[1]

When do not doings become not-doings? Though individuals can insist that what they are doing qualifies as abstinence, the right time and place certainly help legitimate abstinence. A final factor, language, also influences our ability to see abstinence and to recognize it as a social category since we more easily recognize things for which we have a name (Zerubavel 1997, 23). By giving a name to that which individuals do not do, we rely on language to organize abstinence into a meaningful category. Interestingly, the relationship between seeing abstinence and talking about it becomes somewhat symbiotic. That is, while we must first "see" not-doing in order to name it, the language we use to ultimately describe it in turn affects how we perceive abstinence, understand it, and evaluate the decisions and behaviors of others.

Temporal Location

The dimension of time may affect whether a not-doing qualifies as abstinence and, consequently, becomes noticeable in two distinct ways: first, when, or at what point, an individual abstains during his or her life course, and second, on a larger scale, where the abstinence occurs in a larger historical context. Abstinence gains relevance and visibility, then, if it violates norms of individual and/or social time. In other words, abstinence becomes a meaningful category only after the *expectation* of doing arises. Regardless of whether one has previously engaged in the behavior or not,[2] most informants claim that their abstinence became highly visible at certain points in the life course, as others came to regard it as a violation of expected doing.

Lily, a thirty-eight-year-old childfree and single woman, mentions the increasing visibility of her abstinence over time, as she finds it more and more difficult to avoid questions regarding her kids and husband. (She has neither.) Such questions occur at any sort of social event—from graduations to tennis games—where she must interact with people who do not know her. Below she recounts one instance where the inquirers made it quite clear that she was violating an imperative norm:

> I remember once at a club people said, "How old are your kids?" I said, "I don't have any kids." They asked me something about maybe, "What does your husband do?" I said, "I'm not married." Literally, they turned around and walked away. . . . Usually people just sort of go off and try to figure me out.

In a similar way, Sarah believes that her virginity "counts" more as a twenty-six-year-old since she believes that most people engage in sex for the first time either in high school or in college.

Of course, ideas about what are acceptable lengths to abstain within the life course vary over time in the larger historical context of a society as well. Just as some behaviors (and identities based on them) do not come to our attention unless they occur during a particular point in the life course, others have no meaning outside of a given historical context. While some practices occur throughout history, their visibility and salience rise and fall during different eras. For example, sociologists and historians interested in the topic of family note how we become aware of many practices only under the right social conditions. So while children and women have endured violence throughout time, we have only been able to "see" such practices as abuse—as well as their accompanying identity categories: child abuser/molester, "wife beater," and so on—with changes in our understanding of family-related concepts, such as childhood, women's rights, and marriage.[3]

Identities based on abstinence also only gain meaning under specific historical conditions. In fact, many insist that if they were to have abstained in another point in history, their not-doings would not make sense or would pass unnoticed as "normal" behavior. So while Debbie thinks that her decision not to drive may not have been a "big deal" years ago when fewer people in the country as a whole were driving, her abstinence is now more visible during a time when many individuals own cars and daily mobility becomes increasingly difficult in many locations if one does not drive. While Debbie's abstinence is entirely contingent on technology, Georgia, a sexual abstainer, offers an interesting suggestion as to how other abstinences that do not rely exclusively on technological advances may nonetheless be affected by them. Though she abstains from intercourse for different reasons, she muses that sexual abstinence may have declined over time due to advances in birth control that more efficiently protect against pregnancy and sexually transmitted diseases. This perspective raises the intriguing possibility that what eventually comes to be framed as a discourse of "choice" may have origins in specific historical contingencies.

Other abstainers have a less clear sense of how they differ from their predecessors, but they nonetheless perceive their not-doing as remarkable based on the reactions of others. Marla claims that, when others become aware of her virginity, a common reaction is something along the lines of, "people just don't do that [i.e., abstain] anymore. It's so like, 'Oh, you're from the 1950s,' you know?"[4] Jayson sums up this historical uncertainty many abstainers feel toward their not-doing. When I ask him how remarkable he believes his abstinence to be, he replies:

> Um, I don't know because I don't have like, you know, I'd have to go back in a time machine and see and really see myself and see for myself at other points in history how it was or like, you know, I'd have to know more about history and other cultures to see how people understand or something like this, but I think that in this culture that I'm living in it's a fairly out there, crazy thing to do. It's pretty fairly . . . "ridiculous" to abstain from things.

While Jayson's claim that abstaining is both crazy and ridiculous is a matter of opinion, not-doing is, nonetheless, "off track" in a sense. In discussing ideas surrounding entrances and exits into various life events, Lyman and Scott (1989) introduce the term "time tracks" to describe such periods marked by beginnings and endings. Time tracks may be continuous or episodic and are governed by norms of pace and sequence. They powerfully influence our sense of achievement or failure in the life course, as the dominant model of a "successful" life entails both early decision and commitment along a single trajectory (Bateson 1989). Those who get and stay on track earn social points, whereas those who violate norms of either pace (by embarking on a track "too late" or "too early") or sequence (by doing things "out of order") run the risk of various forms of social disapproval, as they appear somehow off track.

Time tracks rely in part on what Robert Merton calls "socially expected durations" (SEDs). In contrast to actual durations or how long something literally lasts, SEDs are "socially prescribed or collectively patterned expectations about temporal durations imbedded in structures of various times" (1976, 265). As ubiquitous social facts, SEDs often pass unnoticed, continually influencing our sense of temporal norms in many areas of everyday life, for example, what constitutes an "acceptable" deadline, an "appropriate" prison sentence, and so on (279). Using the example of Crafttown, erected in 1941, Merton notes how expected durations can carry greater significance than actual durations. In the case of Crafttown, the intention to remain in the town or to leave at some point (i.e., to be a "permanent" or a "transient") manifested itself in very divergent behaviors in community participation. While Merton proposes that the expected durations could be either the independent variable (cause) or dependent variable (effect) in relation to community involvement (274), he nonetheless offers the critical insight that expectations about the future play a key role in present behavior.

Discussions of socially expected durations and time tracks typically focus on doings, but they are relevant to periods of abstinence as well. Though
varying historically and cross-culturally, times clearly exist when one is expected to abstain for specified periods. In addition to differences across time
and place, periods of abstinence may fall at different points in the life course.
Whereas many cultures insist that individuals abstain from sex prior to marriage, occasions for sexual abstinence arise subsequent to marriage, such as
during the period of pregnancy and breastfeeding. In contrast to these instances of anticipated and expected not-doing, the abstainers in this book
differ from such expressions of abstinence in that they appear somehow off
track. Rather than following socially prescribed paths of abstinence, they
abstain for "too long" or from the "wrong things," that is, from acts that
one *should* do given one's position in the life course.

Physical Locale

Where one is also leads others to assume one will participate in an act.
In short, abstinence means different things depending on location. Insisting that "place really does make a difference," Rebecca projects that her refusal to own a cell phone will become a nonissue as she moves from an
urban location in the United States to an indigenous reservation in Costa
Rica to study. In fact, she claims that to own and use a cell phone in the
latter place would be perceived as absurd by both herself and others. On
the other hand, location may allow for abstaining with greater ease, in turn
reducing the marked and visible quality of the abstinence to some extent.
So while Jada feels that her vegetarianism is "very, very remarkable" in the
United States, in Israel she "thought it was the most regular thing ever.
There's a lot of people that are vegetarians [and there is] a very strict separation of the meat stocks and the vegetarian food." Also speaking of his
time spent in Israel, Benjamin says, "It's very strange to me that I don't have
to look hard to find a Kosher restaurant. . . . Not that all the food in Israel
is Kosher—contrary to what a lot of people think—but it's a very different
feeling, you know."

While potential cross-cultural shifts in meaning are perhaps not surprising, finding difference across places need not involve a journey to remote
and distant lands. In fact, geographic moves on a smaller scale—such as between the coasts or even across states within the United States—come with
contrasts. Of her multiple abstinences, for example, Ruth feels that "[not
owning a] car seems to be kind of remarkable in [this state], so it's more
of a context thing. Like in [this state] it's pretty remarkable not to have a

car." Lily adopts a stronger tone when discussing the shift in visibility of her abstinence subsequent to her relocation to the east coast. Not only does she perceive her abstinence to be unique or somehow slightly out of the ordinary in her new city; she believes it to be a total anomaly. With a hint of disbelief in her voice, she says, "I'm the *only* single person I know. I mean, I moved here from [a West Coast city] about four years ago, and here I have two single friends, one much younger and male, and the other one is basically my age, but she is insane, so it doesn't really count. Other than that, everybody I know is or has been married."

Location affects the visibility of abstinence on much smaller scales as well. Social events, too, are often sites saturated with expectations of doing, making one's abstinence stand out more than in everyday situations, as many events highlight the feeling that one should do something. This language of obligation frequently arises among those who abstain from alcohol, as their dry behavior violates what Ciara calls the "traditional way of celebrating certain things." During such instances, Ciara feels particularly aware of her abstinence, as "there are certain times when you are *supposed to drink*," and sometimes she is the "only person standing there with no drink." Her reflections on these moments show the interaction of different notions of place, as she also says that if she were to "move to—where are all the Mormons?—Utah? then [she] wouldn't feel that way" at a similar social event.

Social and professional groups also become sites that affect the significance and visibility of a not-doing. Asia insists that the degree to which one's abstinence seems to count largely "depends on the circles you travel in." Being even more specific, Amelia reports that the strongest response to her vegetarianism comes from those with less education and lower socioeconomic status, suggesting that some abstinences may appear less extraordinary based on one's social position. Ruth, a sociologist, supports Amelia's sentiments, and says that the connection between abstinence and social class often eludes her students. Reflecting on a recent class she taught on social theory, Ruth says, "We had a discussion about vegetarianism when we were reading Bourdieu, and, trying to talk about how different styles, you know, of the different social classes. And some of the girls who were vegetarian really rejected the idea that vegetarianism would be associated with like middle class or something like that. They were sure that this was their personal, individual choice." Social location, then, may not only affect the likelihood of practicing certain forms of abstinence; it can also impact the degree to which others notice and react to it.

A final way that location may affect the visibility of abstinence is by professional location. Craig, whose e-mail abstinence may not seem remarkable in some contexts, says he believes that "statistically, it's pretty unusual given my profession. How unusual I'm not quite sure. People tend to see it as very, very unusual." When I ask if he thinks his abstinence would be less of an issue in another profession, he replies, "I would imagine so. Oh sure. Well, you know, some professions probably don't make use of e-mail at all to the degree that . . . Well, I suppose all professions by now do, so I'd have to be a carpenter or something like that to not truly be dependent on it." Clearly, the remarkableness of abstinence changes across time and space, allowing one's abstinence to stand out or fade into the background. So although abstinence feels abnormal in some regard, the degree to which it does so changes across contexts.

Expectations of doing arise in other ways as well, again leading abstinence to emerge as a violation. For example, Marla notes how it is not simply her age that leads others to generalize about her behavior, but her physical appearance too. She recounts a conversation with a male friend held one night at the art institute where she attended college. The conversation turned to the topic of sex, which she felt was appropriate considering the closeness of their friendship. When he began to ask experience-related questions, Marla felt obligated to tell him that she was a virgin. His immediate reaction was, "But you're so pretty." This was not an isolated event, as Marla notes how "people assume that, you know, if they think that you're attractive, they assume that you've definitely had sex because there's no way that you're still a virgin and blah, blah, blah." It seems, then, that in addition to time and location, *who* engages in not-doing affects its significance as well.

Language

Throughout the book, I will argue that it is imperative to consider the similarity between and consistency across different types of abstinence. After all, an emphasis on similarity carries the advantage of illuminating how larger issues surrounding abstinence transcend its individual manifestations: in a Simmelian sense, how form often overrides content (Simmel 1950). Still, differences undeniably exist in the way we regard and experience different types of abstinence, and I believe we may attribute many of these differences to language and the terms we use (or fail to use) to represent abstinence. Relying heavily on linguistic examples from specific cases of abstinence is in no way an attempt to sidestep or renege on the idea of developing a generic approach to identity. On the contrary, focusing on the language surrounding specific forms allows us to see how systems of linguistic classifications limit or facilitate a comprehensive understanding of identities based on abstinence.

When it comes to doings and not-doings, much of the English language allows us to see the former only. Granted, the terms we do have to refer to abstinence reveal quite a bit about (1) where our collective sentiments lie (measured somewhat crudely by the number of available terms); (2) temporality (Was an abstainer a "doer" in the past? Does he or she plan to abstain permanently?); and (3) directionality (Can one move in and out of abstinence with ease or with little consequence to identity?). With that said, terms to describe abstinence are often either largely unavailable or, if they do exist, fail to capture the complexities and intricacies of not-doing. The former problem appears to be one of invisibility, the latter one of inadequacy.

A comment made by Bryant Gumbel, former coanchor of CBS's *Early Show*, captures both the power of language and the difficulty that arises when terms are inadequate or nonexistent for understanding what someone chooses to do or not-do. Connected to the studio from his assignment at the Democratic Convention on the morning of August 16, 2000, Gumbel expressed his disbelief at Wendy Keller's book *The Cult of the Born-Again Virgin*, in which she claims that it is both possible and desirable to reclaim one's virginity regardless of how often or for how long one has previously engaged in sexual intercourse. Gumbel, overhearing the debate between "experts" with competing views on the topic, quickly summed up his position with his characteristic frankness: "What do you mean?! You can't start again. You either *are* or you *aren't*!"[5] In charging that when one crosses this line between virginity and nonvirginity, one forfeits the potential (or perhaps the *right*) to reclaim a previous virgin identity, Gumbel voiced prevailing sentiments about this form of abstinence.

As I thought further about the various perspectives that morning, I wondered if other forms of abstinence would have incited such an emotionally charged debate. Would Gumbel (and the unconvinced expert interviewed for the segment) object so vehemently had Keller asserted that one can move back to *vegetarianism* after eating meat for any length of time? Would Keller herself feel the need to regard such an individual as a "born-again" vegetarian in order for others to be open to her position? I imagine the answers to both questions to be no.

We often look to the briefest descriptions to tell us a lot about a person, as our expectations of individuals get built into the language we use to refer to different identities. Though the reality may vary, identity markers such as "wife," "Communist," "genius," and "immigrant" serve as mental frames of reference from which we begin to understand a person. Language often takes on a life of its own, coloring our perceptions and shaping our experiences and understandings of ourselves and of others. As the Gumbel exchange shows, we can often not imagine possibilities outside the way our language frames something. While this dilemma applies to identities based on doings and not-doings alike, the limitations of language present an additional burden for abstainers who may already struggle with the task of convincing others of the legitimacy of and logic behind their identity decisions.

Term Dilemmas, Part One: Invisibility

The vast literature on systems of classification—whether the concern is the categorization of food, animals, individuals, or something else—repeatedly suggests that such divisions do not reflect divisions inherently and unambiguously found in nature. As Whorf argues, such categories arise not "because they stare every observer in the face" but instead because "the world . . . has to be organized by our minds—and this means largely by the linguistic systems in our minds" (1956, 213). Cross-cultural variation in the classification and number of terms used to represent diverse entities such as colors, camels, or snow (Newman 2000, 51–54) serves as evidence of this proposition that the "world is a representation of our language categories, not vice versa."[6] As a tool of socialization, language transforms various continua in the physical world into manageable, discontinuous, and, therefore, meaningful categories (Leach 1964; Zerubavel 1991). Through their power to distinguish, words allow us to verbally and mentally elevate socially important figures while leaving the "unimportant" and "meaningless" (what Leach calls "taboo parts" or "non-things") behind as part of a flat and colorless[7] ground.

While most of this literature focuses on "things," the creation of perceivable and meaningful categories through language applies nonetheless to behaviors. Newman suggests that not only do words convey powerful messages about what is meaningful and relevant to a society's members, but that the use of particular words further "reinforces prevailing ideas and suppresses conflicting ideas about the world" (2000, 53, 52). Though certainly not unique to abstinence, the shortage of terms to describe not-doings often poses difficulties. In a language where there are many terms to delineate one's doings, the absence of available referents to one's not-doings complicates the process of projecting a legitimate self based in part on not-doing and the ability of others to perceive it.

There are, of course, both nouns (vegetarian, vegan, teetotaler, and virgin) and adjectives (celibate, sober, clean) that refer to various abstinent practices themselves. Interestingly, these terms do not extend beyond what I previously identified as the three most popular topics of abstinence: sex, food, and substances. In the place of terms specific to a form of abstinence, we must often resort to attaching prefixes of negation (such as "non" and "ex") to words that refer to doings. This practice, then, results in highlighting the doing—rather than the not-doing—as the default category. Thus, terms such as "ex-smoker" or "nondriver" emphasize the negation of the doing instead of recognizing the not-doing as valid in its own right.

In addition to prefixes of negation, we have also extended the grammar of the term "virgin" from its traditional use as a noun to an adjectival form. Referring to anyone who has never participated in the activity at hand, it is becoming more common to hear individuals described as virgin public speakers, virgin fliers, and virgin sushi eaters. Still, the use of "virgin" as an adjective fails to acknowledge the form of abstinence practiced in terms of its unique form. In a different but related example, a quick glimpse through any vegetarian or vegan cookbook reveals countless examples of recipes that borrow terminology from dishes that include meat (or any animal products in the case of veganism) in order to make sense to the reader: vegetarian chili, tofu spare ribs, veggie burgers, vegan ice cream. Though using nonvegetarian or nonvegan food as the reference point, cookbooks and brand names based on packaged, store-bought products do nonetheless frame the vegetarian and vegan options in a positive sense. Whereas in many cases "fake" equals substandard or bad, here imitation takes on a favorable tone.[8]

Having said that we must often refer to a doing in order to comprehend a not-doing, we cannot ignore the fact that terms that recognize abstinence in its own right (rather than as a negation) enter our lexicon from time to time. Interestingly, many of these terms never take off, or they face great resistance not only from the public at large but by groups we might assume would embrace them. In discussing the advent of the term "vegan," Stepaniak (1998) shows the difficulty of adding to or revising available terms. "Vegan," created in the 1940s, appeared a logical term to those involved in such eating practices, as it took the first three (*veg*) and last two letters (*an*) from "vegetarian," in essence "[starting] with vegetarianism and carrying it through its logical conclusion" both linguistically and philosophically.[9] Vegans, then, defied the dichotomy of meat-eaters versus vegetarians by attempting to legitimate a category they presented as a *degree* of vegetarianism (yet different enough to be recognized in its own right). Yet, somewhat to their surprise, even members of the vegetarian community refused to acknowledge the category.[10] Although veganism is now more widely accepted among vegetarians, my experiences suggest that "vegan" remains unfamiliar to many people as both a term and a practice. While my evidence is anecdotal in nature, I frequently receive curious looks or demands for a definition when mentioning vegans (more so than any other category) to those interested in my topic. Furthermore, I cannot help but notice the red squiggly line that appears under the term "vegan" each time I type it—an indication that my computer's spelling and dictionary programs do not recognize the term, despite its almost sixty-five-year existence.

Term Dilemmas, Part Two: Inadequacy

The problems surrounding linguistic terms and abstinence may not end once a name has been given. Frequently, abstainers resort to using terms they believe insufficiently capture the nuances of *how* they practice a particular not-doing. Typification of behavior complicates this problem of inadequate representation.

When describing the role of language in everyday encounters, Berger and Luckmann insist that individuals cannot always and only use terms known to themselves and their intimates if they are to have any degree of successful social interaction. Instead, individuals must make use of the social stock of knowledge, which includes "typified" terms. As a tool of communication with and connection to others, typification allows individuals to situate their personal happenings in a less subjective way by making them comprehensible to others who experience things in similar—but always slightly different—ways (Berger and Luckmann 1966). As an example, while my thirst may subjectively feel a bit different from your thirst (in terms of the amount and type of beverage I desire, the dryness of my mouth, how dehydrated I feel, etc.), I "know what you mean" when you utter the phrase "I'm thirsty." Typification also plays a role in our ability to understand, as Berger and Luckmann say, what to do with the practices and identities of others. While confusion often results from unfamiliarity with a given form of abstinence, problems also surface when an individual practices a recognizable abstinence but does so in a way that defies how most *typically* do so.

As a result, the terms through which individuals must describe and identify their abstinence often fail to capture the nuances (and, at times, glaring differences) between themselves and others of the same "type." In a study specific to vegetarians, Beardsworth and Keil devised a typology of how individuals practice what we lump together as "vegetarianism" in diverse ways and with varying degrees of rigidity. Such attempts at capturing this range of behavior reject blanketing assumptions that "a vegetarian is a vegetarian is a vegetarian." Nonetheless, while researchers may acknowledge the differences, abstainers continue to force themselves into existing categories so as to avoid "appearing to be awkward or eccentric" (Beardsworth and Keil 1992, 271). Consider, for example, Rebecca's reflections on being a "vegetarian": "I would say that I am *not* a vegetarian even though I've probably said it a bunch of times in this interview. I think technically I'm not a vegetarian. In such a meat-based society or meat-centered society, it's just easier if I tell people that I'm a vegetarian." She later offers this revised perspective: "I would call myself a pescatarian, I guess. [She eats fish.] But nobody knows what that is (laughs), so . . . So I don't really use it."

Though also a vegetarian, Ruth faces an additional challenge when disclosing her abstinence to others in that she also practices the principles of "food-combining." In addition to not eating meat, she further abstains from eating certain types of food altogether (such as cheese) or simultaneously (such as starches and proteins). She frequently feels that language fails her on two levels. First, there is no lay term for her type of abstinence; in other words, "food-combining"[11] has not found a place in the social stock of knowledge. The second reason—directly related to the first—has to do with how Schutz and Luckmann (1973) explain individuals' handling of new experiences. They insist that, rather than starting from scratch with each new situation, individuals rely on types constituted in earlier experiences. Since very few people Ruth encounters understand the logistics of food-combining, they automatically interpret her practices exclusively through the lens of vegetarianism. In fact, knowing that "it would be easier to say I'm a vegetarian and I don't eat meat, it's hard to explain why I would prefer not to eat cheese and bread or not eat pizza. People don't actually get that."

Ruth often dreads eating out and describes her frantic scans of menus for "anything interesting . . . to eat besides french fries and salad" as uncomfortable moments. Her fellow diners, not able to grasp her practices beyond the vegetarian element, frequently "point to some pasta dish with lots of cheese on it and say 'Well, here's a vegetarian option.'" At that point, she finds herself forced to resolve the situation anticlimactically by saying something benign such as, "Well, you know, I really don't feel like eating that," a statement that situates her preference *in that moment* rather than in an everyday dietary practice, in essence reducing the potential stigma and bewilderment such a claim might evoke.

Language and the Locus of the Self

In talking about his own decision not to refer to himself as an addict for the rest of his life, Colin tells me, "I'm a big believer in self-talk and the way that you describe yourself to yourself and others in the world is really very much who and what you are."[12] As we have seen, however, abstainers find that words often fail them when trying to describe themselves to others. Limitations of language—whether they be ones of invisibility or inadequacy—pose a fundamental problem for those who base their identities in part on not-doing: an inability to capture the locus of the self. Certainly, this dilemma extends to "doers," as well, since the available terms often force individuals to describe themselves in a cut-and-dried, black-and-white manner, that is, as doers or not-doers.

Bruce, an ex-smoker, finds himself trapped in such semantics, as he struggles for language that accurately represents him. Consider the difficulty he experiences when trying to convey "who he is" to me.

BRUCE: I'm like, *I am a smoker*. I feel it within me.

JM: Even though you don't smoke?

BRUCE: Yeah.

JM: Would you say it's like, I know a lot of people who are in AA [Alcoholics Anonymous] say that you're always an alcoholic even if you don't drink again. Are you that extreme about it?

BRUCE: I wouldn't say that. I mean, I don't even buy that. I mean, it's like I could see like the addictive impulse as sort of a tendency among people, but I don't think that, I don't know. I mean, *I don't feel that I could consider myself a smoker when I don't smoke*. I mean I guess you could say you're an alcoholic, but you're not a drinker. I guess I'm a, I don't know what I'd be, but *I'm not a smoker*. (all emphases added)

Listening to his waffling between identifying as a smoker and not a smoker, I continue to push him to explicate how he thinks about himself now. Unable to categorize himself, he offers this solution: "I don't know. I feel like I have an affinity for smoking. I mean, I just love it so much. *I just don't do it anymore*."

Bruce's comment raises an interesting issue regarding language's role in laying out the connection between "doing" and "being." On the one hand, in order to qualify as "being" a particular identity, one must actively engage in the act. To use Bruce's example, it seems ludicrous to identify oneself as a smoker if one no longer smokes. On the other hand, there are terms available for some abstinences that allow a being to persist in the absence of doing. Thus, one can remain an "alcoholic" while no longer drinking.

There is another side to this equation, however. Just as language may allow us to *be without doing*, language may afford us the opportunity to *do without being*. Consider how the use of "social" and "casual" in front of certain identity terms (such as "smoker," "drinker," etc.) serves to indicate that one's doings should not be treated as indicative of who one is. By saying that I am a "social smoker," I relegate my smoking to context—in essence, bracketing it off—and insist that an occasional cigarette has no impact on what I regard as my "true" self. Such linguistic strategies during moments like this indicate that the "doings" should not be taken as indicative of "beings."

Language may also serve another function in regard to the locus of the self in that certain terms allow others to locate abstainers in terms of temporality. Specifically, some terms identify whether an abstainer has engaged in the act in the past or intends to do so in the future. In terms of sexual abstinence, the term "virgin" locates an abstainer temporally for others, but the terms "chaste" and "celibate" do not.[13] The term "virgin," then, only refers to those who have previously not engaged in sexual intercourse. When others abstain from sex subsequent to doing, they must make use of qualifying terms such as "born-again virgin" or "secondary virgin" or use different terms entirely, such as "celibate."

While some terms locate abstainers unambiguously in regard to time, some do to a lesser extent. To use Raven's example, we know that someone who is "sober" is likely to be someone who plans to *never again* do something (or possibly abstain for a "time-out" period), but this person is absolutely not someone who has *not yet* taken a drink or who *never has and never will*. The use of a given term may also allow or preclude us from locating individuals along the voluntary-involuntary continuum. For example, although they don't tell us much about one's dietary history, the terms "vegetarian" and "vegan" imply voluntary choices about their identities—quite unlike someone referred to with adjectives such as "barren" or "infertile" and nouns such as "old maid" or "spinster." Interestingly, some words may imply either a voluntary or involuntary quality. So while "childfree" refers to an abstinent choice only, the term "childless" applies to both involuntary and voluntary circumstances.[14] Finally, just as language may signify whether one abstains or simply cannot participate in a behavior for involuntary reasons, language may also offer insight into differences in the motivations behind abstaining. For example, refusing to put food into one's body may be a time-out practice for a variety of individuals, perhaps even practiced in similar ways, yet the language surrounding this abstention—a "fast" versus a "diet" versus a "hunger strike" versus an "eating disorder"—tells us something further about the motivation for not-doing.

The Durability of Identity

In addition to its instrumental role in capturing what individuals feel to be the locus of the self, certain terms and phrases also reflect ideas about the durability (or fragility) of identity. Returning to Gumbel's vehement response to the idea of "born-again virgins," it is clear that he perceives virginity to be a piece of the self not able to be regained subsequent to its "loss." Certain forms of abstinence do, in fact, demand unidirectionality, prohibiting convincing returns subsequent to engaging in the act while others appear to allow room for play, for convincing movements back and forth.

An initial explanation of these discrepancies might focus on the degrees to which we envision certain acts as influencing the body. Sex and addiction alter the body in ways we believe other acts, such as watching television, cannot. *Of course* sex transforms us in ways we can never again recover.[15] *Of course* addiction (at least in the eyes of dominant recovery groups such as Alcoholics Anonymous) does the same.[16] Why else would we reject claims to virginity following an act of intercourse and insist that those who now abstain from drugs and alcohol are *recovering* and never *recovered*?[17]

Still, we must situate such ideas culturally. While some may believe "it's no big deal" for a vegetarian to eat meat and subsequently (and convincingly) return to vegetarianism, these may be invalid identity movements elsewhere. It is fathomable, for example, that eating pork among Muslims could significantly impact one's identity, as many Muslims would regard the transformative power of pork as parallel to the way some cultures regard sexual intercourse. In fact, many vegetarians express the opinion that vegetarianism should be a lifelong commitment and are therefore irritated by those who claim to waffle between identifying as vegetarians and meat-eaters.

In addition to the terms used to describe the abstinence specifically, other phrases offer insight into how precarious abstainers believe their selves to be. When describing the moments they decided to abstain, for example, those who quit a behavior of their past often use phrases such as "turning over a new leaf" or "not looking back," implying the need for a complete and convincing break with a previous self. Once practicing abstinence, similar language arises, often expressed in terms of fear or nervousness surrounding the ability to abstain. Now practicing abstinence, individuals worry that other people or certain actions will "corrupt" them, "taint" them, "break" them, or "reverse" their efforts.

If, When, and How We "See" Abstinence

Though abstainers may believe their not-doings to be real and meaningful to them, the ability to and the ease with which others perceive them hinge on issues of time and place. Once recognized, linguistic terms then in turn shape our impressions of abstinence by either acknowledging abstinence in its own right or as a negation of any given doing. In many instances, abstainers feel constrained by time and place and especially by language, as they feel that the available terms either misrepresent what they are, in fact, not-doing, or that others truly do not understand their efforts due to misconceived notions.

The problems and limitations of language, of course, are not unique to those who base their identities around abstinence. Just as language fails to capture the complexities of abstinence, it may also ineffectively portray subtleties within parts of the self based on doings. The advent of new terms alleviates the problem to a degree since "a strongly institutionalized . . . classificatory system makes certain categories readily and legitimately available for the representation of social reality." Yet, such a system may still fall short if it "does not entail that . . . categories will have a significant role in framing perception, orienting action, or shaping self-understanding in everyday life" (Brubaker and Cooper 2000, 27). Nonetheless, the language of abstinence allows for an interesting glimpse into the ways in which we represent the self and its transformations.

Though I will go on to suggest that there is something very modern about the abstainers under examination here, the one thing that remains constant over time is that all individuals who elect to not-do—past, present, or future—face the issues of time, place, and language presented in this chapter. Certainly, the content changes, but the dilemmas persist. In chapter 2, I will take a momentary step back from modern abstainers to explore the importance of time and place in shaping abstinence, specifically to see the various ways in which abstinence has been framed over time. Regardless of where and when one abstains, the current zeitgeist and understandings of the self inform whether others will see abstinence and, if so, the lens through which they will understand it and talk about it.

CHAPTER TWO

Historical Frames of Abstinence

Toward the end of the third century CE, Porphyry of Tyre witnessed the "fall" of his close friend and fellow Platonist philosopher, Firmus Casticius. The nature of the fall? Casticius had "reverted to consuming flesh," an act that, according to Porphyry, clearly violated their earlier agreement that maintaining a vegetarian diet was a key commitment of any dedicated philosopher (Porphyry 2000, 1). Porphyry did not take the news of Casticius's dietary changes lightly and addressed his concerns to his friend in a treatise divided into four books. In it, Porphyry appeals to Casticius on the principles of morality. A moral person, charges Porphyry, "has reasoning in charge at all times, controlling unreason and handling its reins" (48). Therefore, one who engages in the killing and eating of animals fails to control unreason and simultaneously precludes the carrying out of righteousness. Aware that some may scoff at his extension of these principles to animals, Porphyry argues that consuming animals fails to preserve justice because it is done for the sake of pleasure. Believing that when "pleasure is the goal, justice manifestly perishes," Porphyry challenges Casticius to dispute his conclusion that "surely it is obvious that justice is increased by abstinence?" (97).

Though uttered a bit over seventeen hundred years ago, Porphyry's words to Casticius have a timelessness about them, as we have become quite accustomed to thinking about abstinence in terms of justice and other moral terms. Some societies have lauded abstinence so much that their myths reinforce its virtue. In ancient Greek mythology, for example, we are presented with the stories of three celibate goddesses—Hestia, Athena, and Artemis—who struggle against the temptations represented by Aphrodite, the goddess of love and sexual desire. While Hestia wards off suitors and leads a fairly uneventful life, Athena finds herself constantly defending her virginity. The celibacy of Artemis appears even more remarkable, as she longed to preserve her virginity even as a toddler and demanded celibacy from her followers and companions as an adult (E. Abbott 2000, 25–27).

What are we to make of philosophers who write lengthy treatises to close friends on the virtues of abstinence and a culture that creates a goddess concerned with virginity during her first years of life? Do the majority of the documented accounts of abstinence frame the practice as a moral choice based on informed decisions regarding right and wrong? Tracing the various ways in which abstinence has been framed over time shows that not-doing has not always and only been about morality. A look back to abstainers of the past further reveals that even abstinence "crusaders" may not be what they seem at first glance. In other words, while issues of morality creep into many of the frames, and although abstinence is often practiced or promoted in the name of behavior that is "right" or "good," other reasons for abstaining often trump considerations of a moral nature.

Frames are absolutely critical for abstainers, as they organize meaning both for themselves and those around them. The case of Tudor martyrs nicely exemplifies the function of the frame. These martyrs, critics of what they saw as the Catholic Church's overuse of rituals, quickly found themselves all-consumed by rituals to a degree that Byman (1978, 633) charges as obsessive-compulsive. As martyrdom approached, these individuals delved into practices of extreme self-control, such as limiting their sleep and resisting the temptation of an early death (633, 636). Such discipline, they believed, would "keep the prospective martyr on the straight and narrow path to salvation" (632). But it would also do something else: it would quell their own fears and those of others regarding the possibility that their final act would really be one of self-willed suicide (627). According to Byman, "the key, then, was to tread the fine line between suicide and martyrdom," all the while framing it as the latter (628).

Tracing the ways of framing abstinence, of course, cannot be a pure science. The difficulty of dealing with such histories and accounts of abstinence is that often only the most extreme cases have made it to the record in the first place. Nonetheless, piecing together even some of the evidence begins to complicate the abstinence story. While moral crusaders[1] certainly have occupied a large piece of the abstinence narrative, they by no means "own" the story. The story of abstinence is one of shifting frames. At times, abstinence paves the way to a higher spiritual connection. At others, it serves as a method of social protest, a form of entertainment, a way to regain a sense of collective identity in the face of a social crisis, or simply a means of adapting to changing laws and ideology. Though various abstinences may appear similar from an outsider's perspective, the frame in which they occur becomes a crucial tool for understanding the acts from an insider's point of view.

The Religious Frame

The framing of abstinence as a religious act probably fails to surprise many. After all, religion serves as a powerful source of moral guidance, and many look to religion for instruction on both what to do and what not to do in order to remain within the parameters of abiding followers. Mandates of abstinence permeate every religion—past and present—as evidenced in both general principles (as in abstinence from alcohol among Mormons and the "thou shalt not" commandments of Christianity and Judaism), as well as in periodic practices (such as fasts during a particular holiday or time of year). Like taboo, where prohibitions on certain behaviors extend across a group as a whole with no room for negotiation, abstinence often serves as a contingency for group membership. In other words, one cannot identify as part of a particular religion should one choose to violate the required standards of abstinence. At times, such prescriptions arise from religious texts or the history of the group, while at other times an individual leader will influence abstinence practices and the overall reputation of the religion. For example, in his reflections on Puritanism, a religion known for its abstinent practices, Morton Hunt attributes this notoriety to Calvin and proposes that "Puritanism might never have been puritanical . . . had Calvin been a happier or healthier man" (1994, 225).

While there may be something to Hunt's claim, the idea that abstinence in a religious frame results purely from miserably unhappy leaders who impose it on their followers in oppressive ways not only stereotypes but oversimplifies, and it fails to capture the complex relationship between religion and abstinence. Accounts of abstinence in religious contexts illustrate how the decision to not-do need not come as an always-already, top-down, imposed practice. In many instances, individuals appropriate abstinence by their own accord as a means of achieving instrumental ends. While abstainers frame these ends as religious (e.g., salvation), they select their form of abstinence strategically by choosing acts that fall within their own power to reject and that will make powerful statements and effect change. Below I will use the examples of the early Christian ascetics (abstainers from sex) and female medieval fasters (abstainers from food) to illustrate this point of creative agency in the religious abstinence frame.

Early Christian Ascetics

Christianity bears the reputation of an especially continent religion, particularly in terms of sexual behavior. Those who promote abstinence on religious grounds often turn to the Bible for guidance on sexual limits. Yet Kosnik insists that the Bible fails to provide absolute answers regarding sexual prescriptions. Rather, "the teaching of the Bible must be seen against the background of its time, against the cultural and sociological conditions that characterize its era" (Kosnik et al. 1977, 7). Even if one chooses to take the Bible in its literal form and refuses to situate it historically, Kosnik illustrates how the Biblical teachings on sex do not merely fall into the categories of sin and devastation. In Genesis, for example, sex is described as a positive force that brings people together, freeing them from solitude and loneliness (8–9). The first negative associations with sex come from an interest in cultic purity, not morality. This quest for an untainted cultic identity led to several mandates regarding sexual practices such as monogamy and levirate marriages following the death of a woman's husband. Individuals were to abstain from marrying (and having sex with) more than one person not because it was thought to be an inherently deviant act of sexual misbehavior, but because such practices introduced "foreign" wives and, consequently, tainted cultic purity (13).

Levirate marriage—that is, one between a sonless widow and her dead husband's brother in the interest of producing a male heir (thus keeping any inheritance within the family)—also served as a means of maintaining cultic purity. The story of Onan illustrates this point. Kosnik argues that most read the story of Onan (the namesake of "onanism," a term used to refer to masturbation) as a prohibition on masturbation and the wasting of man's seed. Kosnik points out, however, that God's punishment of Onan through a premature death was less related to the fact that he engaged in the "sin" of touching himself than to his refusal to marry his dead brother's wife. Marriage to this woman, Onan knew, would have introduced the possibility of a male heir, preventing his own acquisition of his brother's inheritance. Onan's sin, then, was one of avarice, not wasted seed (Kosnik et al. 1977, 15).

How, then, did sexuality come to bear the burden of a moral failing in Christianity? Kosnik suggests that "under the impact of the prophets, cultic notions of purity were interiorized and transformed into profound moral concepts" (Kosnik et al. 1977, 17). Following the death of Jesus, Saint Paul, influenced by a Stoic[2] morality that framed passion and desire negatively, warned against *aselgeia* (sexual license) and *akatharsia* (impurity or unclean-ness): sins of passion.[3] Saint Paul's admonitions alone could not sustain the norm of sexual continence,[4] and, as coincidence would have it, historical contingencies would be on the side of those who promoted abstinence as a religious act.

Starting in the middle of the second century, the Roman Empire found it-self under almost continual attack by barbarians. Citizens felt helpless amid the presence of rulers who did nothing to stop the invasion of their home-land and turned to Christianity to offer an explanation for the presence of such evil on earth. Convinced that they themselves were in part responsible for the evil around them, individuals turned inward and discovered a way to cope with evil on a personal level, that is, by engaging in voluntary suffering through self-denial (Hunt 1994, 105). During this same time, other Chris-tians rejected the idea that they were accomplices in the injustices and devas-tation around them. Viewing their social conditions through a different lens and seeing themselves as victims of tyrannical rulers, these individuals took a more aggressive approach to the existing social conditions. Interestingly, their path led them to the same destination: abstinence. Fueling the stance of opposition among these Christians was their belief that the coming of Christ signified the end of the present age. According to these ascetics, the "duty of every Christian was to make His victory plain and to hasten the col-lapse of the power of the 'Rulers of the present age'" (P. Brown 1999, 35). Abstinence became the logical solution, as the termination of procreation would preclude the continuation of the present age. Thus, "to halt sexual activity could be regarded as a symbolically stunning gesture" (36).

Medieval Female Fasters

Other periods have produced equally symbolically stunning, religiously mo-tivated gestures of abstinence, ones shaped by the contemporary zeitgeist. The later middle ages (from the late twelfth to early fourteenth century), for example, showed an increase in the use of fasting as a means of merging with Christ. While medieval thinkers had several ways of interpreting the causes of these fasts—as driven by illness, natural causes, fraud, demons, and so on—these prolonged fasts eventually came to be regarded as mira-cles of sorts (Bynum 1987, 208, 195). The actions of one of the best-known female saints, Catherine of Siena, typified the miraculous nature of the fast, as she reportedly ate only herbs and was so committed to abstinence that she put twigs in her throat to prevent forced food from entering her body.

Interestingly, the practice was highly gendered in that it was overwhelmingly women who practiced this form of fasting. Despite the clear connection to spirituality, few men became miracle fasters (Brumberg 1988, 41).

From our present sensibility, women's abstinence from food probably does not warrant a second glance, as we may immediately assume that such practices marked the beginnings of women's struggles with issues of food. A quick psychological diagnosis of such food rejection might simply write off the behavior as just another example of women's self-inflicted punishment and renunciation of their bodies and not a far stretch from current eating disorders. Yet those who study these medieval women demonstrate why we absolutely cannot hastily impose recent historical labels on these fasters, as the abstinence occurred in a context with dramatically different understandings of food and the body.[5]

Medieval women's choice to renounce food rather than something else (such as sex, as in the case of the early Christian ascetics) for religious ascendancy made sense for three reasons. First, medieval Christians were hardly strangers to the practice of fasting. In her exploration of food and medieval women, Caroline Walker Bynum notes that fasting and the Eucharist were the most significant food practices among Christians in general at this time. Regardless of the motivation for fasting—whether it be "in preparation for this Sunday meal [the Eucharist], in Lenten anticipation of the coming of the bridegroom, or in seasonal response to the harvest"—the ultimate goal of the act was "to join with scarcity in order that plenty might come."[6] Second, the view of the body had changed over time. Whereas the early church encouraged fasting as a way to "*escape from* the body that dragged the spirit ever downward" (Bynum 1987, 36; emphasis added), fasts in the medieval context marked a *retreat into* the body as the source of suffering.[7] Bynum powerfully outlines this connection between food, the body, and suffering: "Food most basically meant flesh; flesh meant suffering (sometimes ecstatic, delicious suffering); and suffering meant redemption. Fasting, feeding, and feasting were thus not so much opposites as synonyms. Fasting was flight not from but into physicality" (1987, 250). Finally, the choice of food made sense for women in that it was one of the few resources they controlled. As those in charge of the preparation and serving of food, women "owned" food. Bynum shrewdly observes that, as "human beings can renounce, or deny themselves, only that which they control," it made sense that medieval women gave up food while men renounced the things they owned: money, property, progeny (191–93). By finding this window of opportunity for power in an otherwise oppressive context, women transformed the meaning of fasting by creating a "spirituality which explored areas of Christian discourse/practices which had previously been peripheral but subsequently acquired a certain dominance" (Mellor 1991, 58).

Abstinence, then, reemerges continually throughout history as a component of religion. Certainly, religious texts and leaders often instruct their followers with various "must dos" (or perhaps, more appropriately, "must *not* dos"), yet followers may also appropriate abstinence for their own religiously motivated aims. As illustrated by the early Christian ascetics and the medieval women fasters, the type of abstinence rarely stems from inherent religious beliefs regarding the "rightness" of such practices. Instead, abstainers determine the specifics based on the immediate goal of the abstinence and the forms of resistance most available to them.

The Entertainment Frame

While the religious frame occupies a long-standing and continual presence in the way individuals portray their abstinence, other frames are more transient. The nineteenth century in Europe and North America introduced one such fleeting manifestation of abstinence not present in any previous era: abstinence for profit and entertainment. Though popular at different points in the course of the century, the three main forms of abstinence entertainment—fasting girls, living skeletons, and hunger artists—presented fasting as the choice for public abstinence. Franz Kafka's short story "The Hunger Artist" tells the fate of one such abstinent entertainer, as the reader is introduced to the artist during the point at which he is reluctantly coming to face the end of his career of public self-starvation. The opening lines inform us that the interest in hunger artists has started to wane; whereas spectators once visited him on a daily basis and even held season tickets, it now seemed, "as if by secret agreement, an actual dislike of exhibition fasting had sprung up everywhere" (Kafka 1977, 578). Desperate to reestablish a following, the artist moves his exhibit within the circus to a location where individuals would inevitably pass on their way to other main exhibits. His efforts prove futile, however, as his show never again regains its earlier status. Nonetheless, each day he continues to have his attendants change the tablet marking the number of days that he has fasted, fully aware that no one any longer cares. At the story's end, the hunger artist tells the circus manager that his fasting was not the remarkable feat that others thought it to be: he simply did not eat because he was unable to find food that he enjoyed. With those final words, the artist dies, the circus crew buries him, and a panther becomes the new attraction and occupant of the cage.

The fame of hunger artists as a profession was nearly as short-lived as that of Kafka's protagonist. But, along with their nineteenth-century companions of fasting girls and living skeletons, hunger artists introduced the possibility that abstinence could provide not only a source of pleasure for others through the public spectacle of watching individuals starve themselves to death, but a source of income to those capable of performing such feats. Yet, despite their similarities, fasting girls, living skeletons, and hunger artists were not regarded as mere "entertainers." As we will see, the frame of abstinence as entertainment breaks down further, as observers to these acts relied on a variety of smaller subframes as ways of interpreting the sources of the abilities and talents of these performers. Nonetheless, what these performers collectively highlighted through the public performance of abstinence as entertainment was the concept of *abstinence integrity*—unadulterated performances of abstinence—observed and validated by an audience of objective outsiders.

Fasting girls marked the first appearance of abstinent entertainers, in some sense vestiges of the past phenomenon of fasting medieval women, but removed enough in time and religious intensity to be considered a different type than their predecessors. Fasting girls defied the laws of nature with their claims that they could subsist, in some instances for years, without eating. Unlike living skeletons, who surfaced around the same time at fairs and freak shows, fasting girls performed from the comforts of their homes. Often residents of rural settlements and small towns, the trend of fasting girls arose within communities and families where belief in the possibility of miracles still reigned strong (Brumberg 1988, 91). The printed word, especially pamphlets and newspapers, aided the local and national fame of these "miraculous maids." Such women at times attracted thousands of visitors, including royalty. While some, like the famous Ann Moore, charged an admission fee, many of the other women profited from the informal but established practice of donating money or goods as compensation for the spectacle (Vandereycken and van Deth 1990, 48).

While fasting girls clearly entertained large numbers of visitors and piqued the curiosity of many, they also raised their share of skepticism. Observers to such acts became harsh critics, holding the women to their claims of total abstinence and not accepting arguments of reframing the consumption of certain foods (such as fruits) as not "counting" or somehow constituting "not eating." As one observer scathingly remarked of such women, "You are often deceived by the patient's friends, who will sometimes state that no food has been eaten for days, and who do not consider that beef-tea, milk, or any other liquid should be called food" (Brumberg 1988, 62).

Many fasting girls, however, did not engage in the creative manipulation of reevaluating food and drink but instead stuck to their claims that they were totally abstinent. Such women had the perhaps unfortunate luck of performing such "miraculous" events during a time when scientists and physicians were coming to insist on the empirical observation of "evidence" in phenomena. This quest for evidence led to the eventual watch and around-the-clock surveillance of many of these women, which often resulted in their death. Perhaps the most famous example was the death of "the Welsh fasting girl," Sarah Jacob, whose parents refused to call off a strict watch of her fasting in hopes of "proving" her integrity (Brumberg 1988; Gooldin 2003; Vandereycken and van Deth 1990).

Aside from the collateral outcome of death, the surveillance of these women often led to the exposure of their claims as false and was followed by various forms of public humiliation (begging in front of church on their knees for God's forgiveness, wearing a "Public Impostor" sign, being incarcerated and/or physically tortured; Vandereycken and van Deth 1990, 56). Eventually most of these "miraculous maids" were deemed frauds of some sort. These women, of course, did not defy biological imperatives by abstaining for years on end; in fact, case after case revealed family members' complicity in such conspiracies by slipping the women food in clever manners. Nonetheless, fasting girls were entertaining for the masses of people who witnessed their feats of abstinence, and they were especially awe-inspiring in their unique claim that they could not only abstain from food for lengthy periods of time, but that they simply had *no desire* to eat in the first place. In the latter sense, fasting girls bore a strong similarity to living skeletons, although the latter food-abstinence performers of the early nineteenth century were predominantly male.

Living skeletons, like fasting girls, presented their performance as effortless albeit for a different reason. Unlike fasting girls, living skeletons focused on the naturalness of their thin bodies, *not* on the ease with which they could resist food. In fact, many living skeletons claimed that they did not fast. As in the case of the fasting girls, physicians became interested in the integrity of living skeletons and tried to distinguish "real" living skeletons from individuals who were emaciated due to illness or some other factor. The identifying characteristic and impressive trait of the living skeleton, then, became his ability to carry on and live a seemingly healthy existence despite an outwardly unhealthy appearance (Gooldin 2003, 42).

Since they claimed to have no desire for food or to eat on occasion, fasting girls and living skeletons respectively chose to frame, quite paradoxically, their abstinence performances not as resistance, but as miracles: of divine origin in the case of fasting girls and of nature in the case of living skeletons (Gooldin 2003, 42). This framing stood in stark contrast to that of the hunger artists. Though Kafka's fictional hunger artist chooses to retrospectively present his performances as effortless, the majority of practicing hunger artists framed their abstinence runs as difficult struggles throughout their duration. In an excellent analysis of these three types of abstinence performers, Gooldin suggests why the hunger artists may have appeared to struggle more in their performances than did the fasting girls and living skeletons. Hunger artists, at their peak as spectacles in the late nineteenth century, participated in the most public form of starvation, often spending days and weeks displayed in cages at freak shows, circuses, fairs, and other sites of amusement. For small fees, members of the community could pay to see the artist literally starve himself to a near-death state. The specified duration of the fasts (forty days, for example) and continual public display in their cages precluded the possibility of any "backstage"[8] for hunger artists. These abstinence performers, according to Gooldin, were constantly "counted and accounted for at all times of the day and night" (2003, 49) by attendants who would mark their progress and serve watch, as well as by the visiting spectators who were paying to observe the stunt. Under this unrelenting public gaze, hunger artists were clearly prevented from hiding their struggles from their audiences. Furthermore, around-the-clock surveillance increased the difficulty of fraud on the part of the hunger artists. Whereas fasting girls remained in the privacy of their homes and living skeletons rejected claims to total abstinence, hunger artists had neither of these entrées into a performance of seamless and "effortless" abstinence.

Despite the allegations and documentation of fraud, the disparities between the practices and subframes of these three forms of food abstinence, and their short-lived appearances at different points in the nineteenth century, fasting girls, living skeletons, and hunger artists collectively introduced the possibility that abstinence could occur for purposes of entertainment in a public context. Furthermore, in a way more explicit than in any other period, these displays of abstinence entertainment pointed to the role of others in validating performances of abstinence. Now more than ever, it was not enough to assert one's abstinence: one had to demonstrate it in front of witnesses as well.

The Protest Frame

As we have seen, while the entertainment frame necessitates an audience made up of individuals who will frequently witness and verify the veracity of one's abstinence, the audience members are interchangeable. In other words, *who* is watching matters less than the fact that someone—*anyone*—is watching in the first place. The protest frame, however, absolutely mandates the presence of observers and targets a specific, rather than a generic, audience. Under the protest frame, reform takes center stage, as those abstaining use their refusal of choice as a means of propagating ideas and effecting social change. Regardless of whether individuals undertake the protest alone or with others, react to a current or enduring issue deemed unsatisfactory by them, or ultimately succeed or fail, the original intention of the abstainer focuses on the need for immediate change. In this section, I will use the cases of the original Luddites, the Suffragettes, and Mahatma Gandhi as examples of the variety of approaches to abstinence as a means of social protest.

The Luddites

In its popular use, the term "Luddite" refers to anyone who opposes technological development and the increasingly perceived need for and reliance on such inventions. Perhaps one of the most public and extreme recent cases of Luddite sentiments can be found in Ted Kaczynski, also known as the "Unabomber." Kaczynski, a Harvard and University of Michigan graduate and former math instructor at Berkeley, began writing antitechnology tracts in the 1970s from his cabin in Montana, where he led the life of a hermit. In 1995, following a series of mail bombings carried out by the still-unidentified Kaczynski, the *Washington Post* published his detailed antitechnology stance in his 35,000 word manifesto "Industrial Society and Its Future," more commonly known as "The Unabomber's Manifesto." Starting the manifesto with the claim that "the Industrial Revolution and its consequences have been a disaster for the human race," Kaczynski goes on to draw extreme analogies throughout such as, "the human race with technology is just like an alcoholic with a barrel of wine" (1995, SS1). Despite its sensationalist tone at points, Kaczynski does represent general sentiments of those individuals we often refer to as Luddites in his position that technology increasingly limits personal freedom, autonomy, and independence, as it is a force that is always forward-moving.

Interestingly, the original group of Luddites,[9] for whom those who take an antitechnological stance were named, may not have recognized Kaczynski as an individual who shared their interests. Luddites, a group of textile workers in early nineteenth-century England, are best known not only for their abstinence from certain machinery but for their destruction of the equipment as a demonstration of social protest. The Luddites were hosiery makers engaged in a long-standing English craft. Originally, stocking makers knitted by hand, but most welcomed the invention of the knitting frame. A man-powered mechanical device, the knitting frame could far surpass the quantity of work produced by hand, as it could sew six hundred stitches per minute to a human's one hundred. Contrary to what one might guess, however, the Luddites did not oppose the implementation of this technology, as knitting frame jobs provided a livable income, the ability to work out of the home, as well as set but self-determined hours (Bailey 1998, 3, 5). In a general sense, then, the Luddites were not antitechnology.

What the Luddites *did* oppose was the increasing loss of control they had over their craft. By the early 1800s, rather than owning their machines as they had previously done, many stocking makers now needed to rent frames from manufacturers. Without an established minimum wage to protect their work and economically burdened by the need to rent machinery, the knitters found themselves in deeper financial straits when middlemen (known as "bag hosiers") arrived on the scene, charging an additional fee above and beyond the rental fee required by the manufacturers (Bailey 1998, 7–8).

The straw that broke the camel's back, so to speak, came when the regular knitting frames were replaced with wide-frame knitting machines, which could produce high quantities of lower-quality products in a short amount of time. Meanwhile, men's fashion moved toward trouser pants and away from top-quality stockings, accommodating and encouraging both the profit-oriented spirit of capitalism and the use of wide frames instead of the traditional frames. Poor and on the brink of starvation, the textile workers revolted, breaking the wide-frame machines. Between the years of 1811 and 1816, this practice continued, as the Luddites attacked and destroyed the mills, manufacturing sites, and, at times, the homes of the knitting frame owners (Bailey 1998, 139–40). But it remains critical that the object of the attacks was not the traditional knitting frame but the wide-frame machine. As Brian Bailey notes in his history of the Luddite rebellion,

> Midland framework-knitters were *not* protesting against the introduction of new machines. The domestic stocking-frame had been in use for two hundred years, with relatively little technological improvement. Opposition to machinery *per se* by the framework-knitters would have been cutting the ground from underneath their own feet. It was only the use of wide frames for making cheap merchandise and the undermining of skilled workers' livelihoods that was the object of their violent protests. (1998, 14)

In the end, the revolt largely failed, leaving forty-six rioters dead (thirty-five by execution for their crimes) and mounds of broken machinery (Bailey 1998, 135). The lasting influence of these textile workers, though, can be found in our contemporary use of the term "Luddite" to refer to one who opposes the development of technology and abstains from it as much as possible. Nonetheless, the extension of this term to anyone who takes an antitechnology stance fails to capture the historical circumstances of the original group, namely their strategic response to deteriorating working conditions through abstinence in combination with violent practices, and their ultimate failed social protest.

The Suffragettes

Though the Luddite rebellion failed to achieve the ends desired by the textile workers, other uses of abstinence as social protest have succeeded. In their effort to secure the vote for women in England, the Suffragettes of the early twentieth century began to hunger strike as a way of adding the elements of suffering and sacrifice to their political protest. Other means of protest up until this point had proved ineffective: women could not petition because they could not enter the House of Commons, and their protest efforts could not draw attention as political offenses because the government would not recognize them as such. Frustrated by structural, gender-based inequalities and determined to win the vote for women, Emmeline Pankhurst and her two daughters founded the Women's Social and Political Union (WSPU), the first and largest militant suffrage group in England (Mackenzie 1975, 114, 112–13, ix). Making use of magazines and the national press, the Suffragettes brought attention to the plight of women through their public demonstrations of food refusal.

The strategy behind the hunger strikes was summed up by Constance Lytton, who would emerge as one of the most prominent Suffragettes, in her letter to the editor of the *London Times*: "We shall put before the government by means of hunger-strike four alternatives: to release us in a few days; to inflict violence upon our bodies; to add death to the champions of our cause by leaving us to starve; or, and this is the best and only wise alternative, to give women the vote" (Mackenzie 1975, 135). While ultimately successful, the road to the vote was anything but smooth, the government often resorting to the second of Lytton's proposed responses, that is, force feeding. Known euphemistically as "hospital treatment," the government often called in doctors to forcibly end the hunger strikes by women who were blatantly embarrassing the government, which was facing charges of "allowing women to starve" (Mackenzie 1975, 132, 128). Determined to abstain for their cause, women would resist the attempts to place hoses and other feeding apparatuses up their noses and into their throats by fighting back and placing their fingers in their nostrils and mouths.

As the fight for the vote unfolded, the struggle became an issue of class as well. As upper-class women got involved, the veil was quickly lifted on the government's preferential treatment of them. Constance Lytton, sister to the Earl of Lytton, was forcibly fed eight times until her identity was revealed. (One doctor, with the perfect vision of hindsight, claimed he suspected Lytton to be "of quality" based on the shape of her nose!) It was only subsequent to the revelation of her identity that the force feeding was stopped on account of her "heart condition," a defect curiously overlooked earlier. In other acts of preferential treatment, Lytton, unlike other prisoners, was allowed to receive letters in jail from her mother. Realizing her hunger strike was not drastic enough, Lytton further protested by cutting her chest with shards of glass so that she would be sent to an "ordinary" cell (Mackenzie, Lambert, and Brown 1988).

The interplay between hunger striking and force feeding became a catch-22 of sorts. Just as the protagonist of Heller's novel, Yossarian, could not get out of flying—since one could only be dismissed from the duty if one was crazy, yet asking to get out of the duty made one sane and therefore fit to fly[10]—the British government made similar use of an insanity diagnosis to dampen the crusade of the Suffragettes. The "operation" of force feeding, in short, could only be performed on a woman with her consent unless, of course, she was unable to consent by virtue of insanity (Mackenzie 1975, 126; Mackenzie, Lambert, and Brown 1988). As a result, the government deemed many women insane in order to forcibly feed them, an act that simultaneously discredited the women and terminated their means of protest. Ultimately, however, the Suffragettes claimed victory, as the British government granted the vote in 1918 to women who were over thirty who met certain property requirements and then in 1928 to all women over the age of twenty-one.

Mahatma Gandhi

While the Luddites and Suffragettes took a "power in numbers" approach to reform by working in resistance groups, others, such as Mahatma Gandhi, sought reform by abstaining solo. No stranger to self-denial, Gandhi engaged in a variety of abstinences that would last for differing durations in his life, some for reasons other than political protest. Sometimes others inspired the onset of these abstinences, as in the time prior to his move to London to study law when his mother made him vow not to touch wine, women, or meat (Gandhi 1996, 7). At other times, the decisions were made independently in efforts of self-improvement. In 1906, for example, he took a vow of brahmacharya, a decision to end sexual relations with his wife, as he believed that, "so long as [he] was the slave of lust, [his] faithfulness [to his wife] was worth nothing" (Gandhi 1983, 180). Yet, Gandhi, like his predecessors, recognized that abstinence could inspire social reform in addition to achieving these personal aims. The Luddites and Suffragettes both employed forceful methods of abstinence as a means of social protest and reform; yet the tactics worked unequally for the two groups, as the Luddites failed as a whole while the Suffragettes secured the vote. Despite the success of the latter group, Gandhi opposed the tactic of these contemporary crusaders, deeming it (quite interestingly, given its aggressive nature) a form of passive resistance—a "weapon of the weak"—and, alternatively, he promoted a form of active resistance, exemplified by his model of satyagraha or "Truth-force" (Gandhi 1996, 51, 50).

The idea for satyagraha began in the summer of 1906 following the "Zulu rebellion" in South Africa, which Gandhi declared to be a euphemism for a massacre led by the British government. One month later, the British government in South Africa passed a new form of legislation known by the Indians as the Black Act. This legislation mandated the fingerprinting of all Indians in South Africa and their registration with the police. Upset by the discriminatory and insulting nature of such legislation, Gandhi called a meeting in Johannesburg on September 11, 1906, where he resolved to protest through civil, but nonviolent, disobedience.[11] Shortly after this meeting, Gandhi sought a means of identifying this novel approach of protest and accepted the term "satyagraha" suggested to him by a Gujarati-speaking man. Satyagraha, according to Gandhi, differed from the tactics of the Suffragettes, who practiced passive resistance through their fasts.[12] In contrast, satyagraha called for "intense activity" in the absence of ill-will (Gandhi 1996, 52). In his conceptualization of it, "Satyagraha is pure soul-force. . . . If ill-will were the chief motive-force, the world would have been destroyed long ago. . . . We are alive solely because of love. We are ourselves the proof of this. Deluded by modern western civilization, we have forgotten our ancient civilization and worship the might of arms" (52). In accordance with the law of satyagraha, Gandhi spent the remainder of his life attempting to influence others through fasts. He insisted that framing fasting as coercion is misleading because the act intends to "awaken the conscience" of others rather than to achieve the desired ends through some form of force (89). Fasting, in his view, "is the greatest force because of the limitless scope it affords for self-suffering without causing or intending any physical or material injury to the wrongdoer. The object always is to evoke the best in him. Self-suffering is an appeal to his better nature, as retaliation is to his baser. Fasting under proper circumstances is such an appeal par excellence" (88).

Gandhi used fasting to address a wide variety of causes. On a smaller scale, he fasted occasionally so that his pupils would realize the consequences of their current "moral fall" (Gandhi 1983, 306–7). In another instance, when the Ahmedabad mill hands' commitment to their strike started to wane, Gandhi announced that he would not touch food unless they continued to strike. Awakened to their lapse, the mill workers argued that they, not Gandhi, should fast. Gandhi dissented, arguing that, as a representative of the laborers, it was his duty to fast. The mill owners, touched by his commitment, began negotiations for a settlement, and the strike ended after only three days of fasting (388–90).

On a larger scale, Gandhi fasted in 1932 to protest the separate untouchable electorate because he felt it perpetuated the line between the untouchables and the rest of the Hindu community, and he only agreed to break his fast when the British accepted the Yeravda Pact, which eliminated the separate electorate (Pyarelal [Nayyar], 1956a, 282; 1956b, 290). Also, in 1924, he embarked on the "Great Fast" in Delhi as a response to the almost daily violence and in an effort to move toward Hindu-Muslim unity. Referring to this strategy of nonviolent noncooperation as a "dangerous experiment," Gandhi nonetheless remained convinced that this approach was "a sacred duty at times" and "the only alternative to anarchy and worse" (Andrews 1930, 305). His final fast (beginning on January 13, 1948), following the partitioning of India into two countries, was intended to convince the Indian Union government to pay the government of Pakistan its share of the assets from prior to the partition. The fast—lasting only five days—succeeded; the Indian Union government paid 550,000,000 rupees to Pakistan (Fischer 1956, 455). Less than two weeks later, Nathuram Vinayak Godse shot and assassinated Gandhi, ending the life of one of the world's most effective social protesters through abstinence and other nonviolent tactics.

The "For Your (Our) Own Good" Frame

In most of the frames discussed thus far, abstinence has been presented as a personal decision that individuals choose (albeit with like-minded others at times) for a variety of instrumental aims: religious salvation and validation, personal income or fame, or as a strategy of social protest. Though these abstinence frames continued to persist, the nineteenth and early twentieth centuries introduced a new frame to the scene. While perhaps not in practice, the idea of abstinence—seemingly from everything—came into ideological vogue. Yet, the voices that now predominated were no longer the scattered ones of those *practicing* abstinence: a new chorus of those singing the moral imperative of *abstinence in others* swept the United States and beyond.

As we will see, although the different strands of the crusade to convince individuals to abstain in the nineteenth and early twentieth centuries overlapped on occasion, by no means was there one unified movement. Nonetheless, there appeared to be an emerging consensus that individuals should strive to abstain to some degree in various areas of their lives, including (but not limited to) diet, sexual behavior, and intake of alcohol. The climate of the era increasingly shifted from one of moderation to temperance and restraint, as advocates sought to convince the unconverted that abstinence could pave the way to personal and social health. Relying on advances such as the ability to measure and assess food intake, advocates used principles of "diaetetick management"[13] and other breakthroughs to promote a plan of abstinence.

Despite the claims of abstinence proponents, the push toward abstinence in this era arose neither directly nor purely from any form of scientific enlightenment or advancement. Though these advocates promoted the message that abstinence could achieve a wide range of positive outcomes—ranging from the improved physical health of individuals, the social health of communities, the protection of families, and the prevention of financial ruin and embarrassment, to strides toward equality between the sexes—evidence shows that such responses were ultimately more reactive than proactive. Under the guise of social and personal health for all, the majority of abstinence crusades were direct responses to varying forms of social crises that inspired fear in those who had the most to lose from these impending social changes: the middle class. The examples of dietary management and nutrition, the antimasturbation and sexual abstinence crusade, and Prohibition and the passing of the Eighteenth Amendment illustrate how, under certain conditions, the decision to abstain originated not from the abstainers themselves but from outside and somewhat informal recommendations rooted in medical or scientific "evidence" or from formal and codified means of enforcement, such as the passage of new laws. Under the "for your own good" frame, then, we see the possibility that even those who encourage abstinence in others may not necessarily do so because they believe in the moral rightness of not-doing but because they believe it will help them regain control over rapidly changing social conditions.

Diet

The interest in medical regimens surrounding diet was well established by the time abstinence took off in the eighteenth and nineteenth centuries. The obsession with monitoring one's diet arose during the unique critical junction of the late seventeenth and early eighteenth centuries, nestled between established religious tenets and a newly developing system of capitalism. Due to practices in religious orders and monasteries, many were familiar with the association of health with bodily discipline and religious duty (Turner 1982b, 23–32). The advent of early capitalism offered a new metaphor—the body as machine—that would continue the tradition of viewing the body as in need of discipline while gradually divorcing such practices from their roots in the institution of religion. The dismantling of the linkage between bodily discipline and religion did not happen overnight, of course, but the demands of capitalism helped to sever the two more rapidly.

As Weber's (1994) well-known argument on the relationship between the Protestant ethic and the ethos of capitalism suggests, capitalism would reap the benefits of the insecurities posed by the Protestant faith. Aware of God's plan for the "chosen ones" but unaware of who those ones might be, God's followers could, at best, hope they were predestined for his grace and, in the meantime, act "as if" by throwing themselves into their work. Sober and disciplined workers function as clear assets in a capitalist context, as the presence of a healthy workforce guarantees high levels of production. Yet the values of health and bodily temperance were not merely promoted among the working classes most directly involved in production; such responsibility for physical health permeated the upper classes as well. In a context where many were still reluctant to accept scientific propositions such as germ theory and instead clung to the belief that intemperance was the leading culprit of disease and other physical ailments, discourse on bodily discipline and the avoidance of overindulgence found a captivated audience in various segments of the population (Turner 1982b, 27).

Starting with the target audience of the upper class at the turn of the eighteenth century, George Cheyne sought to address the social problem he viewed both among himself and fellow members of his class: corpulence. Subscribing to the parallel between the physical body and the machine, Cheyne proposed a system of bodily surveillance through his principles of "Diaetetick Management." The diseases of civilization, he insisted, were diseases of abundance, not scarcity (Turner 1982a, 261, 262). Whether the source was overcrowding, the importing of spicy, exotic foods, or the influx of liquor, the health of England's upper classes (i.e., those who could afford to indulge in these new temptations) faced a serious threat.

In addition to his recommendation of "a light diet, a regular vomit, horse-riding, and a regular pattern of sleep" (Turner 1982b, 26), Cheyne assisted his followers by developing a list of common foods divided into "easy" and "less easy" to digest for quick reference. Furthermore, he proposed a dietary plan that spanned the life course of the individual. The plan was one of increasing abstinence, a gradual cutting back and eventual cutting out of various substances, mainly animal products and fermented liquors. The plan for those who had passed their sixtieth year presented the strictest regimen of all: "to give up all animal Food; and then every Ten years after to lessen about a quarter of the Quantity of their vegetable Food; and thus gradually descend out of Life as they ascended into it" (Turner 1982a, 264).

The perceived necessity of monitoring one's diet extended along both the dimensions of place and time, as other proponents of a scrutinized diet appeared in the United States and well into the nineteenth century. Perhaps the best known promoter of dietary abstinence was Sylvester Graham, a member of the Northeastern purity advocates, a group committed to health reform in America beginning in the 1830s. Graham and his fellow reformers believed America to be in a state of upheaval and thought that the surest and most efficient way to restore order was through the reestablishment of authority within individual members of society (Sokolow 1983, 40). As a result, Graham and his fellow colleagues in the Northeastern group set about to conquer the triumvirate of vices in food, sex, and alcohol. Though Graham did lecture occasionally on the negative effects of alcohol on the body, his original program focused largely on individuals' sexual and nutritional habits (56). Over time, Graham's crusade narrowed to an exclusive commitment to nutrition and personal hygiene, as Graham believed that hunger, like sexual desire, could have deleterious effects on the body as it moved farther away from its "natural" state (100).

According to Graham, pure hunger only occurred in the presence of a stomach that was in a "perfectly normal, healthy, and undepraved state."[14] Consequently, the Grahamite diet aimed to achieve this normal condition of the stomach by promoting a modest diet that excluded meat. A vegetarian himself, Graham insisted that cravings for meat did not emanate directly from one's body; instead, the desire for meat reflected the development of immoral habits encouraged by the depravity of modern civilization itself

(Sokolow 1983, 101, 103). In her historical analysis of the Northeastern purity advocates, Sokolow argues that the promotion of vegetarianism "was not simply a nineteenth-century expression of a perennial condemnation of gluttony that substituted vegetarian arguments for a mixed diet" (121). Rather than serving as the latest fad diet, Graham and his followers' promotion of vegetarianism developed as a logical response to the latest understanding of the body. In a mindset that encouraged the perception of the body as a "self-sustaining organism whose sensitivity protected [individuals] against urban life," succumbing to the unnatural urge of excessive hunger through the satiation of meat could result in disaster for the human and social body (121).

Sex

Cravings for meat and other "dangerous" foods were not the only temptations that threatened to ruin individuals; according to the thinking of the time, sex could produce equally devastating consequences. In fact, many of the proscriptions for various food abstinences over time often have resulted not entirely from a desire to avoid the negative effects of the specific food but rather from a wish to squelch the sexual desire thought to be incited by the consumption of such food. The Grahamites, for example, warned that "overstimulating" food could cause excessive intercourse and lead to masturbation, both of which came with their own detriments. While abstinence proponents of the time varied in their opinions of which foods were especially "overstimulating," commonly cited foods included those that were highly spiced, as well as meat, shellfish, and all alcoholic drinks (Moran 2000, 7). Such fears were not particular to the nineteenth century. Yet, the climate of self-improvement in the name of social salvation particular to the nineteenth century allowed the fears surrounding indulgence in food and sex to further intensify and entangle with one another.

In addition to avoiding such culinary "triggers" of one's sexual appetite, individuals (especially males) were to abstain from "onanism"—masturbation.[15] Though physicians, scientists, and other social thinkers debated precisely how masturbation affected individuals, they unanimously concurred on its harm not only to individuals but to society as a whole. In fact, some argued that the effects of lust on the individual caused such devastation that men should not merely avoid carnal acts but strive to eliminate them entirely from their thoughts and even their dreams (Moran 2000, 5).

What was so devastating about masturbation and other sexual acts that one had to aim for total self-control over one's thoughts and acts even during moments of unconsciousness? While an increasingly open conversation on the Hidden Scourge (i.e., sexually transmitted diseases such as gonorrhea and syphilis; Pankhurst 1999, 134) and a greater understanding of and ability to detect sexually transmitted diseases through inventions such as the Wassermann test for syphilis (Fleck 1979) could account for a piece of this mandate of self-control, it alone cannot sufficiently explain this emphasis, especially in the case of masturbation. Prohibitions on masturbation revealed deeper social fears than the spread of sexually transmitted disease; the troubling question of class began to plague Americans. Not able to rely on secure and identifiable class positions (as in places with a more well-defined system) and threatened by the influx of immigrants around this time, members of the somewhat amorphous middle class sought out other means of distinguishing themselves from "common" people of lower classes (Moran 2000, 11). Science and the arrival of a new public morality extended a helping hand during the middle class's time of need.

The understanding of the body in the nineteenth century also relied heavily on the principles of a "fixed-energy" system. In such a framework, the body has a finite amount of energy, and overexertion by one part of the body depletes the energy from other areas. As Emily Martin shows in her analysis of menstruation, in centuries prior to the nineteenth, bodily secretions were looked on favorably, as they counterbalanced fluids taken in by the body (1992, 31). The nineteenth century, however, brought about a change in the conceptualization of balance between intake and outgo, as physicians came to view the body with the assistance of borrowed economic metaphors. Spending-saving metaphors replaced ones of intake-outgo, and with this shift came warnings of expenditure. The result, according to Martin, was a culture obsessed with conservation of limited resources (34). For women, the expenditures of menstruation justified their exclusion from participation in other activities of expenditure: the paid labor force, political participation, and education to name a few. Martin argues that this shift marked the first time where male and female secretions came to be regarded differently, as there was no analogous pathological process in males (34). Indeed, while the loss of fluid via masturbatory and other forms of ejaculation was not used as a means to justify men's exclusion from participation in the public sphere, such losses were nonetheless interpreted through the models of fixed energy and spending-saving. Thus, the same principles that were designed to keep women from entering public life and higher education also served to keep men from pleasuring themselves.

Physicians, reformers, and religious figures warned males about the consequences of upsetting the balance of such systems, and the 1830s marked not only an increase in the number of writings on the topic but a shift in tone as well, as the admonitions regarding the consequences of "self-abuse" became severe in tone. Most subscribed to what Barker-Benfield calls the logic of the "spermatic economy" (Frankel 2003, 308, 309). Sokolow summarizes this model: "Using an economic analogy, self-control, self-denial, and the postponement of sexual gratification were the biological and physiological equivalents of economic savings and capital accumulation. The reckless 'spending' of sperm led to moral and physical bankruptcy" (1983, 85), and the physical effect of seminal bankruptcy meant the loss of an individual's finite amount of sperm. Trudgill notes that, until the end of the nineteenth century, a colloquialism for orgasm was "to spend," yet it was unclear exactly how much was being spent (1976, 17). Unlike the developing dietary science that was becoming increasing quantified through measurable amounts such as protein and calories, calculating sexual processes was more amorphous (Turner 1982b, 29; Trudgill 1976, 27). While many believed sperm to be finite, it was difficult if not impossible to know precisely how much sperm an individual possessed. In an attempt to convince young males of the severity of seminal loss in spite of the uncertainty of its limits, physicians resorted to somewhat arbitrary calculations, such as that of eighteenth-century French physician Samuel August Tissot, who suggested that one ounce of sperm was as concentrated as forty ounces of blood (Moran 2000, 9).

Masturbation, in short, was serious business. Popular horror stories of the nineteenth and twentieth centuries detailed other possibilities, including that told to G. Stanley Hall, who would later become known as the "father of modern adolescence," as a young child by his father. As an installment in his routine lectures to his family on sexual hygiene, Hall's father recounted the tale of the boy who engaged in a sexual sin, became an idiot, and contracted a disease that ate away at his nose until only two holes were left in his face for nostrils. The story inspired such fear in Hall that he rigged homemade apparatuses in an attempt to keep himself from succumbing to any form of self-abuse. When those methods failed, he prayed furiously (Frankel 2003, 310–11).

But masturbation was serious business in another sense as well, that is, as a commercial venture. Hall was far from alone in his fear of moral bankruptcy and physical debilitation, and doctors capitalized on such panic. Doctors' orders came to include, but were not limited to, prescriptions such as applying "spermatorrhoeal rings" to prevent nocturnal emissions, placing plaster strips along the back of a boy's penis, and tying his hands to bedposts (Moran 2000, 10). Should such measures fail, doctors and the ever-present quacks of the era also specialized in the area of "seminal loss," and many young boys responded to ads in newspapers and magazines in hopes of reversing or preventing such dire consequences (Frankel 2003, 310). The effects of this draining on the body were not only thought to leave men physically weak, but could, over time, threaten their lives. Fear of the fatal effects of the loss of semen in general and of masturbation in particular led phrenologist Orson S. Fowler to lament that "few of [his] own sex wholly escape this snare while thousands on thousands die annually from this one cause!" (Moran 2000, 8).

While the fear of debilitation, the depletion of sperm, and even death through masturbation somewhat logically grew out of the philosophy of fixed energy and economic thought, such concerns surfaced outside the United States too. Across the Atlantic, individuals such as British Suffragette Christabel Pankhurst protested the wasting of seminal fluid and declared it unfortunate for individuals and society since the energy lost through such immorality could alternatively be put into other endeavors (Pankhurst 1999, 135). French doctors Fournier and Béguin also admonished against the individual and social consequences of onanism in youth, insisting that masturbation

> is all the more fatal since it strikes *society* in its element, so to speak, and tends to destroy it by enervating, from their first steps, the subjects who would efficaciously contribute to its preservation and splendor. How often we see these weakened, pallid beings, equally feeble of body and mind, owing only to masturbation, principal object of their thoughts, the state of languor and exhaustion to which they have sunk! (Rosario 1999, 139)

Common to these places was a social crisis of sorts. In France, the fear of a declining birth rate led crusaders to promote the conservation of sperm (Rosario 1999, 140). In England, social stratification was becoming increasingly complicated, as all strata were trying to distinguish themselves from those directly below (Trudgill 1976, 20). Similarly, in the United States, individuals were seeking means by which they could distinguish themselves in a muddy class system. In all cases, by rejecting the supposed libidinous and uninhibited ways of the lower classes and by exercising self-restraint, individuals could preserve their class and outwardly signify their social position in a society that offered few other reliable indicators.

Masturbation, of course, was not the only means by which individuals depleted their limited reserve of sperm; sexual intercourse was perceived as equally dangerous. Sex education programs developed in the United States in the early part of the twentieth century not only as a result of the recognition of the stage of adolescence in the life course and the rise of public schools,[16] but in response to the need for middle-class individuals to distinguish themselves from members of the lower classes (including the latest wave of immigrants). The economy of sperm philosophy combined with lingering Victorian beliefs that character had to be created, and the idea that the male self was especially unruly, ultimately set the stage for a program of self-control through abstinence. According to Hall and other theorists of adolescence, a "civilized" individual had the capacity to develop a system of inhibitions during puberty, and such a mark would distinguish him from his "savage" counterparts (Moran 2000, 5, 17).

The economy of sperm principles that guided the middle class during this era translated into the preservation of real assets as well. In 1798, Malthus had published his treatise on population in which he argued that lack of sexual self-restraint of the masses would lead to a population that exceeded the means of feeding itself (Trudgill 1976, 31). From that point on, the members of the middle class worked not only to prevent the economic collapse of the institution of the family but to distinguish themselves from the class of the sexually unrestrained and to prevent slippage into those classes since "unchecked sexual indulgence in a largely pre-contraceptive age could lead to financial embarrassment" (17). At the same time, it was equally disastrous for the middle class to severely limit procreation. Therefore, men needed to decipher how to "enter upon sexual relations with full potency" (Freud 1999, 142), but only during "appropriate" times. In this social environment guided simultaneously by Malthusian and Victorian principles, crusaders devised their detailed plan hinging on the economy of sperm as a means of assisting the middle class (males, in particular) in navigating through the delicate dance of when to abstain and how.

Alcohol

From our current standpoint, it is not surprising to find examples from the past where individuals promoted and enforced by law abstinence from alcohol. After all, we live in an age of "anonymous" groups—Overeaters Anonymous, Narcotics Anonymous, Debtors Anonymous—all of which model themselves after the original group, Alcoholics Anonymous (AA). As extensions of AA, these groups base their philosophies and prescriptions for recovery on assumptions of an addiction. In fact, the first step for any anonymous group involves one's acknowledgment of powerlessness to that addiction (Alcoholics Anonymous 1976, 59). In a time where addiction seems to loom at every corner and threatens to permeate our eating and drinking behaviors, substance use, spending habits, sexual practices, and other behaviors, historical promotions of abstinence from alcohol, arguably the original addiction, fail to surprise us.

Having said that, we should not allow our current dispositions to color our understanding of past crusades for alcohol temperance. In fact, the most noted and widespread push to encourage (and demand) abstinence from alcohol—Prohibition and the passing of the Eighteenth Amendment to the Constitution—predated the disease model of addiction. Rather than insisting on abstinence from alcohol for reasons of physical health, the movement of the mid-nineteenth to early twentieth centuries framed temperance as a shrewd moral move. Under this lens, drinkers were not sick or disease-ridden; they were immoral sinners (Gusfield 1963, 30). Charges of sinful immorality immediately evoke associations with religion. Religion did, in fact, play a clear role in the promotion of the value of temperance at this time, a point illustrated both by the name of a predominant temperance organization, the Women's Christian Temperance Union (WCTU), and their common practice of entering saloons and praying for their closing (74). In his fascinating analysis of the temperance movement as a symbolic crusade, Joseph R. Gusfield acknowledges the role religion has always played in recruiting leaders, rallying support, and establishing a moral code in American temperance. Nonetheless, while proponents of temperance relied on widespread religious principles to foster the development and acceptance of the movement, Gusfield argues that the goals of the crusaders had little or nothing to do with religiously motivated ends. Instead, as in the cases of dietary and sexual abstinences of this era, the drive for alcohol abstinence stemmed from a sense of impending social crisis, namely that of a changing status system (12).

Shaken by the effects of the American Revolution, which had left class an amorphous entity, many were further threatened by the settling of frontiers, the rise in non-Protestant religious practices, and the increasing number of independent farmers and artisans (Gusfield 1963, 5). Needing a way to distinguish themselves from other members of society, middle-class members took on abstinence as a means of marking their class status. As a status movement, the goals of temperance lay more in the interest of making symbolic gestures than in furthering instrumental goals (20–21). In such forms of crusade, Gusfield insists, "the goal is reached in the behavior itself rather than in any state which it brings about" (21).

Interestingly, while temperance began as a means of *identifying* the middle class, the emphasis quickly shifted to one of assimilation and reform of lower classes and immigrants, that is, to guiding them away from their misled habits. Relying on remnants of Malthusian thinking, crusaders extended the association between abstinence and economic prosperity beyond the realm of sex and into the area of drinking. Personal sobriety became the sign of respectability, as abstinent individuals were sure to steer clear of the economic ruin of the prototypical drunkard, immortalized in part by temperance fiction of the time. Organizations such as the WCTU had alliances with labor unions, and many crusaders focused their efforts on how to convince lower-class workers that the copying of middle-class habits (i.e., abstaining) could lead to economic success (Gusfield 1963, 45, 78, 81). Gusfield emphasizes that, while crusaders believed in the connection between economic success and abstinence, they shared their messages disproportionately with workers, not employers, who, under this thinking, would also logically benefit from a sober workforce. In presenting their case, "the argument addressed to the worker went somewhat as follows: Economic success is a result of reputability and efficiency at work. Drinking destroys both reputation and ability. Abstinence assures the person of his reputation and also prevents the decrease in abilities brought on by chronic or episodic alcoholism. The man interested in his economic welfare has an interest in being abstinent" (Gusfield 1963, 82).

When such assimilative efforts fell short, the reformers shifted to a plan of coercion. Throughout the history of temperance, there had been a scattering of legislation passed with the intent of forcing lower-class citizens to abide by the ideal of alcohol abstinence. One such example (and the earliest major temperance bill) was the Fifteen-Gallon Law, passed by the Massachusetts legislature in 1838. True to its name, the Fifteen-Gallon Law prevented the purchase of liquor in quantities below fifteen gallons. Clearly, this legislation played a role in curbing the consumption of the lower classes and poor since they were the individuals least able to afford such amounts (Gusfield 1963, 52–53). From 1838 on, legislation came and went, but the ratification of the Eighteenth Amendment by thirty-six states in 1919 and its implementation in 1920 for the first time prohibited the sale or consumption of alcohol to all members of society, regardless of class.

But coercion, too, would fail. As Gusfield notes, the passage of the Eighteenth Amendment did little to eradicate the sale of liquor, and many continued to hold anti-Temperance sentiments (1963, 118). Furthermore, the amendment was short-lived and consequently repealed in 1933, as the Depression Era "made issues of status secondary to economic and class issues" (127). Despite these initial setbacks, the later passage of the Eighteenth Amendment marked a symbolic "victory of the rural, Protestant American over the secular, urban, and non-Protestant immigrant. It was the triumph of respectability over its opposite. It quieted the fear that the abstainer's culture was not really the criterion by which respectability was judged in the dominant areas of the total society" (110).

The Importance of Framing

When individuals abstain, others want to know why. In fact, when telling others about my research, the issue of "Why?" was a top contender with "Are they religious?" for the most frequently asked question. Frames begin to answer the eternal "why" question of abstinence, as they provide a reference point from which we can begin to understand the choices behind individuals' decisions not to do something. Yet, individuals do not possess total freedom over the choices regarding which acts will be framed as abstinence and the ways in which they will be framed. In a society where murder is a felony offense and one of the most deviant acts one can perform, no one is impressed by my "abstinence" from murder, and most would probably scoff at the suggestion that it constitutes abstinence in the first place. As a felony crime and violation of social norm, everyone should not do it. At the same time, should I choose to abstain from a behavior in which most people engage, I must select a frame that makes sense in the context of my historical circumstances and cultural context. Abstinence must be voluntary in order for me to frame it as such; therefore, it seems ludicrous to make food abstinence claims for the purpose of entertainment, for example, in the context of extreme poverty and food shortages within the relevant social group.[17]

As we have seen, some of the frames have enjoyed a relatively short life. Although the entertainment frame peaked in the nineteenth century, there are signs that there may be piecemeal efforts to revive it. As I write this chapter, for example, David Blaine, one of the most renowned magicians of our time, has recently completed his public forty-four-day fast in a clear box suspended over the Thames River in London. When asked about the stunt in a pre-event interview with CNN anchors Thomas Roberts and Heidi Collins, Blaine stated that he thought of it "as kind of [a] performance art piece." Claiming that he "thought it would be amazing to see a human being framed in a glass case, almost like [a] butterfly that [he has in his] apartment," Blaine also admitted that the idea originated in part with Kafka's story of the hunger artist. Like the hunger artists of the nineteenth century, Blaine insisted on constant surveillance: "They can come at all times to see it, and it's lit up in the nighttime, and it's—it'll be obviously visible all day, and it's in an open space where everybody can watch it."[18]

And come they did. Many Londoners watched firsthand, and others around the world witnessed via media coverage. Many admired his somewhat incomprehensible abstinence. Yet just as many scorned Blaine firsthand—with eggs, grilled burgers, and verbal abuse—and, from afar, through scathing commentary. Headlines in the print media throughout the month-and-a-half ordeal captured the mockery of Blaine and his inability to impress others with titles such as "The Blaine That Nobody Noticed" (*New Statesman*; Thomas 2003), "Blaine Isn't New, Even Buddha Warned Us Against Publicity-Hungry Fasters" (*London Times*; Armesto 2003), and the one that most pathologized Blaine's actions, "As Headline-Grabbing Illusionist David Blaine Begins a Risky Survival Stunt in London, We Look at His Troubled Childhood, His Tortured Obsessions and Ask . . . Just How Far Will This Man Go?" (*Express*; Edge 2003). Thus, while it appears as though Blaine successfully completed his stunt, he was ultimately unsuccessful in his attempt to revive the frame of abstinence as entertainment.

Other frames, such as the religious one, enjoy a long history and show no signs of waning, suggesting their continued perceived legitimacy. But frames may persist due to the difficulty of challenging them. As the exchange I share in the introduction to this book demonstrates, viewing abstinence through a moral lens, too, remains a popular way of framing it. It is true, of course, that some people abstain (or do not abstain) because they believe it the "right" thing to do. But explaining behavior in terms of right and wrong takes us nowhere and precludes our understanding of how abstinence works as a generic process of everyday life since, as Dan Savage asks, "Who can argue with good?" (2002, 2).

The moral frame remains interesting, however, because it introduces the possibility of using one frame as a guise for another. Since claims of morality frequently and effectively shut down conversation, framing abstinence as a moral issue often glosses over evidence that the abstinence serves other purposes. Returning to the example of Porphyry at the start of this chapter, we can see how moral claims of rightness (in this case, not eating meat) can serve to separate, distinguish, and elevate individuals or groups over others. Consider Porphyry's words to Casticius:

> It is not surprising that *ordinary* people think meat-eating contributes to health, for they are just the people who think that enjoyment and sex preserve health, whereas these things have never profited anyone. . . . The *ordinary* person does not understand what is advantageous either to the individual or the community, and cannot discriminate between *low and civilised behaviour*. (2000, 51–52; all emphases added)

While I have presented these frames as mutually exclusive, they may operate better as heuristic and analytic devices than as representations of "real life." Frames overlap, cover up, and entangle with one another. Does this suggest their meaninglessness? Not at all. As we will see in chapters 6 and 7, how individuals not-do varies little across types of abstinence: abstainers from food, driving, sex, and technology may engage in similar identity strategies. Yet it is the frame that both answers the "why" question and distinguishes them as modern abstainers, different from their historical predecessors despite their common decisions to embark on a path of not-doing.

While historical accounts of abstinence provide a glimpse into some of the ways individuals have framed not-doing over time, they tend to derive from a history of squeaky-wheel moral crusaders and prominent historical figures rather than from the common, everyday practices of individuals. Even so, this history leaves us with a few lingering questions: What frames are no longer available? What (if any) new frames exist? Has abstinence, as Gusfield argues, lost its ability to confer esteem (1963, 4), or do others continue to recognize it as a legitimate identity decision? In the next chapter, I will give center stage to contemporary abstainers who engage in abstinence as an everyday practice—individuals who, while distinct from their predecessors, tell an equally compelling identity story.

CHAPTER THREE

Contemporary Abstainers

In the previous chapter, I traced some of the frames through which abstainers have presented and enacted their not-doing over time, including abstinence as a way of merging with Christ or achieving other religious ends, as a shocking form of entertainment, as a method of social protest, and as a means of social segregation. Despite their diversity in time, place, and motivation, these abstinence performances share the common element of using abstinence as an instrument by which individuals could distinguish themselves from the masses: as revolutionaries, as miracles, as exemplary moral beings. But there is a strikingly different feel to the choices made by current abstainers from those of their predecessors. To begin to answer the question of what it means to abstain in contemporary times, we must first consider what shifts have occurred in the ways in which we both understand and experience personal identity.

Much of the thinking surrounding identity in high modernity documents the exceptional degree of freedom individuals enjoy in creating themselves. Indeed, one of the hallmarks of contemporary identity is choice. In his discussion of the changing sensibility that accompanies a shift from traditional to industrial society, Daniel Bell cites a revolution in the way we conceive of the self.[1] In the former type of society, "a traditional man would say, 'I am the son of my father'" when asked "the classic question of identity 'Who are you?'" In contrast, contemporary individuals respond along the vein of "I am I, I come out of myself, and in choice and action I make myself." For the first time, we no longer have our identity dictated by tradition or authority, but instead create ourselves by virtue of our own experiences (Bell 1978, 89). Such freedom, Bell warns, may come at the risk of uncertainty and anxiety:

The sociological problem of reality in our time—in terms of social location and identity—arises because individuals have left old anchorages, no longer follow inherited ways, are constantly faced with the problems of choice . . . and no longer find the authoritative standards or critics to guide them. The change from family and class to generation as the "structural" source of confirmation thus creates new strains in identity. . . . But this change is, also, the source of an "identity crisis." (1978, 90)

This "crisis" results in part from the increasingly public nature of the self that began in the nineteenth century. According to Richard Sennett, up until the eighteenth century, individuals viewed public and private as distinct and held both in equal regard. While one could "make" the self in public, it was only in private that one could "realize" the self (Sennett 1978, 18). With the rise of capitalism in the nineteenth century, individuals found that they needed to shield themselves from the public and, as a result, elevated private life to a level morally superior to public life. Still, public appearances became vital, as the prevailing belief held that anything one did could signify what lay beneath: in other words, actions were seen as an indicator of who one *was*.

Contemporary theorists suggest that the belief that any of one's actions could "count" as a delimiter of "self" has increased anxiety and led to narcissism among social actors. Narcissism, according to Sennett, is not, as pop psychology would suggest, about excessive self-love. Instead, narcissism is about an extreme concern for and absorption with the self—both of which injure the self and prevent gratification.[2] Some reject the term "narcissism," as well as the idea that anxiety is higher now than in times past. Nonetheless, they believe in the notion of the self as somewhat amorphous and tenuous (Giddens 1991, 52) and insist that the openness of daily life means that choice becomes increasingly important as a constituent of self-identity. To use the language of Anthony Giddens, the self must be reflexively made (5, 3).

It is important to note that the element of control over one's self is not entirely unique to modern abstainers. Certainly medieval fasters, Christian sexual ascetics, and hunger strikers alike engaged in highly stylized forms of bodily control. Yet abstinence in times past was largely a deliberate attempt to regain control in the face of crisis and/or in the context of limited options. The unfortunate paradox of the contemporary and unprecedented degree of freedom is that individuals receive little guidance as to how to navigate the vast sea of identity options.[3] As Roger Gottleib notes,

It is liberating, but also frightening and difficult, that in our time people are supposed to find the meaning of their lives by themselves: to sift throughout a nearly limitless range of occupational, relational, ideological, and even geographic options and say with confidence: "This is what I stand for, what I identify with, what I will work and sacrifice for to know that my life means something." Our parents, the supportive ones at least, tell us: "You can be anything you choose to be." And they usually have no idea how frightening that statement is. For one implication is that if we don't choose to be something, we won't be anything. Our being something depends on our choosing and our continuing to substantiate that choice over and over again. (2003, 64)

Finding one's self in a world of possibilities, then, becomes "an exacting task" (Bellah et al. 1991, 19). The result of this identity journey without a map means that the onus of choosing a particular lifestyle as a way to give form to our narrative of identity lies squarely on our own shoulders (Giddens 1991, 81).

As we saw in the previous chapter, by the end of the nineteenth century, abstinence had become a "must" among various segments of American society. This mandate of not-doing led to its paradox, that is, that abstinence "was no longer voluntary; instead it was a coercive weapon of a social group whose own style of life was no longer ascendant" (Bell 1978, 64). This form of morality would soon be replaced by a new one inspired by the rise of consumer culture. As urban areas developed more and more over the start of the twentieth century, consumption flourished, emphasizing the need to spend and own, all the while "undermining the traditional value system, with its emphasis on thrift, frugality, self-control, and impulse renunciation" (64–65). This trend continued to gain momentum through subsequent decades, and, as Bell notes, by the 1950s American culture witnessed a change from the "good morality" to the "fun morality." Whereas at one point indulgence raised eyebrows and called for self-examination, the new morality suggested that the *failure* to indulge now did the same (70–71).

Though the overarching message in identity self-construction dictates that individuals can design their selves by choosing from a bottomless pool of options, apparently picking one option alone does not suffice. We live in an era where more is seen as better, where talk of being "*all* you can be," getting *more* for your money, and other phrases that conflate consumption and personal fulfillment reign.[4] Such ideology, however, clearly extends beyond the accumulation of "things." In recent decades, we have been inculcated with new terms that express the valuing of *doing* more (rather than merely *having* more) as well. We find ourselves surrounded by exemplary cases of "doers," ranging from those who are able to "multitask" in a given situation to those whose masterful doing has become a more permanent mark of their identities, those who "do it all" (think "supermoms"). Identity multiplicity, or the ability to be many things at once, then, is a relatively recent historical value.

Where did these changes in our sensibilities surrounding the self leave abstinence? The overlap between the rise in a narcissistic culture and a consumer culture—in short, a concern with both the self and excess—would seemingly discourage abstinence as an identity practice. Yet the connection is not so cut-and-dried. As Featherstone notes, although consumer culture fostered a distaste for asceticism on the one hand, it failed to replace asceticism with hedonism entirely (1982, 21). Instead, Featherstone argues, the total abolishment of asceticism lies more in the realm of cultural imagery while, in reality, individuals engage in strategies of what Jacoby calls "calculated hedonism" (18). Nonetheless, the cultural imagery regarding the reign of hedonism leads us to question those who appear to retract from it. To use an analogy in line with consumer culture, in a time when individuals can "shop" for identity, why would anyone choose to leave the cart at the door?

Understanding identity in this way unquestionably affects the ways in which we view abstinence, and those who choose to *not-do* become suspect in a context where the valuing of self-creation through doings is triumphant. One interpretation of the decision to abstain, captured in Gottleib's quote above, entails viewing these "failures" to commit as identity-nullifying moves, a *lack* of sorts. Popular thinking echoes this sentiment, as evidenced by strategies used by those attempting to convince teens to abstain from sex or drug and alcohol use. Campaigns must highlight not only the value of abstinence, but work extra hard to play up its ability to confer identity and not simply the lack of one. As one antismoking commercial touted in recent years, "I don't smoke because sometimes what you don't do . . . that makes who you are."[5]

Another possible approach—one not totally divorced from the first—validates resistance as a strategy of being while concomitantly pathologizing its origin. Popular treatments of abstinence reflect such sentiments in their seeming disbelief that abstinence can be a chosen identity path. In perhaps unsurprisingly sensationalist reports on abstinence, media stories rarely stop at mere coverage of the individuals' decisions, but instead probe further into *why* anyone would make such a choice, in essence relegating abstinence to psychological and perhaps even medical realms.

Some answer the "why" question by framing abstinence as a response of fear. While supposedly having the opportunity to make ourselves through various doings, we also witness the negative consequences of *overdoing* in the presence of a consumption-driven zeitgeist. (One only need look at the overwhelming number of "anonymous" groups designed to help individuals manage a variety of "addictions" of excess.) In such a context, it becomes easy to perceive abstinence as a panic response, an effort to gain control in an overwhelming world. In a recent *Newsweek* article on virginity, for example, the writers introduce Latoya, identified as the "survivor" among the various types of virgins ("beauty queen," "ring bearer," and "renewed virgin"). Latoya, we are told, "lives in a chaotic world: so far this year, more than a dozen people have been murdered in her neighborhood. It's a life that makes her sexuality seem like one of the few things she can actually control" (Ali and Scelfo 2002, 63). In another magazine published around the same time, a woman reflects on her own abstinence decisions in her essay on teetotaling. Initially resistant to how she believes a psychiatrist might frame her choice to abstain (i.e., as fearing a loss of control), the author confesses that she now concurs with this assessment, arguing that "it's harder to embarrass yourself while drinking a Tab" (Marx 2002, 148). The fourth edition of the *Diagnostic and Statistical Manual* (*DSM-IV*) for clinicians and counselors further fuels such perceptions by providing us with a host of abstinence-related diagnoses, captured by the increasing number of "phobias" and "avoidance disorders" (American Psychiatric Association 1994). If abstaining is not about lack or absence, so the logic goes, the avoidance inherent in it must come down to some form of irrational fear.

There are several dangers in focusing exclusively on the psychology of those who abstain, one being the potential elevation of individuals' not-doing to a master status of sorts. As historical accounts of abstinence offer us a glimpse only into the most remarkable cases of abstinence, that is, stories of those for whom abstinence overshadowed and trumped other ways of identifying the self, this assumption of the importance of abstinence may not seem far-fetched. In the present study, too, some abstainers speak of their not-doing as being at the "core" of who they are (Colin's term) through the use of phrases such as "abstinence IS me" (Lisa). Nonetheless, most echo Raven's sentiment that abstinence is only one piece of her identity, and that, while all of these things "make up who [she is, she is] not any one of them, but the combination." A purely psychological focus on abstinence also effectively removes the behavior from its social context and roots it in the bodies and minds of individuals.[6] A concern with the psychology of abstinence, then, renders irrelevant the relationship between the decision to not-do and its current context, and context, as we saw in the previous chapter, can be everything when it comes to understanding abstinence.

Let me be clear that I am not writing off the use of psychology in understanding abstinence. For many abstainers, a fear of losing control lies at the heart of their decisions to not-do. As the subsequent chapters will show, many individuals decide to abstain following battles with addiction and other bad experiences. For them, not-doing allows them to regain a sense of power over a part of their lives they previously perceived as out of control. Yet, even here, abstinence hinges on a rational decision based on past experiences and not an irrational fear. It is equally important to note that for many others, abstinence has little or nothing to do with a fear of any sort. What these individuals offer is an alternative way of understanding what it means to abstain. In this perspective, abstinence is not a lack or a phobic retreat, but simply one more viable choice among the range of possibilities. If it is in fact true that we hold responsibility for our self-creation while often lacking the tools and training for its design, abstainers offer a glimpse into one means of achieving a relatively high degree of identity control at a minimal cost.

Contemporary Frames of Not-Doing

While I have outlined some of the larger structural changes that influence identity in general and abstinence in particular, the question remains as to how individuals themselves frame their not-doing. Perhaps not surprisingly, one frame that continues to enjoy cultural legitimacy is that of religion. Despite an increasingly secular society, many continue to root their abstinence in religious origins. Another popular way of framing abstinence is through the lens of physical health. As a society moving toward the recognition of the dangers of excess, the appearance of abstinence as a health strategy becomes a logical outcome.

But there remains something remarkable about the ways in which individuals discuss their participation in not-doing. Even when they invoke religion, health, or some other frame, abstainers appear to be "good moderns" in that they overwhelmingly use the language of choice. This highly personal way of framing abstinence persists even in instances where not-doing appears mandated to an extent. When I ask Charles and Lisa, who are Jehovah's Witnesses, to what degree they feel their abstinence is voluntary, they both insist that abstinence is 100 percent their choice. Lisa tells me that everything they do, they do willingly. Charles, too, points out that they are not forced to do anything, but that "you're given choices, and . . . basically we're making our own decisions."

Why bother framing abstinence as religion or health (or anything, for that matter) if it is the case that abstainers, with their highly modern sensibilities, feel that personal choice is reason enough to not-do? One answer is that some clearly believe in the continued integrity of these frames. For others, however, such frames serve as convenient, ready-made cultural referents, tools for explaining their abstinence to others in ways now deemed socially acceptable. Marta is an interesting example of the combination of the two approaches, that is, someone who frames her abstinence from sugar in the context of health both due to her conviction that her body cannot tolerate sugar *and* due to her realization that such an explanation satisfies others without requiring she reveal what she considers to be more intimate details of her life story. At the beginning of our conversation, Marta tells me that she cut sugar due to migraines and other negative effects of intake (mood swings, "food comas"). Guessing this was in part due to medical advice, I ask her if a doctor diagnosed her condition. She responds by saying, "I never actually went to the glucose tolerance test because to me it was pretty clear that's what it is. It's kind of like going to the doctor when you know you have a cold to have them tell you that you have a cold. I mean, it was pretty clear. . . . It was so obvious that I have low blood sugar." Later in the interview, Marta reveals that she is also an ex-smoker and a recovering alcoholic, and, throughout the course of our conversation, it becomes increasingly clear that her decision to cut sugar was in part due to her reluctance to face her self-proclaimed addictions to alcohol and nicotine. In her mind, she thought the other substances were "not too important to get rid of," and she continued to drink in modified ways due to her new sugar abstinence. She tells me, "Well, at first, when I would drink, I would have grapefruit juice and vodka—not like rum and coke (laughs). I used sugar a while as my problem, but in truth . . ." For Marta, the health reasons behind abstaining from sugar are real and legitimate, but in presenting her reasons to me initially (and others generally), she chooses to present her abstinence through what she views as a legitimate cultural frame.

Others echo the usefulness of established frames. In discussing her past experimentations with food abstinences, Sarah says that certain practices demanded an explanation given how noticeable they became in the presence of others. Rather than launching into a full account of her reasons, she found that she could just state that she abstained for religious reasons. Sarah had no intention of misleading others, as her Judaism played a role in her not-doings; however, such accounts served to package abstinence in an acceptable way for curious observers. Jada comments at length about how others may demand socially acceptable explanations for abstinence and the use of "real" frames. Recounting a friend's practice of celibacy, she recalls that others had trouble accepting her decision as a legitimate one. Jada believes that if her friend

> said that she was a nun, people would still make fun of it because people still don't know what to do with that idea, but it would be a lot easier for people to come to terms with than, you know, that she has some eccentric Buddhist take on it. I don't know. I mean, I think that people are more respectful of decisions that are based on some like practical explanation of something . . . "I don't eat milk because my stomach blows up" [or] "I'm lactose intolerant, so I drink soy milk instead." "Oh, of course." But like if you have soy milk in your cupboards instead of milk because you just choose not to drink milk, it's like kind of odd, you know. People have opinions about that.

Maya provides an example of how using an accepted cultural frame can dramatically alter the nature of the interaction and the ease with which individuals can publicly abstain. When we sat down to talk, Maya was in the early stages of her first pregnancy and not visibly showing, so she was still at a point at which she could decide how to frame her abstinence in social situations. Though she initially wanted to wait longer to tell others of her pregnancy, Maya found it difficult to convince others that she simply did not want to drink. Realizing that most people care and are curious when others do not drink, Maya has decided to reveal her pregnancy in such situations. Below she describes how framing her abstinence as a health issue for herself and her future child satisfies others without question:

> There are a few people who don't know [that I am pregnant], and when we are out at a bar or restaurant, they'll be like, "Oh, you're not drinking?" I'll say, "No, you know, I'm pregnant," and that's almost like that's a really acceptable answer among a lot of people, pretty much everybody. But, you know, that's more acceptable than saying you're not pregnant, you're going out and you just don't want to drink because you don't want to drink. And it seems like you get a lot more slack and a lot more hassle, people bothering you that way than, "Oh, she's pregnant."

Maya later points out how the ability to use health as an acceptable frame to explain abstinence during pregnancy is a fairly contemporary one, as women as recent as her mom's generation could not have made use of such an explanation. In a conversation with her mother, Maya says that her mom told her that women of her generation rarely worried about intake levels of caffeine, calories, alcohol, or nicotine when pregnant. While only one example, the historical and medical shifts in our beliefs regarding appropriate times to do or not-do clearly influence the ability of individuals to use particular frames as ways to explain and comprehend abstinence.

The decision to present abstinence from within a given framework depends on a variety of factors, ranging from individuals' own opinions regarding a frame's integrity to its perceived utility in successfully managing social situations. At the end of the day, however, individuals insist that the decision to abstain is a personal choice made from a host of available possibilities. Regardless of how they choose to frame their abstinence in a given moment, all find that they continue to contend with assumptions concerning the motivations behind their decisions, their own psychology, and what it means to abstain in the first place. Given the history of abstinence over time, ranging from its periodic association with morality to its current relation to the consumption ethic, it hardly surprises us to hear not-doing framed in terms of both purity and lack. As we will see below, abstainers strongly reject the notion that not-doing involves a lack of sorts. On the other hand, individuals embrace the language of purity when describing their definitions of abstinence, albeit in a creative and interesting way, one that challenges our commonsense notion that purity is about "goodness."

Acting, Not Lacking

In the early 1980s, Adam Ant broke into the music scene with "Goody Two Shoes." Quickly topping the charts, the song became best known for its catchy tune and the opening line to the chorus: "Don't drink, don't smoke / What do you do?" Never revealing the intended target of the song, Ant tells us all we need to know about this person while capturing several assumptions regarding abstinence. First, the name of the song itself—"Goody Two Shoes"—links abstinence and morality. Second, by abstaining from both drinking and smoking, this person violates an expectation of doing. Finally, in a context where identity hinges largely on visible behaviors, this nonparticipation appears to constitute some sort of lack. Conflating abstinence with absence, Ant's "What do you do?" expresses both astonishment and curiosity surrounding this "lack." Why would one deny oneself such "pleasures"?

Not wishing to overanalyze a hit from the 1980s, I mention Ant's song because it captures many of our popular conceptions regarding abstinence, namely that lack, inactivity, and morality serve as the key ingredients in its makeup. Interestingly, however, these criteria fail to capture what it means to abstain from the perspective of those engaged in the process. In elaborating on their personal definitions of abstinence, abstainers are quick to point out what they believe it is *not*. Questions along the lines of "what do you do?" arise often, and most abstainers infer the message to be that they are somehow "missing out" on something. While there may be a "lack" of children to discuss at a cocktail party or no drink in one's hand at the same event, abstainers overwhelmingly reject the implication that their lives are somehow incomplete or unfulfilled.

While some individuals plan to abstain indefinitely, others anticipate "exiting" abstinence or at least consider it a viable option in their futures. However, even among those who find themselves considering the possibility of terminating their abstinence at some point, the general sentiment is that a feeling of missing out will *not* be the impetus behind their decision. Eve, a forty-year-old professor, sums up this sentiment when discussing her ambivalence about having children:

> I think it comes down to one thing and that is I feel no absence. I don't feel anything missing, and I always assumed that when one had a child it was a sense that you wanted to enrich your life in certain ways and had a yearning for something or a longing for something . . . just a sense that you are reaching out for something additional. I don't feel any of that. I just don't. . . . So I think that fullness, that sense that our life is already kind of brimming, is the major reason we haven't had kids to this point.

Denis, a sixty-five-year-old retiree who practices simple living (a collection of abstinences aimed at moving away from participation in a mass consumer society),[7] echoes this stance that one's life can not only be complete but "brimming" when he tells me that in no day does he complete all that he hopes to accomplish, leaving him no time to "sit around thinking about, 'Oh, there's this thing that I gave up which I wish I could do.'"

While abstainers resist associations between abstinence and lack, others may continue to draw the connection and react with a tinge of scorn at times. Jane, a childless woman, says, "I don't think of myself as 'not a mother'; that doesn't come into it at all." When I ask her if she thinks her self-concept differs from how others view her, she replies, "Yes, I do. I think others perceive me as a woman who is of a certain age who does not have children. In fact, I've been called a, what is it? A DINK [Double-Income, No Kids]. Do you know that one?"

An assumption of a dull, boring life often accompanies the association of lack. Georgia sums up her own experiences, as well as those of others, when she tells me that people basically say, "That sucks; that's not going to be any fun" when learning of her decision to abstain from sex. In a similar way, Todd, a recovering alcoholic and addict, says that others frequently ask him, "What do you do if you're clean? I don't understand. What's there to do?" When he answers their queries with a list of things he enjoys doing, a typical response is, "Well, I like doing that, too, but I like drinking beer when I do that."

As an extension of their frustration with associations drawn between abstinence and lack, abstainers urge a reconsideration of abstinence as performance similar to doings. Benjamin, an Orthodox Jew and Hillel director,[8] believes that perceptions of abstinence as lack rather than as active doing may stem from mere misunderstanding on the part of observers rather than a malicious attempt to mischaracterize. Sometimes this unintentional reading of abstinence may have further unsuspected origins, such as translation issues. To illustrate this point, he offers the example of Sabbath practices:

> You know, it's interesting because one of the areas most people define with how you keep the Sabbath is by talking about abstinence: that you don't do this, you don't . . . You know, it's true that you don't, you abstain from work, but work is not a real good translation of what you don't do. It, it kind of means using energy creatively. . . . It's really a joyous, fun time. But to the outsider, to the observer, you notice the abstinence.

The element of active doing seems logical in instances where abstaining entails overcoming some form of chemical addiction, as one must initially contend with physical withdrawal and urges to satiate desires one's body has come to depend on. Yet the work of abstinence is often not limited to these first days, weeks, or perhaps months of recovery. Individuals who have remained clean for several years continue to use the language of *working* the program (often Narcotics Anonymous or Alcoholics Anonymous), *taking* it "one day at a time,"[9] always *remembering* (so as to avoid "slips"), or following other strategies described with similarly active language. Ken, a thirty-eight-year-old recovering addict, describes the possibility of addiction "losing its patience" (i.e., leading to relapse) when recovering addicts get to a point where they feel that abstinence no longer requires effort. When I ask him to follow up on this interesting concept of an addiction's (im)patience, he tells me:

> A lot of people forget all the bad times, so you know, you need to go to a meeting [AA/NA] and maybe you need to hear a person's story who only has thirty days clean because their pain is fresh and you can relate to a lot of the things that they are talking about, and it may trigger your experiences. . . . If you don't do the things that you did in early recovery, you know, as far as . . . Okay, when you get that eighteen years, maybe it's maintenance, okay, but you still need, you need to do that.

Noting the distinction between "maintenance" and the early stages of recovery, Ken insists that the active resistance against old behaviors extends well beyond the time needed for the body to cleanse itself of substances, suggesting a performative dimension extending beyond the period of physical withdrawal.

Abstinence and Purity

At first glance, mention of the connection between abstinence and purity may seem curious given my claim that it is possible to discuss abstinence in a way that divorces it from moral considerations. The language of purity resurfaces time and time again in descriptions of abstinence, but it does so in ways we might not initially expect. While occasionally arising in the sense of goodness, more often descriptions of an abstinence-purity connection arise in a different context and rely on three alternative (but not always mutually exclusive) conceptions of purity: as a lack of contamination, as a contrast to an innocent state, and as a strategy of order.

Purity as a Lack of Contamination

The first (but least common) use of the concept of purity *does* involve an idea of abstinence as an untainted, unadulterated, or "clean" state. This notion of purity may or may not be accompanied by a sense of goodness or righteousness. It is more often the case, however, that such descriptions are devoid of any sense of moral standing. Those using purity in the sense of contamination rarely refer to spiritual or moral hygiene, but instead describe abstinence as a vehicle to a physical cleansing of the body. Denis, as part of living more simply, often fasts as both a means of controlling his total food intake (despite his love of eating) and purifying his body. Insisting that fasting is "virtually one of the most basic health treatments for people who have ailments," he goes on to note the positive consequences for healthy individuals, as well: "As I understand it, the body is an extraordinarily well-organized, if we can say, intelligent system, and so when it is deprived of a constant flow of nourishment, it uses its excess or damaging materials to keep the vital functions going." Emily, a Jehovah's Witness, offers a similar explanation of why Witnesses do not smoke. She tells me that "the body's almost like a temple. You keep it clean and keep it sacred, and by smoking you're defiling the body." While her language bears heavy religious overtones suggesting a motivation quite different from Denis' description of fasting, the ultimate aim of both remains a purification of the body.

Such rituals are not limited to the level of the individual. Charles, another Witness, elaborates on how this practice of avoiding defilement extends beyond individuals' physical bodies to the body of the congregation. The practice of disfellowshipping members, [10] he tells me, is a "loving thing for people" because, in addition to serving as a form of discipline, "it keeps the congregation clean." Yet, the body of the "group" may be less tangible than a church congregation. Kids who claim a "straight edge" [11] identity but later engage in behavior that defies its principles (by smoking, drinking, using drugs, etc.) receive a similar response. Although straight edge is not an organization with membership or initiation rites, the slang for one who later violates the standards of not putting what Jayson calls "poisons" into one's body is that of "excommunication."

Abstainers claim that others worry about "corrupting" them, a word that embodies this notion of purity not only on a moral level but also in the sense of contamination. While such associations between purity (as cleanliness and/or goodness) and abstinence exist, most reject the assumption that they engage in such practices in order to achieve some form of moral superiority. Ciara, who abstains from alcohol, tells me with a hint of irritation in her voice, "The thing that I don't like is I feel like people are very condescending like 'Oh, you're so good. You're so pure. You're so . . .' I don't know, and it's like, for me, that's not what it's about. I don't appreciate when people label me that way." Ciara is not alone in her disdain for such reactions. Shelley says that many people are aware of her virginity because she informs them but that others "can just tell" because they think she looks like a "good girl." She finds the term "good girl" ("whatever that is supposed to mean") incredibly insulting because of the heavy moral implications it carries. Expressing her anger at those who use the language of good and bad to distinguish virgins from nonvirgins, Kia, too, claims that she "[hates] that part of it."

Purity as a Contrast to Innocence

A second use of the term "purity" involves a contrast to an alternative state of not-doing: innocence. *Quantitatively*, at least, the states of "innocent" and "pure" appear similar in that they both involve "zero" performance of the behavior. *Qualitatively*, however, these two states have a very different feel to them. The arrival of an expectation of doing marks the difference between *innocent* "not doing" and *pure* not-doing. Innocence, then, as a nonperformative not doing, exists prior to an awareness of some expectation of doing. Subsequent to this "awakening,"[12] individuals who performatively resist doing shift from innocent to pure. In his discussion of the distinction between pure and fallen women—a popular topic of Victorian literature—Lloyd Davis offers the following useful distinction between the two concepts: "Purity is not the untried innocence of childhood, but the sustained virtue that passes unpolluted through the temptations of maturity . . . we cannot say of a woman that she is pure until she has passed through the fire" (1993, 10).

While abstinence appears to concern purity only, it indirectly relies on innocence. Retrospectively, innocence gains meaning in that its end marks the point at which individuals decide to transform not doing into not-doing. Some not doings, of course, never gain significance in one's identity by becoming not-doings. Instead, they persist as present but noninfluential parts of who one is. Consider Rebecca's response when I ask her if there are other behaviors from which she abstains. She says, "What else don't I do? (long pause) . . . I mean there are tons of things that I haven't done, but I'm not saving for them. Like I've never been snow skiing and I've never been scuba diving, but . . . (laugh)." It is interesting that she distinguishes between those things she simply has not done with those things she perceives herself as "saving for," the latter belonging to the realm of innocence and purity. Innocence often remains invisible while it is occurring because the acts involved are simply not yet deemed appropriate for individuals for a particular category, especially those of a certain age. As an example, consider the fact that we do not refer to children as "virgins," "childfree," or "single" despite their similarity (strictly in terms of the absence of doing) to adults in these categories.

Those who pass directly from a state of innocence to one of purity (that is, with no "doing" in between) often label defining moments as points where they consciously decide to continue along the path previously followed. The defining moment marks the point in one's narrative where the awareness of an expectation of doing enters and one deliberately chooses to resist. Marla notes her surprise when she was forced to realize at the age of thirteen that the possibility of sex "was starting to become an issue" and she had to make decisions regarding her stance. Sandy, also a virgin, tells me how her parents waited to have any conversations about sex with her until she was fourteen. Describing herself as a child who was a bookworm with few friends, she says her parents probably did not feel the "big talk" was necessary until she started "noticing guys." The word choice of "noticing" is telling in that it reminds us that these boys were present all along, but it took some sort of cognitive shift for them to come to her attention.

Raven, a recovering addict, elaborates on how her current alcohol- and drug-free state differs from the time before she began to use. Illustrating the contrast between innocence and purity, not doing and not-doing, she responds to my question regarding any differences between being sober now and the time before she began to drink. She says, "You mean before I ever had my first drink? Well, I don't think, I would not call it abstinence because I wasn't abstaining from anything. I just hadn't had it yet. It's like, you know, I've never had tripe, but I'm not abstaining from it."

Purity as a Strategy of Order

The third use of the concept of purity also entails a cognitive element in that it relies on perceptions of order. This final depiction of purity resonates with what Mary Douglas documents as the original use of the term. Douglas insists that our association of purity with a quest to avoid dirt and pathogens and to preserve hygiene (as in the previous section on purity as a lack of contamination) is a relatively new use of the term. Our present conceptualization of dirt stems from the nineteenth-century discovery of the transmission of disease through bacteria. This breakthrough in the understanding of illness and the presence of pathogenic organisms has affected us so much, Douglas argues, that "it is difficult to think of dirt except in the context of pathogenicity." She challenges us to rid ourselves of the association between dirt and germs and to revisit what she terms "the old definition" of dirt, that is, "matter out of place" (1966, 36, 35). Dirt, Douglas argues,

> implies two conditions: a set of ordered relations and a contravention of that
> order. Dirt then, is never a unique, isolated event. Where there is dirt, there
> is a system. Dirt is the by-product of a systematic ordering and classification

of matter, in so far as ordering involves rejecting inappropriate elements. This idea of dirt takes us straight into the field of symbolism and promises a link-up with more obviously symbolic systems of purity. (35)

Douglas shows how certain objects are not inherently dirty; rather, when they appear in places they do not belong, we designate such disorder as "dirt." Such examples include shoes on the dining room table, food in the bedroom, outdoor things indoors (35–36).

Just as we prevent disorder in these areas of our lives, abstainers struggle to keep their identities in order by avoiding behaviors, substances, and associations that would threaten the perceived validity of their abstinence. Consider what Lisa, a Jehovah's Witness, says about the need to keep the sacred and profane separate, as the profane carries the potential to "spoil" the sacred: "In First Corinthians it says that 'Bad association spoils useful habits.' So all these good habits we have, if you hang around people who do the direct opposite, *you're going to do what they do; they're not going to [not-] do what you don't do*" (emphasis added). Lisa's passage stresses the need to continually engage in identity work, to avoid associations that may challenge her abstinence. I emphasize the end of this passage as a way of showing both the performative aspect and difficulty involved in abstaining. Charles, another Witnesss, offers an analogy that reinforces Lisa's point: "You can illustrate it in a way that if somebody were to go out in a white suit and roll around on the ground, that white suit will get dirty before that dirt on the ground will get cleaned up."

While a sense of good and bad acts exists in the statements of these Witnesses, it is not the case that all abstainers put themselves on a moral high ground vis-à-vis those who engage in the acts. In fact, many abstainers criticize other abstainers for engaging in acts deemed inconsistent, reinforcing Douglas's point that purity is a process of maintaining a coherent system. While abstainers agree that abstinence must remain a coherent system of sorts, there remains less agreement as to what constitutes "consistent" or "inconsistent" behavior. Below, Jada provides an example of what she deems inconsistent behavior as she discusses her frustration with self-proclaimed vegans who occasionally eat pizza simply because they "like the taste." Jada tells me,

> I feel closer to a guy I know in New York who is like very committed to hunting and his way of living, his belief system, than to those vegans that eat pizza sometimes, you know, because what they're doing is backing out on the belief-system commitments they've made. People who eat meat always

think that it's like vegetarians will just clump themselves together with all the other nonmeat eaters and be like, "Well, you guys are bad because you eat meat." But I actually have more respect for someone eating meat with like an ethic behind it than I do for someone who is not with no ethic behind it.

The New Abstainers

There are many reasons why abstinence may change over time. First, while some frames enjoy longevity, many pass quickly in and out of fashion depending on the current social climate. Second, shifting understandings of the nature of the self may also influence how individuals perceive and experience abstinence. Finally, abstinence changes by virtue of there being more things from which to abstain over time, especially in an increasingly technological age. Put another way, with each development in ways to travel, communicate, interact, work on our bodies, and so on, we encounter a potential new site of abstinence.[13] Such factors remind us that we must not readily assume that abstinence in the present mirrors that of the past in either form or content. Referring to the case of fasting medieval women, Joan Brumberg cautions us not to inaccurately transfer and superimpose our understandings of the symbolic meaning of a behavior (here, restricted eating habits) in one time to the same behavior in an entirely different context. Whether examining fasting medieval women or those who abstain from technology hundreds of years later on the other side of the globe, we need to strive to detail the contextual *geist* of a given time in order to avoid misrepresenting the meaning and experience of abstinence.[14]

Ironically, in trying to identify the ways in which abstinence may be unique at this moment, the current zeitgeist itself reinforces the notion that abstainers try to combat, that is, that they are "lifestylers,"[15] identifying first and foremost by what they choose not to do. Abstainers express at least some awareness of the extent to which the current social environment, with its emphasis on excess and choice, may lead others to assume they lack something or are on some obsessively focused crusade. Their decision to not-do in a context where doings matter so much not only highlights their abstinence but makes it appear a zealous yet fearful retreat from the world of endless possibilities. On the contrary, the abstainers paint quite a different portrait of what it means to abstain. They illustrate how the decision to abstain can serve as one more way of being from among a vast array of options, a deliberate choice, distinct from other forms of mere "not doing." In this sense, then, these abstainers are thoroughly modern and narcissistic in ways that their predecessors were not. Time, then, matters in shaping abstinence at every step of the way, ranging from initial considerations and understand-ings of the meaning of not-doing to its eventual carrying out. As the next chapter will show, time matters on yet another level, that of individual bi-ography. One's experience with abstinence personally hinges largely on the point at which one elects to not-do. Just as understanding abstinence frames over time allows us to situate contemporary abstinence, abstainers' own past experiences and future expectations shape how they not-do in the present.

CHAPTER FOUR

"You Gotta Run the Whole Tape": Pathways to Abstinence

Preparing to leave the coffee shop following my conversation with Jayson, I feel energized and excited by what we have covered. Jayson is a straight edge kid, which for him means he identifies as a hardcore punk yet abstains from alcohol, drugs, cigarettes, and promiscuous sex and is vegan and pacifist. My first time talking to someone who identifies as straight edge, I am fascinated not only by the various forms of abstinence involved but also by the ways in which Jayson negotiates multiple not-doings. Eager to see the transcript of our meeting, I nonetheless worry about what may have been missed when the tape recorder was on, as his soft voice competed with the loud noises of the shop: televisions, cappuccino machines, and other conversations. Little did I know that I was about to learn the lesson that most interviewers do at some point, that is, that sometimes the most interesting moments take place outside the structure of the interview itself, often when the recording device is off (Powney and Watts 1987).

Two of the voices in particular I fear will overpower Jayson's are those of college students sitting at the table next to us. As we leave, one of the guys says that he could not help overhearing parts of our conversation and wonders if I am doing a project on straight edge. Less interested in my very brief answer, he turns to Jayson and says (with a cigarette in hand), "I used to be straight edge." Having learned Jayson's feelings about people who "used to be straight edge," I feel my heart race even before he has his turn at a brief response: "Adorable." Both men at the table hesitate and look puzzled, and I quickly initiate our exit before the confusion of our neighbors could transform into anger.

While this one-word reaction expresses his disdain for those who decide to "experiment" with straight edge, it also captures the conflicting interpretations between Jayson and the cigarette-bearing observer regarding what it means to practice this form of abstinence. For the latter, straight edge was a phase, a temporary stop in his life trajectory, whereas for Jayson truly being straight edge entails a lifelong commitment. Clearly, Jayson's perspective on what it means to be straight edge, its seriousness, and its degree of permanence contrasts sharply with that of the onlooker to our interview. As he explains:

> The idea behind straight edge is that it's for the rest of your life and that if you stop, like if you were to start smoking or something like that, it's not just like you're not straight edge anymore, but like you never really were and you were just confused. If you have the attitude that makes you straight edge, then that's just it. You're just never going to decide to do that again for the rest of your life. If you didn't, you know, you just didn't understand. Maybe you told people you were straight edge and you told yourself that you were straight edge, [but] you just didn't know yourself and you just made a mistake and, you know, you weren't really straight edge.

It was not until a much later point—specifically, when I started to consider pathways to abstinence—that I came to fully realize the richness of this brief encounter between the former and current straight edgers and to realize that their perspectives were perhaps not as irreconcilable as I originally thought. I began to wonder if the cigarette-smoking guy who "used to be straight edge" might have offered a point of view very similar to that currently given by Jayson had I interviewed him during his straight edge period. By saying this, of course, I am in no way claiming to know how the former would have told his story during his straight edge period, nor am I predicting that Jayson is "confused" (to use his language) and will change his behavior and attitude regarding straight edge in the future. Nonetheless, I am haunted by the possibility that, at some point in the past, this observer did not view straight edge as a "phase," something that he would one day in a coffee shop causally refer to as a "used-to-be" piece of his identity. Though I cannot substantiate these ruminations in any way, even their potentiality forces me to acknowledge the implications of narrative events.

In the previous chapters, I have explored how abstinence may hinge on temporal dimensions in that the historical era to a degree shapes both how individuals will abstain and the frames available for their not-doing. Our encounter with this ex–straight edger points to the importance of temporality on another level, however: that of personal biography. In addition to larger social time, individuals may choose to abstain at a variety of points throughout their behavioral (or nonbehavioral) careers, and these points gain meaning not only by the decision to abstain in the present, but through past experiences and future intentions. In other words, factors such as whether one's abstinence is a continuation of or break from one's past in combination with the expected duration of not-doing carry strong identity implications in the present.

While the coffee shop encounter highlights this issue of temporality on an individual level, it simultaneously illustrates that *how one speaks of abstinence in the present is precisely that* and perhaps no more. Though Jayson's attitude toward straight edge as a permanent choice echoes how most straight edgers approach their decisions, the high number of those who "break edge" coupled with our coffee shop run-in reminds us that, quite frankly, things may change. The possibility of change does not speak to a failing on the part of abstainers, but simply reflects the potential fluidity of any identity voluntarily elected. For this reason, though we may be tempted to speak of the "stories" or the "narratives" of abstinence, we must remember that they more likely resemble "snapshots." For sure, these snapshot moments refer to and rely on ideas about the past and the future, but they ultimately tell us more about how the present shapes our ideas about what lies before it and after it rather than serving as unadulterated glimpses in either direction.

While my larger goal in studying abstinence is to explore the commonality between abstainers despite variation in type (dietary, sexual, etc.), there remains something distinctly different between some abstainers that does not hinge on what type of abstinence they practice. Instead, the differences among abstainers lie in how they tell their stories of abstinence. The shape of these stories, in turn, depends directly on two factors: how abstainers behaved in the past and how they anticipate behaving in the future. Based on these dimensions of past participation (or lack of) and claims regarding intentions to abstain on a temporary or permanent basis, abstainers fall into the following four categories:

	Perceived duration of abstinence	
	Temporary	Permanent
Previously engaged in behavior?		
No	Waiters	Nevers
Yes	Time-outers	Quitters

These four types arise from individuals' own ideas about expected durations and may or may not coincide with socially expected durations, time tracks, and related phenomena. While socially expected durations (R. Merton 1976) certainly influence their experience of abstinence, their individually expected durations may be equally (if not more) influential in the construction of their accounts and the descriptions of how they arrived at their current state of abstinence. For example, when we hear the term "virgin," we likely assume the so-named person will engage in sex at some point in the future since "virgin" brings to mind a "waiter." Yet, virgins may also be "nevers" in that they may plan to embark on a course of lifelong abstinence. Though an individual who is simply waiting and one who is anticipating permanent abstinence share similar pasts in regard to the absence of any doing, their differential future plans may lead the two to tell very different stories of abstinence. Personal understandings of the past and present, as well as expectations regarding the future, strongly influence the type of narrative devices individuals will use when describing their paths to abstinence.

Narrative Tools

As with any narration, the stories we choose to tell about ourselves—our autobiographical accounts—are not mirrored, untainted reflections of our experiences.[1] Instead, we tend to present our story of self "as a sequence of unique, unrepeatable events" (Freeman 2001, 284) that progress along a linear timetable. Of course, trajectories are often neither continuous nor unidirectional, and individuals must resolve such dilemmas by selecting and highlighting events as significant in their narratives and by engaging in the process of "mythological rearranging" (Hankiss 1981, 204).

Not only do storytellers possess the ability to rearrange their narratives, they also decide where breaks in the narratives occur. Although not on the level of the individual, a glimpse into the periodization of history sheds light on the ability to create discontinuity out of what are in actuality continuous and, at times, overlapping events. As Kubler insists, any historian of narrative "always has the privilege of deciding that continuity cuts better into certain lengths than others. He is never required to defend his cut, because history cuts anywhere with equal ease, and a good story can begin anywhere the teller chooses" (1962, 2). Using the example of art periods, Kubler notes that, although Renoir and Picasso knew each other's work in 1908 Paris, Renoir belonged to the "old" class of Impressionism, while Picasso belonged to the "new" era of Cubism (1962, 56). Such curious divisions result from our continual efforts to "periodize" history by regarding "conventional historical periods as essentially homogeneous blocks of time and keep[ing] them separate in our minds, even if . . . they are actually contiguous" (Zerubavel 1998, 317).

On a smaller scale, as tellers of our own stories, we similarly have a lot of discretion in how our stories will unfold. Not only can we engage in mythological rearranging by controlling the order of the events of our story; we also decide how we will divide the narrative we create. Despite the fact that what we identify as beginnings and endings may in reality flow into one another and overlap, we segment our lives in ways that make sense to us. Narrative markers serve as one useful tool in this design, namely, originating events, defining moments (or "anchoring events"), and turning points.

Originating events are useful narrative tools in that they offer a sense of "when, where, and how 'it all began'" (Pillemer 1998, 71). Like other narrative site markers, they are often constructed retrospectively as attempts to explain one's current position by offering a point of origin through which one can imagine a continuous line to the present. According to Pillemer, such events "convey a sense of enduring influence and even causality" (1998, 73). In order to operate effectively as markers of beginnings, originating events must erase what precedes them through the cognitive strategy of amnesia Zerubavel terms "mnemonic decapitation" (2003, 93). In ways similar to those used by writers of historical narratives, mnemonic decapitation implores us to forget by putting into place "phenomenological brackets" that "relegate [prior] events to social irrelevance" and imply that they lie "outside the official [personal] narrative" (94).

Unlike originating events, which mark a clear and often early (in terms of the chronological life course) start to the path to one's current position, defining moments (or what Pillemer calls "anchoring moments") suggest less focused origins. Rather than serving as *the* moment of deciding to embark along a particular path, defining moments identify the site at which one's current trajectory is clarified. Frequently (but not always), defining moments imply a sense of destiny, a belief that one was headed in a direction all along, often unaware of one's path until this revelatory moment. The defining moment, then, raises the veil, sheds light on, or opens one's eyes to what is perceived to be one's "true" path (Traas 2000, 14, 15).

On first glance, turning points appear to be a variation of originating events in that they, too, mark the beginning of a trajectory. The difference, however, is that they mark a point of radical departure from a prior trajectory. While I use the language of "points" and "moments," such shifts may in reality look more like a process. Turning points—whether they are of longer or shorter duration—result in "course corrections" of some sort (Hareven and Masaoka 1988, 274). In order to conceptually visualize turning points,

Andrew Abbott offers the mathematical analogy of lines and slopes, suggesting that turning points mark the moment when the slope of a line changes, moving from positive to negative or vice versa. Nonetheless, while a change in slope is a necessary component of a turning point, it is not always sufficient, as Abbott suggests that a turning point often requires substantial time along the new path in order to distinguish itself from what might instead be a "minor ripple" along the old path.[2]

Though varying in their approaches and conclusions, researchers illuminate how individuals often rely on the past as a means to explain their present situations. Curiously absent from such analyses of narrative construction and others like it, however, is the consideration of how ideas about the *future* affect the shape narratives take. Perhaps this neglect results from the assumption that the future will be a direct extension of the present,[3] particularly if the present is thought to be positive in some way. For example, Traas (2000) uses the "coming out" narratives of gays and lesbians as the prototypical defining moment, the implication being that one's sexual identity has been and will continue to be constant over time. Yet, if, as Daniel Bell argues, an orientation toward the future is one of the central changes that come with modernity, then we need to take the future seriously in its ability to influence the present. Even if we construct a coherent past and future in the effort to gain authenticity in the present, this coherence need not imply that the future will be a direct extension of the present (May and Cooper 1995, 78). In fact, evoking defining moments to draw connections between the past and present need not preclude change in the future. As the abstainers who are waiters show, many individuals not only allow for the possibility of change in the future but anticipate it.

"That's a Never Have, Won't 'til Later": Waiters

Of the four types explored here, the waiters and the quitters receive the most attention in the literature on identity. Interestingly, in the case of waiters, the focus lies heavily on preventative strategies or what successfully helps individuals *delay* or *prevent* exiting abstinence. These studies often rely on samples of teens and young adults and focus on issues such as losing one's virginity, getting married, having children, and other transitions associated with these groups.[4] When looking at these individuals, rarely do researchers consider how individuals *come to abstain*; rather, the emphasis is on *how to keep them there once they arrive.*

As discussed in the previous chapter, the shift from innocence to purity marks the site where individuals become aware of the importance of a particular act or the expectation to perform. This shift may or may not be accompanied by a decision at that moment to abstain. Though individuals often remember their reactions to learning about sex, drugs, or whatever the topic may be, there is rarely a clear decision made at this time, as the issue still feels remote from their own lives. So while individuals undergo the shift from innocence to purity, they typically make a more deliberate, conscious decision to abstain at a later point in time.

Sandy illustrates the distinction between these two moments. When detailing her shift from innocence to purity, she tells me that she "had no idea" about sex before her sex education lessons in school. Not feeling satisfied by her basic lesson on sex (boys in one room, girls in the other), Sandy probed her friends for further information. Her friends, in turn, did not offer a much clearer description of sex, as they simply told her that what boys have and what girls have "sort of lock like a puzzle." Perplexed by the puzzle analogy, Sandy decided that she "didn't like this growing up thing" and that she just "want[ed] to be a kid again." Despite the shift from innocence to purity at age eight, Sandy's defining moment did not occur until she was fourteen or fifteen and a close high school friend became pregnant. Seeing the effects motherhood had on her friend, Sandy decided that she "[didn't] even want to play with that" and chose not to engage in intercourse.

Embedded in part of this passage but not cited above is Sandy's succinct statement on having to worry about issues of pregnancy and potential motherhood: "That's not me." These three words allude to the belief that abstinence may have been a part of her "character" that only became visible when called to the surface by outside events. This perspective consistently runs throughout the narratives of waiters. Also referring to his decision to abstain from sex, James tells me that it is only when his girlfriend initiates a conversation about "doing something" that he thinks "maybe I shouldn't do that." When I ask if he had thought about his position before, he says, "I think subconsciously the decision was maybe already made—does that make sense?—and maybe I just had to bring it up."[5]

Although abstainers characterize defining moments as one-time events rather than processes, other instances arise from time to time as opportunities to reaffirm or revise their positions. Such smaller, "intensifying moments" may occur on either side of what they identify as the larger defining moment. In discussing her decision not to drink, Shelley frames her behavior as abstinence—despite the fact that she is legally underage—since drinking is so prevalent on her college campus. Having originally reached her decision through the desire to abide by religious doctrine (specifically, "to obey the law of the land" as a Christian), Shelley remarks how her decision has been intensified at various points, such as when watching a family member struggle with alcoholism.

Again, while individuals often characterize these defining moments and intensifying moments as *characteristic of, in sync with, or typical of* "who they are," this seeming essentialism only applies to the past and the present. As they claim abstinence falls in line with their core selves, they simultaneously allow for change in the future, as they envision themselves engaging in sex, drinking, or otherwise exiting abstinence at some point down the road. It is precisely this openness to change that distinguishes the waiters from the nevers.

"I'm Not Going to Bother With It": Nevers

Whereas waiters have said "no" to doing in the past and "yes" to the future, those who consider themselves nevers say "no" to both. At first glance, these narratives appear to offer a simple, uncomplicated path to abstinence. Yet these stories are quite intriguing on closer examination precisely because of their "flatness" and seemingly unremarkable qualities. Unlike the waiters— who offer a past filled with growing awareness of expected doings, defining moments, and intensifying moments, as well as a projected future of doing—the nevers offer none of this. Their stories, in short, appear to be the Great Plains of narrative, having no peaks or valleys, only an unmarked and level surface.

What is particularly fascinating in the construction of these narratives is that the flatness does not manifest itself in a constant, driving struggle to abstain throughout one's life. Instead, individuals construct the evenness of these narratives by claiming, quite fittingly, that abstaining *never has* and *never will* require any work on their part. Though abstaining may be hard in a *practical* sense (for example, eating a vegetarian diet in certain locations), there is no mention of temptation or any consideration of exiting abstinence throughout the narrative. As a result, phrases like "I just don't prefer 'em" or "I've never felt the urge" run through these narratives. Unlike the waiters (who describe abstinence as a marked, pre-doing in their life trajectory), the quitters (who define it as a marked post-doing), or the time-outers (who see it as a marked "stop along the way" of an identity otherwise based on doing), the nevers view abstinence as an unmarked, unremarkable yet persistent part of the self.

As a strategy to demonstrate how abstinence is a "natural" part of who they are, some reject—in a way that rings of essentialism—the idea that they are capable of feeling temptation or being swayed. Others are more open to the possibility that their abstinence was "planted in them" in some way, usually during childhood experiences and socialization. Amelia, a vegetarian who has never eaten meat at any point in her life, discusses her transition to moving away from a situation of "forced" vegetarianism (i.e., in her parents' vegetarian household) to the experience of living on her own. She tells me, "Yeah, I could have strayed, and even now that I could make my own decisions, I would still choose not to. I have no desire to eat meat. Like the thought of it just . . . I have no desire to eat meat." The Jehovah's Witnesses present their abstinence in similar terms. Abstinence guided by religious doctrine may appear less voluntary on the surface, but, even for those raised as Witnesses, the opportunity to make one's own decisions regarding the faith and its practices of abstinence presented itself on leaving home. As Lisa tells me, "You can always make that choice. Even when you're raised in the truth, you're around truth or Witnesses, you still make your own choice whether you actually want to serve Jehovah. 'Cause you could actually grow up around Witnesses and decide 'I don't want to be one.'" Emily, another Witness, reinforces Lisa's statement, as she, too, believes she could have chosen a different path once on her own. Instead, she found herself continuing on the path set for her by her parents, as her attitude at the time was "I didn't bother to do it [when younger], so I'm not going to bother with it now."[6] This statement makes the interesting suggestion that there are appropriate times in the life course to experiment with or introduce certain behaviors and that if one fails to do so, there is little point in "bothering" with them later.

Despite an awareness of their choices to continue abstaining, the nevers describe how abstinence becomes a seemingly natural and invisible part of their daily lives or, as Emily describes in the following passage, "automatic."

> I think a lot of the decisions we make are subconscious. . . . We do things and don't think about it because we just do things. Because from the time you're young . . . you just learn from the Bible at whatever age you start. You just know this from the Bible, and it just stays with you. So you might think, "I like this dress, but there's too high of a slit and I don't think it's appropriate." There's a lot of decisions we make, and in the back of our mind it's because we're abstaining from certain things. It's so automatic to us to make these decisions. It's just a part of our life. We don't even think about it sometimes.

Again, Emily's point is not that abstaining is part of her "nature" in an essentialist sense of the term, but that the repetition and rhythm of not-doing become so routine as to be almost, to use her term, "subconscious."

"I'm Just So Over It": Quitters

In her study of what she calls a sociologically unique role, Helen Ebaugh interviews ex-nuns, divorcees, widows, retirees, and other seemingly diverse identities in order to develop a generic understanding of the process of becoming an "ex." The ex role, she suggests, differs from other roles in that it entails a different form of socialization and relies largely on one's past identification, the latter often resulting in what she labels "hangover identity" (1988, 6, 5). Despite the wide variation among substantive areas of their former identities, Ebaugh finds that the exes pass through very predictable stages, starting with a period of first doubts and subsequently moving through an exploration of alternatives, a turning point, and, finally, the development of the ex role. The turning point, however, "is a critical phase of this process, as it is an event that mobilizes and focuses awareness that old lines of action are complete, have failed, have been disrupted, or are no longer personally satisfying and provides individuals with the opportunity to do something different with their lives" (123). Quitters, too, overwhelmingly mention turning points in the path from doing to abstaining, but the language used to describe these moments suggests subtle differences between them. Colin describes his turning point away from drugs and alcohol as "coming to a crossroads of either having everything be great and work out, which they did, or blowing up." The image of a crossroads implies knowledge of both the journey and the point at which he needed to make decisions regarding the future. This reflection on his turning point is quite different from Asia's, as she tells me her decision to become a vegetarian happened rapidly after her mother killed and served a duck that had been given to her family. For Asia, this was not the foreseen culmination of a journey, but a moment when something "just kind of clicked . . . kind of a switch that went on that allowed me to see things in a very different way, differently than I had seen them before."

In addition to the use of crossroads and "light switch" moments, a third way quitters describe their turning points is through the language of full capacity. Marta, who cut sugar out of her diet ten years ago, decided that she "was just so over it."[7] Growing up in a household with a mother who did not cook but often took her and her sister to Mayberry and allowed them to eat ice cream for dinner ("mint chocolate chip with hot fudge on top . . . my favorite"), Marta reached a point where she felt she had had enough. This theme of maximum capacity pervades many of the interviews, as Todd often tells people who continue to ask him why he does not drink at all that he used to drink "a whole lot" by which he implies his past, present, and future will average out to a "normal" amount of consumption. Ken, also a recovering addict, tells me that he only "decided to do something about it" after he had "exhausted all means . . . and all avenues, you know, of getting high."

Even when individuals come to a crossroads, experience a revelation, or feel that they are simply "over" engaging in a particular behavior, exiting may not be instantaneous. While she acknowledges that people may become vegetarian overnight, Jada feels that this was not possible for her. Instead, she describes the process as a gradual "pulling back" from meat. Interestingly, she did not come to identify herself as vegetarian on her last meal of meat, but months later. She says that although she had "been in that phase [of not eating meat] for a couple months . . . all of a sudden I was like, 'Yeah, I'm a vegetarian.'"[8]

Jada's passage highlights a critical aspect of turning points often not recognized, that is, that cognition and behavior must coincide. While she engaged in what most would interpret as behavior characteristic of a vegetarian, Jada was unable to perceive herself as such until she made the complete cognitive shift as well. This narrative strategy of recognizing turning points appears frequently among recovering addicts. In a style modeled after recovery narratives associated with the "anonymous" groups, many of those recovering refer to hitting their "bottom," an intriguing metaphor for turning points, as the only possibilities are either to stay at the bottom or to change directions, so to speak, by making the necessary cognitive and behavioral changes to start moving up. Just as the period prior to turning points—that is, where cognition and behavior meet—may be characterized by moments of not-doing *without* the necessary cognitive shift, the reverse may be true, as well. As an example, Jayson illustrates how the cognitive may *precede* the behavioral in his claim that, while straight edge "totally fell into line with the way [he] was thinking," it was only after he quit smoking that he felt he had made the shift.

While the difficulties of getting cognition and behavior to fall into sync are sometimes due to personal factors, often it is the case that external factors beyond an individual's control delay the turning point. Ray, an eighteen-year-old straight edger, characterizes his cognitive turn toward vegetarianism in terms of the instantaneous light switch model offered above. Describing this moment, he says, "I guess I was like eleven at the time. And like I was in the mall somewhere and I saw a 'Meat is murder' sticker, and I really thought about it. It got to me, it really did." Yet, as an eleven-year-old living at home with his parents to cook for him, he found it was impossible to make the shift at this time.

"At This Point, I Just Can't": Time-Outers

Whereas the previous three groups gravitate toward a particular style of narrative, this final group of abstainers offers less stylistic coherence. While the pathways differ, most mention arriving at abstinence in an anticlimactic way. Some, like Carol, use the language of drift in describing her transition to celibacy eleven years ago.[9] A professional dancer who participated in what she describes as a very sexual climate in earlier decades, Carol felt a need to abstain after rapidly losing many friends to AIDS. Unlike some of the quitters discussed above, she resists the idea that it was a well-defined, clear-cut decision, but instead frames sex as "something that [she no longer wanted] to indulge in." She describes herself as "pulling back" from the scene, and she also is unclear about how long she will abstain. She tells me that "it was more like a phase. I knew that I'd probably get over it (laughs). I did, you know, but there was this eight or nine years where I just couldn't sleep with anyone, and that was my own choice." Her reference to "getting over it" signals her willingness to exit abstinence at this point. Though she has yet to do so, Carol feels that she would consider having sex with someone if the conditions were right. Still, in her mind, she has not set a timeline for her exit, as have many of the waiters.

Some time-outers describe their path to abstinence as a shift from *involuntary* not doing to *voluntary* not-doing. Beth and Ruth both currently do not own cars by their own choosing, yet they both recount a point where this was strictly a financial matter. Over time, however, they both realized some of the advantages of not owning a car. Both acknowledge the expected practical and financial pluses, including freedom from the expenses associated with maintenance and repair, yet Ruth points out the somewhat unexpected consequences when she says that not owning a car "almost becomes like a badge of honor" earning her (pun perhaps intended) "social mileage and good storytelling." Like Carol, Beth and Ruth expect to exit their abstinence one day, in this case because they feel that it will become increasingly difficult to continue without cars where they currently live.

As they say "yes" to both the past and the future in terms of engaging in a given act, time-outers offer a conception of abstinence not typical of the other three types, that is, cyclical abstinence. Though the time-outers interviewed do not explicitly mention the possibility of abstinence subsequent to their next phase of doing, it is not a far stretch to imagine such a return.

Thinking Outside the Box: Recurrent Abstinence

In the fictional work *Confessions of Zeno*,[10] Italo Svevo's title character chronicles his own attempts to quit smoking. Each time he vows to "never again" smoke, he ritualizes the last cigarette, finding a way to highlight its significance. The first "last" cigarette comes with the memory of the peer who introduced him to smoking. Some last cigarettes arrive during periods of illness, others at celebratory rites of passage (such as the one to mark his decision to leave canon law for science, as well as the subsequent decision to leave science to return again to law). Still other last cigarettes occur on dates Zeno has twisted into importance: the ninth day of the ninth month, in the year 1899 ("Surely a most significant date!") or the third day of the sixth month, in the year 1912, at 24 o'clock ("It sounds as if each number doubled the one before"). He soon realizes that "there is no lack of dates in the calendar, and with a little imagination, each of them might be adapted to a good resolution." He eventually gives up searching for the unique aroma and taste he believes lie in the last cigarette and stops calling these many cigarettes "the last." He rationalizes this move as follows:

> In order to make it seem a little less foolish I tried to give a philosophic content to the malady of "the last cigarette." You strike a noble attitude, and say, "Never again!" But what becomes of the attitude if you keep your word? You can only preserve it if you keep on renewing your resolution. And then Time, for me, is not that unimaginable thing which never stops. For me, but only for me, it comes again. (Svevo 1930, 17)

On the surface, Zeno's story may seem a quaint, fictional account of one man's repeated failures in his attempts to quit smoking. Still, in his ultimate institution of the "last cigarette" as a regular ritual, Zeno introduces the possibility of abstinence as a recurring phenomenon, entered often and sandwiched between identifiable periods of doing. Recurrent abstinence reminds us that, while these categories are useful analytical tools for studying how abstainers arrive at their current form of abstinence, they are not the only options. Taken alone, the four categories suggest a linear, forward-moving path, having said "yes" or "no" in the past and planning to say one of the two in the future. But narratives may also take a cyclical form. Though individuals' lives proceed in a linear manner chronologically, they may appear to "rhyme" experientially. The phenomenon of the past rearing its head into the present in similar yet different ways not only leads to a sense of déjà vu; it also demands the construction of a different form of narrative structure: the "recurrence narrative" (Zerubavel 2003, 25).

The stories offered by various abstainers, particularly those who have struggled continually with addiction, offer a more complex narrative than strictly linear ones by showing that, while the intended goal may be a forward progression into eternal not-doing, this movement more often appears circular as one moves in and out of periods of abstinence. Narratives of quitters hint at previous cyclical movement, as they detail earlier unsuccessful attempts to abstain. Quitters often frame such circular movement as unintentional and due to forces beyond their control (e.g., *not being able* to quit smoking). Yet, individuals may also *deliberately* institute cycles of abstinence. Jake offers a glimpse into how intentional cyclical abstinence might look.

A thirty-four-year-old administrator, Jake became a vegetarian when he was seventeen, so he has been practicing this form of abstinence for half of his life. His entry into abstinence was sparked by a 1985 album by the band Boston in which a few lines on vegetarianism appeared. The band also supplied information on PETA (People for the Ethical Treatment of Animals), and he decided to write to the organization for information. He tells me that it is curious that he decided to abstain at this point, as he was then living with his brother, whom he describes as a "huge meat eater." On his entrance into vegetarianism, Jake believed his abstinence would be temporary, at first thinking it would last for a week or so. He says that soon a week became a month, a month a year, and so on. While this is an interesting example of a shift between cells in the matrix (from a time-outer to a quitter), the narrative does not stop here. About seven years ago, Jake installed a vegan period that lasts from October 26 to Thanksgiving. Wanting to eat a vegan diet for part of the year, Jake chose this period because it precedes a period during which he believes it would be very difficult to abstain, that is, the holiday season of cookies and other foods he enjoys that contain animal products.

Yet Jake selects this period for another reason as well. Each year on the anniversary of his switch to vegetarianism, Jake observes "meat day." This day, celebrated with friends, is meat-focused, and Jake allows himself to eat many of the foods he claims to miss throughout the year, such as hot dogs. Despite the installed periods of meat day and its immediate successor, his vegan period, Jake's dominant identity (at least in terms of dietary practices) remains that of a vegetarian. In this sense, then, meat day, a period of doing, becomes the time-out period from an otherwise year of abstaining (albeit to varying degrees). While similar in structure to the time-outers, Jake's abstinence differs in that it is deliberately cyclical and the deviation is *from abstaining*, rather than *from engaging* in the act. This well-instituted cycle does not preclude flexibility and improvisation within it. In fact, when I interviewed Jake in late April, I commented to him that he was very tan, and he told me that he had just begun a disciplined exercise regimen of running. In addition to running, he was also instituting a two-month off-schedule period of veganism. Wanting to prepare for an upcoming trip to Europe, Jake felt it appropriate to improvise by adding another period of veganism within his usual annual cycle.

Jake's practices—more so than those of the other abstainers—allow us to more fully understand the occasional decisions made by individuals to abstain who would otherwise not consider themselves "abstainers." Though frequently invoked throughout this book, the distinction between doing and not-doing and between abstainers and nonabstainers is often a false dichotomy. At some point, all of us are likely to engage in abstinence, yet we often consider such abstinence to be "normal" in the sense that it is expected in some way. Often, this normal abstinence takes on a cyclical form. So not only are we not surprised, then, to hear that a woman is abstaining from drugs and alcohol during her current pregnancy, but we also expect that she will implement another such phase of abstinence should she become pregnant again in the future.

What is considered a form of a normal cyclical time-out varies, of course, among various groups, but it nonetheless enjoys a long history. Some matrons in ancient Greece, for example, participated in an annual three-day chaste event for women at the Festival of Thesmophoria. During this period, the women, separated from men, would sleep on willow to calm their sexual appetites, dress plainly and without make-up, and fast. Though most would assume the active sexuality of these women as wives, they participated in such practices annually in order to defy the stereotype that all unguarded women were whorish (E. Abbott 2000, 34–35).

History also provides examples of how institutions may encourage or require abstinent time-out periods. In his published journals, Thomas Merton writes frequently of the various vows of silence he has taken in his career as a monk. Capturing a lot of what it means to abstain, Merton frames this form of not-doing as active in some way: "It is not simply a question of 'existing' alone but of doing, with joy and understanding, 'work of the cell'" (1999,

249). This form of a time-out period carries utmost importance according to Merton in that "it is the cocoon that masks the transition stage between what crawls and what flies" (209). For Merton, then, temporary abstinence serves as an aid in the transformation from one state to the next. Though he charges these periods as constituting a "false identity," he claims that they nonetheless possess "a temporary meaning and validity" (209).

Many Christians, too, engage in cyclical abstinence during the six-week period of Lent that begins on Ash Wednesday and ends on Easter Sunday. During this time, some Christians will "give up" things they deem tempting or bad for them in some way. Lent serves as a telling example of recurrent or cyclical abstinence for a further reason. Though the practice of giving up something during the spring season of Lent is in and of itself a cyclical process, within this month-and-a-half-long period, there may be smaller cycles as well. Some of these "cycles within cycles" may occur on a weekly basis, for example. Therefore, while an individual might choose to abstain from sweets for the entire six-week period, he or she might also abstain from meat every Friday throughout the period.

A final example of "normal" recurrent abstinence is the New Year's Resolution. Each year, news programs, commercials, and individuals themselves all obsess about how to stick to New Year's resolutions. Perhaps this fixation stems from the high rate of failure people experience with their resolutions each year. It does not take a particularly sensitive eye and ear to see how quickly individuals' vows to "never again" engage in a behavior such as smoking or overeating quickly dissipate into a time-out period from doing, sometimes only lasting hours! Such rapid transformations are especially poignant in that they reveal the importance of the potential limitations of only capturing individuals' intentions at a given moment. In the case of New Year's resolutions, a dramatic difference may exist between one's practice of abstinence on January 1 and on January 2.

Those who identify as abstainers offer perspective into these everyday forms of "normal abstinence" in that they show how narratives can change over time. While abstainers as a whole do not come off as whimsical in their decisions to enter and exit abstinence, changes of heart do occur. As Jake's story illustrates, one's present identification can conflict with those of the past. In a similar way, those of the present cannot predict future classifications with 100 percent accuracy. As an example, Eve, who is forty and childless, currently identifies herself as a waiter, but realizes that in the future this status may change whether it be for voluntary (i.e., she decides with her husband that they prefer the childfree life) or involuntary (i.e., she is unable to conceive) reasons. The move from a voluntary abstinence to an involuntary not doing also introduces the possibility that one may exit the matrix entirely since an act of not-doing only qualifies as abstinence if chosen freely.

Come Together: Conjoint and Contingent Abstinence

Deciding to abstain entails a voluntary refusal or resistance of a thing or behavior. But the journey down the route to abstinence need not be one of isolation. Though the informants map out their own courses to not-doing, they enter the story of abstinence at varying points throughout their lives. In addition to purely individual decisions to not-do, individuals may choose to abstain in the presence of others in one of two main ways. First, individuals can choose to abstain in conjunction with another person or group of people. Second, they may decide to abstain in order to join a group or organization that demands abstinence as a prerequisite. The former path is one of conjoint abstinence, the latter contingent.

Conjoint abstinence generally operates under the principle that, when it comes to restraint, power lies in numbers. Granted, some individuals will choose to abstain temporarily simply as an expression of support. Though a wife may intend to return to cupcakes and cigarettes after her husband loses twenty pounds and quits smoking, she may abstain for the duration of his "toughening up" period, the time during which he builds up his resistance against the temptations these things bring for him. On the other hand, both or all (in instances where more than two people are involved) may possess full resolve to abstain. While such commitments are common among dyadic partnerships (and reinforced by two-for-one offers on gym memberships, hypnosis sessions to quit smoking, etc.), they extend to larger groups as well.

Like conjoint abstinence, contingent abstinence often occurs in the company of others. In this case, individuals do not abstain because they believe a group effort is a more powerful one; instead, the group requires abstinence for all members. More so than conjoint not-doing, contingent not-doing appears less volitional, and, as a result, not abstinence at all. Admittedly, the choice here differs from other types of abstinence in that one must accept abstinence and group affiliation as a package deal. The choice is one of all or nothing: group membership *and* abstinence or neither. Ray illustrates his decision when discussing his coming to practice multiple abstinences: "Well, I always like said I was never going to do hard drugs and shit, but pretty much I decided I [was] going to go straight edge. I didn't first say, 'I'm going to quit doing this' and then I said 'I'm going to quit doing that; now I can go straight edge.'"

Religious affiliation is perhaps the most recognizable form of contingent abstinence and one that often appears to offer individuals the least degree of choice in determining their abstinences. Emily, a Jehovah's Witness, explains that, while it is true that some things are forbidden practices within her religion, general principles guide—but do not determine—their behavior. She elaborates on what she sees as an important distinction between the two:

> Well, actually, when it comes to interpretation, there's really only one interpretation of the Bible, and God gives his own interpretation within it. It's not as if we have to read it and say, "What do you think?" He has ways that he basically wants us to live by. He shows us by laws, and laws are just black and white—you know, no murdering, no adultery, no fornication. That is very straight. You don't have to wonder.
>
> But then you have principles. Like the scripture on not defiling the body. So you reason on that, and that helps you say, "Well, I'm not going to smoke." You won't find a scripture that says "don't smoke." But those are principles you can reason on, so [you say], "I won't smoke; I won't use drugs or abuse them." And then you have a conscience. And we have a Bible-trained conscience because we've been studying.

But principles can become laws over time, placing abstinence again closer to the forced side of the elected-mandated continuum. Charles takes Emily's same example when describing such a transformation: "It's interesting that until relatively recently, as an organization, smoking was allowed. But after doing research and looking further into the subject, it was deemed that smoking was not permissible. So individuals were given six months in which to quit smoking, and it is an excommunicating offense."

Religions and other organizations that have similar operating dynamics can vary in the degree to which they require abstinence of their members. Some offer principles while other mandate abstinence without exception. In societies that grant relatively high levels of freedom, however, adult members still ultimately *choose* to belong to such groups and organizations. Generally, when they do so, they feel a strong commitment to both the affiliation and the abstinence itself. As Charles says, it is "really not a reason [to say] 'I'm abstaining because I'm a Jehovah's Witness.' One thing I'm thankful for [is that] as an organization we are taught *why* we abstain from things."

Telling the Story of Abstinence: It's About Time

When telling the stories of their not-doings, abstainers make use of narrative tools in order to create a past that is consistent with their present location. Yet equally important in this telling is the simultaneous invocation and construction of the future. For them, the present story of abstinence gleans a lot of its significance from its use to forecast what will happen in the months and years to come. The issue of time bears so much potency, in fact, that it appears to trump the type of abstinence one practices in shaping the ways in which one describes one's pathway to abstinence.

Clearly, some patterns emerge when considering whether one has engaged in a given behavior in the past and whether one plans to participate in it in the future. Specifically, quitters tend to use turning points to highlight what they see as a permanent end to an old self of engagement, while waiters opt for the highlighting of defining moments as a way of making their current abstinence distinguishable from a prior period of "innocence" in which one lacked awareness of what later came to be a significant act of not-doing. Those who are taking a time-out from doing offer less consistency in describing their pathways to abstinence. For a variety of reasons, they arrive at abstinence from a past of doing and with the intention to return to that doing in the future. Nonetheless, abstinence significantly contributes to their sense of who they are at this moment in light of where they have been and where they plan to go. Finally, having never participated in an act *and* never intending to do so necessitates little storytelling. Having neither a past nor a future of doing to contrast to their current abstinence, these abstainers produce relatively flat narratives. Taken together, these differences in narrative structure defy a tendency to assume that sexual abstinence tells a juicier story than nondriving, for example. Instead, the presence of peaks and valleys versus a level narrative without texture depends more on temporal location than on any inherent features of the type of abstinence itself.

Despite the fact that particular narrative styles often coincide with being a quitter, waiter, time-outer, or never, it is important to keep in mind that individuals may describe their paths to abstinence in ways that strongly depart from those of others of the same group. While it may be accurate to say that quitters are more likely to frame abstinence as a result of a turning point, for example, this is certainly not always the case. To illustrate this variation, Jane, a childless woman, tells me that her desire to have children was not consistent throughout her life. Unlike many of the nevers who express a lifelong lack of desire, Jane says that her abstinence marked a turning point since, at one point, she wanted "a whole mess of children."

Jane's transformation was not behavioral—since she and her husband have prevented pregnancy throughout their marriage—but cognitive. It was only when her behavior and cognition coincided that Jane recognized a turning point in her narrative.

Looking farther into Jane's narrative, the aptness of the title of this chapter, "You Gotta Run the Whole Tape" (offered by Todd, a recovering addict), becomes evident. Going farther back into her story, Jane tells me that, as the oldest child of a widower, she spent many years burdened as a caretaker for her siblings and step-siblings. Reflecting on this experience in light of her final decision on children, she reinterprets her previous desire *to have children* as uncharacteristic, rather than her desire *not to have children*. "Running the whole tape," then, allows us to get a better understanding of how people view their current abstinence as characteristic or uncharacteristic of "who they are." Of course, sometimes running the whole tape means starting with the present, as individuals express uncertainly about their paths to abstinence. While such narratives do not offer much insight into how one came to abstain, they still allow us to see how individuals construct the future as well as the present. Running the whole tape also permits us to see the other actors behind one's decisions. Choosing to abstain with others who share common goals (conjoint abstinence) or accepting abstinence as part of an affiliation with a desired group (contingent abstinence) also undoubtedly influences the ways in which individuals understand, experience, talk about, and practice abstinence.

Regardless of the degree of clarity in one's pathway narrative, however, all abstainers offer a glimpse into the process of abstaining in the present. Whether abstainers will continue along the path they set for themselves remains to be seen. Surely some will, while others will change courses for a whole host of reasons, perhaps only again facing their once-held views on abstinence years later in a coffee shop encounter. Nonetheless, when it comes to understanding the decision to abstain, on both a personal and a social level, timing is, in fact, almost everything.

PART II

Doing Not-Doing

CHAPTER FIVE

Determining What Counts:
Abstinence Thresholds

While documenting the "official" story of the sexual revolution in his 1973 book *The Rape of the A*P*E* (American Puritan Ethic)*, Allan Sherman includes a joke in which the protagonist decides to form an organized religion, the Great Institution of Man. (He elects himself God by a vote of one to zero.) He details the process of one of his first duties—issuing commandments—as follows:

I decided to only have one Commandment. I would make it not only easy to follow, but hard to break. Carefully, I planned it so that a sinner would have to go far out of his way to violate my Commandment—and even then there wouldn't be any fun in doing so. It was the most absurd taboo my imagination could produce. I wrote it down, brought it to the local stonecutter and asked him to carve it on a great stone tablet.

THOU SHALT NOT STUFF FORTY-SEVEN
TENNIS BALLS INTO THY TOILET BOWL.

"I'm sorry," the stonecutter said, "but I just won't print that."

"Why not?" I asked. "What's wrong?"

"I refuse, for the good of mankind," he said.

"What do you mean?"

"Well, my friend," he said, "if I don't print this here Commandment of yours, the world will never know about it and things will go along as usual, with the usual madness and stupidity, but nothing special. But if I do print it and your new religion catches on, do you have the slightest idea what will happen?"

"No," I said.

"Within three days there will be a worldwide shortage of tennis balls."

"No!" I cried.

"Without question. And by the end of the week every average person in America will have forty-seven tennis balls stuffed into his toilet."

"You mean the Sinners?"

"Nope. Sinners will have forty-eight. Hopeless Degenerates will have forty-nine."

"Good Lord! Well, thank heaven for the God-fearing people."

"Yes, they'll only have forty-six. They play according to the rules." (Sherman 1973, 125–26)

Though some may take this abbreviated version of Sherman's joke to be a statement on organized religion, it also highlights the sometimes arbitrary and whimsical nature of thresholds and classification schemes. Whereas Sinners and God-fearers receive their sense of identity by virtue of not being each other, the commandment of this proposed new religion highlights the fine line dividing them, a difference of two tennis balls.

Just as the God-fearers must keep their tennis ball count at forty-six and no higher, we are accustomed to rules governing our potential *maximums*, the numbers under which we are told we must remain in order to avoid danger or penalty. Signs on elevators inform us how many pounds or what number of riders may cause the machinery to malfunction. Speed limit postings remind us how many miles per hour we must not surpass on a highway if we want to remain law-abiding drivers. Cities often enforce construction regulations that limit the total height of new buildings. But lower limit and minimum level thresholds also shape our experiences. Sometimes these minimums are based more in nature and the physiology of our bodies, such as the point at which we are able to detect certain colors, perceive sound, or feel a sensation. Others are almost entirely subjective and individual, such as the thresholds surrounding the points at which we sense physical pain or discomfort. Still others appear entirely constructed: traditional height and weight requirements for specific occupations such as firefighting, the income level at which individuals become liable to pay state and federal taxes, and the ages that determine when people may elect to participate in a variety of activities, ranging from registering to vote and obtaining a driver's license to joining the armed forces, purchasing alcohol or cigarettes, and renting a car.

Despite their frequently random and capricious quality, thresholds serve the important purpose of establishing meaning by identifying at what point a person or thing becomes identifiable (and, therefore, meaningful), whether it be as a territory, a sensory perception, or a personal identity. Through the use of dividing lines, thresholds cognitively inflate the mental space between entities that may be quite close in reality. With the establishment of thresholds, we "see" the gap between children and adults (although a member of the former category may be seventeen years old while a member of the latter is only eighteen), the distinction between the poor and everyone else (despite a potentially nominal difference in income),[1] and the difference between weight classes in wrestling (while only a few pounds may separate the wrestlers).[2] As Zerubavel argues, "such a tendency to mentally 'stretch' distances often overrides even the ubiquitous 'law of proximity' that normally leads us to perceive things that are close to one another as parts of a single entity" (1991, 25). Though most definitions associate thresholds with lower limits, they nonetheless imply upper limits, as they operate together with the thresholds in the category above them in order to decide at which point a person or thing can no longer belong to a given category.

When it comes to abstinence, thresholds seem nonnegotiable and perhaps even irrelevant. After all, common sense tells us that, in numeric terms, abstinence means an absolute zero. We assume that both the lower and upper limits of abstinence lie squarely at zero and that the line distinguishing abstainers from nonabstainers falls between doing something zero times and doing it once. Like the difference between forty-six and forty-eight tennis balls, this space remains rather small, but we assign great importance to it, assuming that one instance of doing threatens to expel someone from the category of not-doers. In this sense, then, the space between zero and one has a larger feel to us than that of other comparable metric spaces.[3] Whereas the difference between doing something eight versus nine times or two thousand versus two thousand and one times may pass unnoticed, crossing over from never doing something to doing it for the first time[4] may bring with it a sense of change ranging, at a minimum, from a noticeable transformation to, in some instances, a permanent, irreversible alteration of status (Mullaney 1999, 5). In short, we believe the move from zero to one strips us of our behavioral virginity in a literal or figurative way.

When abstainers define their abstinence, they, too, highlight the space between zero and one as the threshold at which the site of transformation resides. In a way that is consistent with Mary Douglas's (1966) theme of achieving cognitive ordering and creating coherence in a system, most abstainers have a clear sense of what would be "going too far" or violating a sense of order in regard to their identities. Yet, the language of "going too far" evokes the imagery of travel and movement, a curious and seemingly inconsistent notion within the concept of abstinence. A discussion of what counts as abstinence may appear odd or even moot. After all, abstinence, in the strictest definition of the term, entails stasis, in that any move toward doing nullifies its credibility. Or does it?

The insistence that one can go too far in not-doing (or doing for that matter) suggests that there may be room for creative license in defining abstinence, and, indeed, individuals evaluate what counts as abstinence in two distinct ways. For some, not-doing lies exclusively in the narrow set point of zero where *any* doing disqualifies one's claim to abstinence. They insist that abstinence must entail the absolute *absence* of doing. For others, the space between zero and one affords the opportunity for playing creatively, for stretching the boundaries of abstinence while maintaining its integrity, thereby allowing for a lot of flexibility in terms of performing abstinence.

The difference between these two conceptualizations can be thought of as the contrast between abstinence as a point and abstinence as a zone. This distinction between abstinence as a set point versus abstinence as a zone is *not* inconsequential. As subsequent chapters will show, how one defines what "counts" as abstinence bears critical influence on how abstainers report performing or "doing" not-doing. The story does not end at the level of personal interpretation, however. While individuals' definitions surely impact the ways in which they perform abstinence, abstinent thresholds need not always and only fall between zero and one. Experiences with observers to abstinence, as well as institutionalized thresholds, can also determine what successfully qualifies as "real" abstinence. Thus, our commonsense notions may fail us. Entering abstinence and maintaining its integrity may at times be more complicated than the binary distinction between zero and one, doing and not-doing, suggests at first glance.

Abstinence as Point

If we conceptualize behavior in simple numeric terms, it may seem that abstinence would have the value 0 while any doing would qualify as a positive integer of 1 or higher. Those who believe abstinence is a set point adopt precisely this point of view. For them, behavior can be translated into integers that represent the degree of doing, and abstinence, in order to stay meaningful, must reside at zero. Assigning abstinence a value of 0 may appear to revert to the association between abstinence and lack, but individuals who take this perspective view zero solely as a description of the absolute absence of behavior devoid of the judgment associated with the concept of lack. Under this conceptualization, the difference between doing and not-doing becomes a binary distinction between black and white, and any doing threatens to expel individuals from the realm of not-doing. Such rigid notions in principle leave no room for experimentation with doing, time-out periods from abstinence, or other moments of exception. When an individual engages in an act of doing within such a framework, she or he becomes a "hypocrite," behaving in an "inconsistent" way with little or no possibility of writing off the behavior, excusing it, justifying it, or accounting for it in some other way.[5]

As an example of someone who defines abstinence in this manner, Marta believes that abstaining from smoking and drinking means completely refraining from such acts and often feels disappointed when people tell her that they "don't drink" but order a beer at a bar or have a drink on "special" occasions. Ciara offers an even stronger emotional reaction to such contradictory behavior, saying it "so pisses [her] off." Though she realizes that others may not support her views, as she is "just being very extreme and very literal," she elaborates on the rationale behind her position: "In theory, if someone were saying, 'Oh, I don't drink, but I have a sip here and there' or whatever, to me that's not abstaining. That's just drinking infrequently or whatever . . . I feel like if you're saying that you don't do something then you never do it." Bruce initially appears to disagree with such a literal definition of abstinence when he answers my question as to whether one can smoke once in a while and still make valid claims that one is abstinent with "I guess." Nonetheless, he quickly follows up with, "Well, it depends on what you mean by abstinence, which is . . . by definition it means you don't do it, right? You could do it once in a while, but you're not really abstaining." Many other abstainers feel similarly in that they see those who claim to be abstinent while engaging in the behavior from time to time as "kind of lying" (Ray's language).

Classifying behavior as either abstinent or not reflects what Eviatar Zerubavel terms "rigid-mindedness." Those who see the world through the lens of rigidity adhere to a system of mutually exclusive categorization; in short, an object, person, geographic region, or any other entity may belong to category A *or* B, but under no conditions to both. Such an approach in effect "segregate[s] islands of meaning from one another so as to preserve their insular character" and results in the process of creating "discrete 'mental ghettos' that never 'touch' one another" (Zerubavel 1991, 34). Colin sums up the rigid-minded, point approach to abstinence when he tells me, "If someone says they are abstinent, they either are or they aren't. It's very binary. Anything else is a description . . . it's either a hypocritical description or it's a description of moderation."

Abstinence as Zone

In the second conceptualization of what counts as abstinence, individuals express skepticism toward the binary, black-and-white approach and instead offer a glimpse into shades of gray. In other words, while binary thinkers cling to the zero pole as the home of abstinence, these more flexible thinkers recognize the space *between* zero and one. Though they validate the "true" abstinence of complete not-doing, they challenge the notion that whole integers alone can capture the full meaning of behavior. Whereas the first conceptualization of abstinence plays up the poles of zero and one, acknowledging the space in between as useful only in its ability to separate the two, those who see abstinence as a zone give center stage to that space, highlighting the gradations on the way from one ideal-typical pole to the next. This difference becomes one of decimals over whole numbers. Rather than believing that only an absolute zero constitutes a legitimate claim to abstinence, here the range from 0 to .9999 . . . may qualify.

Adopting this more fluid, gray, and negotiable approach to abstinence opens up the possibilities for what constitutes legitimate not-doing and allows individuals to engage in acts that would unquestionably expel them from abstinence under the former, point conceptualization of not-doing. These abstainers provide themselves, then, with the potential to practice abstinence between the poles rather than forcing themselves to cling to one side of the continuum. To give a dietary example, on occasion some abstainers will allow things they normally would not eat or drink to enter their diets if the percentage (or frequency of doing) is small. For example, abstainers might on occasion eat a dessert with a small percentage of alcohol in it or eat something that has been cooked in wine (despite an alcohol abstinence) or, say—as Jayson does about once a week—"ah, fuck it" if "something says it has less than 2 percent eggs in it" (despite an abstinence from all animal products).

Abstainers also note how this more flexible approach operates in a qualitative sense as well. In addition to playing with the percentages of egg or alcohol in a product, some abstainers also show some signs of leniency and creativity in terms of establishing what *types* of acts will not violate the integrity of their abstinence. For example, someone with a binary conception of doing and not-doing might lump various sexual acts such as oral sex, anal sex, and vaginal intercourse under the category "sex," and thus would not consider someone who engages in any of these acts sexually "abstinent." In contrast, those who recognize degrees or even some form of hierarchy within sexuality institute a system that allows them to participate in oral sex, for example, while remaining "virgins."[6] Beth illustrates this alternate perspective when she admits that, despite her own refusal to own a car as a way to slow down the pace of life, she will borrow the car of a friend and drive on occasion. In her mind this is not hypocritical since she proclaims that she has not "committed [herself] to never trying to get anywhere except on public transportation or walking." Similarly, when asked about other abstinences, Bruce insists that he does not take "hard" drugs, drawing a line that separates marijuana and mushrooms from all other drugs.

Abstainers also realize that others of the same type (e.g., virgins, non-smokers, recovering addicts) may define not-doing in different ways, as others may have varying criteria.[7] Asia, for example, realizes that some vegetarians will not use dairy or wear fabrics such as wool, leather, or silk; however, she has a complicated fit in this scheme. Though she does drink soy milk, she tells me, "I don't plan to give up half-and-half. I like that in my coffee." She also does not wear much leather, but finds that she must often buy leather shoes because she has exceptionally small feet. Finally, she tells me that "*of course*" (her words, my emphasis) she does not have fur, but that she does wear wool.

This flexibility in terms of both quantity and quality stands in stark contrast to the rigidity of the abstinence-as-point perspective. Rather than forcing particular behaviors into set categories of abstinent or not, those with flexible mindsets allow for the possibility of a "plastic notion of meaning" and avoid "freezing entities [or behaviors] in any one mental context by assigning them fixed meanings."[8] Still, it is important to point out that flexibility does not imply the complete lack of any parameters or boundaries. Like most zones, lower and upper limits exist. Applied to abstinence, those who operate somewhere in the space between zero and one still believe there is a point at which one can no longer claim abstinence; yet, as Lineya tells me, "that's your own choice where you draw that line." Furthermore, where one draws this line can vary within an individual's own abstinence over time. Sarah, a virgin, offers a nice generic glimpse into the nuances within the space between doing and not-doing, while explaining her changing views about what "counts" as abstinence. She says, "It's just that I took it a few steps forward and then I took a few steps back. And I'm still changing, and I think I will always change, but that's where it is right now."

Abstainers range from playing with their lines on a regular basis to changing them gradually over time to not moving them at all. Such decisions hinge not necessarily on the degree of seriousness in their commitments to abstinence but instead on their feelings regarding a given abstinence. We can clearly see the effects of one's perceptions on a certain type of abstinence among those who are multiple or "polygamous" abstainers. Jayson's willingness to say "fuck it" when eating a product with a small percentage of eggs in it at first glance seems to correspond to his claims at other points in our conversation that he is "not going for this unrealistic, ridiculous ideal of purity" and that "the ideal . . . is to do the most that you can." Yet when we discuss some of his other abstinences, he flips to the binary conceptualization of behavior, insisting, for example, that even one puff of a cigarette would preclude his ability to assert a straight edge identity. Lines serve as necessary tools as he moves back and forth from viewing abstinence as a point and as a zone according to the abstinence. The difference between the two conceptualizations, then, lies not in the willingness or unwillingness to draw lines—both perspectives necessitate the drawing of lines—but, rather, in the placement of and the degree to which one will negotiate those boundaries.

Alternative Thresholds

Abstainers vary in terms of where exactly they pinpoint the threshold of abstinence; nonetheless, whether they adhere to the point or zone approach, they all agree that this threshold lies somewhere between zero and one. Yet, the importance of thresholds extends beyond the actual carrying out of abstinence. Experiences with outsiders to abstinence suggest that what counts as abstinence and the ability to be a convincing abstainer are not totally solo acts, as they are often determined in part by others. Furthermore, these experiences suggest that *entrances* to abstinence—whether one has engaged in the behavior before (a "quitter" or "time-outer") or not (a "never" or a "waiter")—sometimes do not gain legitimacy unless the person has crossed a threshold of a different sort.

While many abstainers, especially those who conceive of abstinence as a point, feel that doing to any extent would spoil their abstinent identities, others imply that at times certain doings will carry no permanent identity implications. In fact, abstainers claim that others invite them to "try" a given act. At first glance, we may mistake such invitations as attempts to taint or nullify an individual's claim to abstinence. Yet, the language of *trying* suggests reversibility and the possibility of later returning to abstinence. "Just try it" encounters are common with those who have never engaged in a particular act (that is, "waiters" and "nevers"), the implication being that one cannot make informed decisions about what one prefers *not* to do if one has never tried it in the first place.

In one vein, this sort of reaction suggests that the type of substance, act, et cetera that one tries may allow one to safely experiment without ill effects on one's abstinence. In suggesting this, others may also make implications about where the specific parameters lie *quantitatively*. Specifically, the language of "trying" often comes with an emphasis on *one* rather than multiples. Shelley and Ciara, who both abstain from alcohol, claim that others often try to convince them to drink with phrases such as "Not just once?" and "Oh, come on, just one," respectively. The insinuation here, of course, is that one time is no big deal in the larger scheme of abstinence. Of course, the type of abstinence practiced directly influences the responses of others, as limits remain on the ability to convincingly use the language of experimentation with particular forms. So while someone may tell a non–sugar eater to try a sweet just one time, the same language would sound ludicrous to someone who is childless or a virgin, as we perceive exits from this form of abstinence to be largely unidirectional and irreversible. Thus, while the tactics available to others vary, they are limited and further constrained by larger social understandings of the specific abstinent identity—understandings that may entirely preclude the possibility of experimentation.

While many observers to abstinence urge individuals to try something one time, others push abstainers to engage in an act more than one time or insist that larger amounts (e.g., more than one bite, sip, etc.) will not adversely ruin one's abstinence. So while Debbie says that others often tell her to have *a* drink, at times they go so far as to say, "Have *some*." In other instances, the focus lies not on amount (a quantitative measure) but on the type of act (a qualitative one). Shelley recounts one incident where others tried to convince her that *what* she drank rather than *how much* would allow her to engage in drinking without tainting her abstinence. In this situation, someone told her explicitly that drinking would not affect her, as she would be drinking *lite* beer! Such offers to engage in what is seen as alternate or less potent ways of doing clearly raise the issue of what counts as abstinence (or what would disqualify one from claiming such an identity) in a qualitative sense rather than a strictly numeric one.

Regardless of whether the emphasis is on amount or type, attempts to convince an abstainer to try something complicate our understanding of the abstinence threshold. Whereas abstainers identify the most significant distinction between doing and not-doing as the difference between doing something zero versus one time, audiences to abstinence performances suggest that the threshold may lie elsewhere. For example, the insistence that one must try an act at least once in order to make a convincing and informed decision to abstain suggests that some perceive the line between doing and not-doing as falling between *one and two* rather than *zero and one*. Contrary to abstainers' arguments that genuine abstainers are those who cling to the complete absence of doing or get close to doing but never close enough to negate one's abstinence, this alternative perspective on abstinence insists that those who actually *cross* the line between one and two before deciding to abstain may be the most convincing abstainers.

The expansion of the zero-one dichotomy into the zero-one-two trichotomy should not come as a surprise since we tend to live in a culture of "don't knock it until you try it." Perhaps in part due to desperation—but also in an attempt to teach their children to make informed decisions—parents, of course, often resort to this tactic. Rather than allowing children to flat out refuse something, parents frequently establish the rule that their kids must taste the Brussels sprouts or try on an article of clothing at a store before they may effectively protest. It is the simple act of trying something once on the part of children that appeases most parents.

The significance of the line between one and two appears in more permanent situations as well. In an effort to curb population growth, many countries are now instituting informal or formal means of encouraging couples to limit their offspring to one child. Interestingly, while it would certainly help the population if some couples were to have *no* children, the emphasis remains on one. Such standards likely stem from an intersection of the need for population control with the persistent norms of parenthood, especially motherhood, in that it may be an "unfeminine" act not to have children at all but a contribution to the social problem of overpopulation to have more than one child.

And, as some of the above responses to abstinence suggest, the threshold may lie in other places besides the line between one and two. The insistence to try *some* implies that the abstinence threshold may lie somewhere beyond the space between one and two. Though, from the outside, it may not appear to be abstinence, many participate in acts to a limited extent so that they may frame their doing as abstinence from something else. Returning to the above example of having children, some couples feel that they should have only two children and no more. Living in a place where there are no formal (or even strong informal) demands to limit the number of children they may have, these couples believe that it is appropriate to only reproduce themselves (numerically, at least) as a strategy of population control. So while they are by no means abstaining from having children, they are abstaining from contributing to what they identify to be a global problem: overpopulation.

In addition to the tendency of demanding that individuals try something before making claims to "real" abstinence, we also hold those who are exiting a history of doing to a trial period of sorts. Though recovery groups such as Alcoholics Anonymous grant recognition chips of sobriety to users who can abstain for even one day—since staying clean for even twenty-four hours in the face of addiction is thought to be remarkable—in many other instances we demand a substantial passing of time before we perceive the abstinence as convincing in some way. In this sense, then, thresholds become important tools for marking the passage from doer to current and legitimate abstainer.

Unlike the one-two threshold discussed above, the thresholds of quitting (whether permanently or temporarily) are not solely the focus of outside observers to abstinence. Abstainers, too, hold strong ideas regarding when abstinence gets juxtaposed to a doing-laden past. Though Colin believes that any abstinence from drugs and alcohol is remarkable when one has struggled with addiction, he nonetheless thinks that "a year seems to be a real magical thing" and claims that other recovering addicts share his point of view.

The power of time comes through most tellingly in discussions of acts that we normally assume transform individuals in permanent ways, such as sex. Until recently, the loss of one's virginity could only be a one-time event. Having sex, so the logic went, altered individuals irreversibly, and individuals could not oscillate between virginity and a nonvirginal status as one might between vegetarian and omnivore. The recent crusades to promote abstinence among teens, however, gave birth to the identity of the born-again or secondary virgin, someone who could reclaim virginity in the face of a sexual past. In conversations with Sandy and James—both virgins—the topic of the born-again virgin arises. When I ask Sandy if she thinks it's possible to make a convincing return to virginity after having sex, this is how she responds:

SANDY: I think maybe if they waited long enough. Like if they were having sex when they were little—when I say little I mean fourteen or fifteen—and they realized that they didn't want to do that and maybe stopped when they were like eighteen and didn't do it again until they got married when they were like twenty-eight or something, that's like convincing. But somebody that, you know, has dated and has had sex for a long time and just decides you know, I'm not going to have sex for a while, and then has sex a year and a half later, it's not very convincing.

JM: So it's more about demonstrating that you can really resist for a period of time?

SANDY: Yeah, I would think if somebody had sex and completely abstained from it until they were married, for like ten years or something like that. That would be sort of convincing; I would accept that. But somebody who just says, "I'm a born-again virgin" and they don't have sex for two years, then they date someone and have sex again, I don't think that's really convincing.

James thinks that the concept of a born-again virgin "has its pros and cons." On the one hand, he claims, "it's really good" to regret a past move and decide not to do something anymore. "On the other hand," he tells me, "it's like, it's just kind of funny, I guess it's kind of ironic, especially if you had lots of sex, and you're like, 'Oh, sex, I'm a virgin again; I'm born again.'" When I ask him if being born again is ever convincing, he acknowledges that it can be, but that the concept in general remains a bit strange in and of itself. Thinking it through out loud with me, he says,

> If I compare it to . . . I guess it would be more realistic to me if I compare it to drug and alcohol abuse. I mean if you do a ridiculous amount of drugs and then you stop, that's really great, that's convincing, that's really good, especially if you don't do anything ever again. That's fantastic, but it's funny to say "born again." You don't say "I'm born-again sober." You just say "I've been sober for this many years." But yeah, I guess it would be convincing.

Though he fails to provide a set point or threshold at which abstinence legitimates a born-again identity, James nonetheless implies that time is a necessary requirement for a convincing exit from doing.

The Need for Thresholds

Whether they identify as abstainers or not, individuals establish and make use of boundaries as reliable ways of identifying themselves. Sometimes these boundaries have more physical properties, as in the instances of an arch, a crossroad, or a threshold over which a groom traditionally carries his bride.[9] At other times, the boundaries are less cut-and-dried, more negotiable and subject to change. Ultimately, however, both upper and lower limits serve to couch identity in the spaces in between.

In the instance of identities based largely on individuals' actions, thresholds highlight the point at which one may no longer make claims to abstinence. With that said, they also identify "normal" levels of doing from excessive doing. A consideration of thresholds for those who do not make claims to total abstinence may seem a moot point in the context of this discussion, as they clearly engage in a given act. Another way of regarding these individuals is as "pseudo-abstainers." Though they may eat or drink a particular food or beverage, have sex, drive, or participate in an act, they nonetheless pride themselves in their ability to abstain from doing to an excessive or unnecessary degree. Again, these individuals in no way deny their own participation in an act. Instead, they insist that the ability not to cross over other meaningful thresholds is just as important as the one between total abstinence and doing.

In Italo Svevo's book *Confessions of Zeno*, the protagonist takes the reader through his struggles to quit smoking, detailing his history with and love of smoking and discussing his personal threshold between ten and eleven cigarettes in the process. He reflects that, though it would take a full hour to feel the impact of another hour's worth of smoking, he recognizes his limits and dares not smoke one cigarette past ten while waiting for the others to take effect. Crossing that line between ten and eleven cigarettes invariably turned him into "a perfect terror." Though a piece of fiction, Svevo's work reminds us of the real-life examples in which individuals set thresholds to mark their not-doing within their doings (not becoming a "terror," alcoholic, nymphomaniac, or whatever the case might be). Consider an example from the area of drinking. The issue of underage alcohol use continues to be a primary concern on college campuses. Perhaps recognizing the unrealistic goal of having completely dry campuses nationwide, the focus has instead shifted to how to prevent serious episodes of "binge drinking" among college students. In trying to identify the line at which social drinking or "normal" partying transforms into binge drinking, many alcohol researchers resort to quantitative measures. Specifically, they identify binge drinking in terms of the number of drinks consumed on one occasion (five in a row for men, four for women) or the number of consecutive days (usually two) in which a person fails to complete other activities in order to consume alcohol. Taking such definitions seriously, the *Journal of Studies on Alcohol* recommends that researchers adhere to a conceptualization of binging as "an extended period of intoxication with concomitant neglect of activities/obligations." Authors who have used the word "binge" to describe behavior that does not meet such criteria, the journal urges, should now use alternative terminology. While it remains to be seen whether individuals internalize these quotas, it is very possible that students whose universities have implemented such standards could use them as a way to frame their drinking as abstention from binging and, therefore, not problematic.

Just as there are thresholds marking the difference between doing and not-doing in general and between doing and doing excessively, so too are there lines between not-doing and not-doing in a problematic matter. In the instance of eating disorders, for example, a sometimes blurry line arises between the reduction of food intake through dieting—which has become increasingly normal in an overweight nation such as the United States—and the practices associated with anorexia nervosa. In a study of women recovering from eating disorders, one woman explained her personal method for upholding normal abstinence while warding off the diagnosis (at least on her own terms) of a disorder. For her, losing ten pounds at a time constituted a "diet" whereas losing anything in excess of that amount pushed her over the line into the realm of problematic eating (or, perhaps more aptly, not eating).[10]

Despite the varying points at which individuals locate their personal thresholds and the different reasons for which they do so, the fact remains that, for most abstainers, they themselves validate the "logical" line between doing something zero times and doing it once. Still, they enjoy a large degree of freedom in choosing whether they will employ the use of a more rigid set-point definition or a more flexible zone-like conceptualization of not-doing. As Craig notes, when it comes to a given behavior, "you have to deal with the question of . . . to what degree you'll give into it or whether you're just going to be authoritarian and not give into it at all." As the next chapters will show, however, this decision ultimately holds great importance in influencing how abstainers actually not-do. Although abstinence performances in the past (as in the cases of hunger artists and fasting girls) often demanded that *others* monitor the authenticity of their abstinence performances, the use of points or zones in accordance with lines affords individuals the opportunity to evaluate the integrity of their *own* practices of not-doing. Chapters 6 and 7 will introduce two possible behavioral strategies, "fire walking" and "fence building" respectively, the former relying on an abstinence-as-zone conceptualization of not-doing, the latter being associated with viewing abstinence as a set point.

CHAPTER SIX

Fire Walking

Starting in the late 1990s, "reality" shows began to sweep network television. In such programs, ordinary individuals could achieve fame through their willingness to be stranded in a remote location without the luxuries of home (*Survivor*); push the limits of their bodies and minds through such stunts as jumping off tall buildings, being covered in tarantulas, and eating horse rectum (*Fear Factor*); date twenty people simultaneously with the hopes of finding Mr. or Ms. Right (*The Bachelor, The Bachelorette*); sing and subject themselves to sometimes scathing public criticism (*American Idol*);[1] or temporarily leave their current (and typically successful) careers in an attempt to secure a job working for tycoons like Donald Trump (*The Apprentice*). Millions of Americans watched (and continue to watch) these shows weekly, seemingly intoxicated by the trials of people "just like them" and the tricks to which the producers of the shows subject their unsuspecting stars (a far-from-rich "Joe Millionaire," a busload of "Average Joes" in place of the exceedingly gorgeous dating contestants on what had already become the "regular" reality dating shows). While we appear to be addicted to the possibility of stardom for everyday people, we also appear to be captivated by their bamboozlement and suffering.

No show better captured this voyeuristic fascination with others' trials than Fox Network's *Temptation Island*.[2] Aired in 2001, *Temptation Island* (now known as *Temptation Island I* to distinguish it from its sequels) took four unmarried couples that were in long-term relationships "to a remote Caribbean island to test their devotion to one another and answer the ultimate question, 'Have I found "The One" or is there someone better out there?'"[3] On arrival, the men and women were separated and taken to separate sides of the island. At this point, the game began with the four couples and twenty-six "hot" singles (thirteen men, thirteen women) together on the island. While the contestants would occasionally see their mates, they were not allowed to communicate with them throughout the two-week trial.

The degree of physical and emotional intimacy that took place over the course of their stay on the island looked a lot like what many would call "cheating." But not on this reality show. After all, temptation was literally the name of the game. One need only glance at websites for all three versions of the show, filled with sounds of lapping waves and chirping birds accompanied by images of silhouetted, bikini-clad, taut bodies to understand the stakes of the game. The show's logic implied that the couples themselves needed to endure such temptations in order to test the strength of their relationships, as well as their boundaries and resiliency, seeing just how far they could pull away from their long-term partnerships without causing them to snap. Yet, even in this setting of condoned temptation, there were limits to what the contestants were expected to tolerate. At the start of the game, the rules dictated that the women and men could immediately remove one of the single players of the opposite sex, terminating that person's participation for the entire game. As individuals, the players could also "block" one of the singles from dating their partners in "real life" by assigning that person a sign of prohibition: a necklace of the same color worn by the couple. Even in pseudo-fantasy worlds, such as that of Temptation Island, it appears that limits exist.

During the final episode of *Temptation Island I*, viewers watched to see if temptation or true love triumphed for each of the remaining three couples.[4] Huddled around a bonfire—an appropriate symbol for a show on temptation—each partner in turn revealed his or her decision to terminate or continue the relationship. In spite of their confessed attractions to and involvement with other players, all three couples chose to stay together.[5] A transcript of the exchange between the final couple, Valerie and Kaya, dramatically sums up the lessons learned in the course of the first season:

> Valerie pulls out a piece of paper from her pocket, something she has written to read to Kaya. She begins, "You and I both know that in my past relationships I sometimes acted on temptation. Obviously I must have found something exhilarating about acting on them, but now I derive my exhilaration from my relationship with you." Valerie's voice starts to crack; the tears run down her face. Her voice is wrecked with emotion as she continues, "And not from acting on those temptations." She finishes and bows her head down to her knees sobbing.

Fox's follow-up on the couples reported that temptation had, in fact, made their relationships stronger. Kaya and Valerie moved to Los Angeles together after a week-long reconnection in Miami, Billy and Mandy decided to give "a passionate long-distance relationship" a try, and Shannon accepted Andy's proposal ten minutes after their trip to the bonfire.[6] Temptation proved to be an auspicious test for love.

Some who watched the first season of the show expressed both disappointment and surprise when all three couples chose to remain in their long-term relationships rather than exploring further possibilities with the singles. While the absence of such a dramatic ending (i.e., a couple deciding to break up) led to disappointment, the element of surprise likely stemmed from the fact that these couples had at times engaged in acts that some might perceive as deadly to a relationship. Yet, in the minds of the couples on the island, temptation and the acts it led them to commit were positive forces, ways of validating their relationships with their partners. In this sense, they were deftly fire walking.

As an abstinence identity strategy, fire walking brings with it two main assumptions. First, when fire walking, abstainers may participate in a level of doing without discrediting their claims to abstinence. In other words, what one avoids when fire walking is not necessarily the act of doing (or degrees of doing) but the *symbolic meaning* typically associated with a given act. In the previous chapter, I made a distinction between defining abstinence as a zone rather than a point. Whereas conceptualizing abstinence as a point requires that individuals remain "total abstainers" who do not engage in the act to any degree, seeing abstinence as a more amorphous, zone-like quality pushes the boundaries of abstinence away from absolute zero. Not surprisingly, when abstainers fire walk, they invoke this latter conceptualization of abstinence, that is, as a zone rather than a point. The second assumption is that temptation comes with high merit. In so closely approaching the thing that they renounce, temptation becomes a pressing issue with which these abstainers must contend. Rather than viewing temptation as a destructive, external force, those who fire walk appreciate its ability to reaffirm identity and "prove" the integrity of their abstinence.

The Dark Cloud of Temptation?

When we think of temptation, we likely think of things that are bad for us in some way. After all, the primary definition of temptation is not simply about desire in general, but about cravings or longings for something that is "wrong." Despite the pleasure associated with a given act or thing, something deemed tempting comes with consequences. The concept of temptation hinges in part on a notion of resistance, then, as it exists in the space between an acceptable not-doing and an unacceptable doing. Consequently, discussions of temptation evoke simultaneous conversations regarding willpower, resolve, strength of body and mind, self-control, self-discipline.

This discourse of resistance is not surprising given the rich history on the dangers of temptation. The Greek maiden Pandora offers us perhaps the first lesson in temptation. Most are familiar with her infamous act of disobedience: opening the forbidden box. Overcome by her curiosity and unable to resist, Pandora unleashed "plagues innumerable, sorrow, and mischief for mankind."[7] A perhaps lesser-known fact regarding Pandora is that she herself was also a source of temptation. Created by Zeus—the father of men and gods—and showered with gifts from other gods, Pandora, with her unparalleled beauty and maidenly qualities, became a source of temptation for men and gods alike, as well as the representation of the evil and tempting nature of womankind.

In addition to mythology, religion offers a host of warnings on the perils of temptation. Christianity takes an especially strong stance regarding temptation's dangerous nature, collapsing it with evil and personifying it in the form of the devil. The Lord's Prayer includes the line, "And lead us not into temptation, but deliver us from evil," and the Bible is filled with passages on temptation.[8] In Genesis, the very first book of the Bible, Adam and Eve, the first humans created by God, make their notorious fall to temptation in the Garden of Eden. The season of Lent, the forty-day period preceding Easter Sunday, is intended to recognize Jesus's continual temptation by the devil. Luke 4:1–13 tells the story of this lengthy series of trials in which the devil tempts Jesus—who abstained from food during the entire course of this encounter—with the prospect of bread, all the kingdoms of the world, and the chance to jump from a temple top with the hope that angels will guard the fall. Jesus resists, as the scriptures of the Bible encourage its followers to do. As 1 Peter 5:8–11 cautions, the devil "prowls around like a roaring lion looking for someone to devour." Consequently, it is one's duty to constantly "be self-controlled and alert" and to "resist him." First Corinthians 10:12–13, too, urges, "Be careful that you don't fall!" Yet, should temptation rear its ugly head, "God is faithful; he will not let you be tempted beyond what you can bear. But when you are tempted, he will also provide a way out so that you can stand up under it." Ephesians 6:13–17 perhaps offers the most powerful statement on the absolute need to protect oneself from the destructive force of temptation:

> Therefore put on the *full armor* of God, so that when the day of evil comes, you may be able to stand your ground, and after you have done everything,

to stand. Stand firm, then, with the *belt of truth* buckled around your waist, with the *breastplate of righteousness* in place, and with your feet fitted with the readiness that comes from the gospel of peace. In addition to all this, take up the *shield of faith*, with which you can extinguish all the flaming arrows of the evil one. Take the *helmet of salvation* and the *sword of the spirit*, which is the word of God. (all emphases added)

Current secular representations of temptation borrow from religious models in presenting temptation as "evil," a malicious desire to engage in something "sinful." Scores of song lyrics offer a glimpse into what it means to be tempted. In "Blood of Eden" (referring, of course, to the original sin), Peter Gabriel sings about "the darkness in my heart," the "heated and the holy," the untying of "knotted chords," slipping grips, and "a moment of forgetting" to slip into "bliss." Johnny Cash, in perhaps one of his best-known hits, "I Walk the Line," offers strategies for resisting temptation: keeping "a close watch on this heart of mine," keeping "my eyes wide open all the time." Borrowing closely from Oscar Wilde's quote "I can resist anything but temptation," Rush's song "Resist" opens with a similar line[9] and follows up with "I can learn to compromise anything but my desires." Other songs deal with more specific temptations, substances being a popular choice. The Velvet Underground, for example, make no attempts to mask the source of temptation at hand in their song "Heroin," in which the subject wishes he could be a sailor, safe "from the big city where a man cannot be free of all the evils of this town," especially heroin ("it's my wife and it's my life"). Fugazi sings of the battles of temptation with the same drug in "Glue Man." Here, however, the addict succumbs to temptation when he "holds his home [heroin bag] in the palm of his hand, and he says, he says, 'You are my everyone, you are my anyone, you are my anytime, you are my every time, you are my everywhere, you are my anywhere.'"[10]

The overarching message from a variety of sources is that temptation is an ominous, lifelike force that lures in its victims. Succumbing to temptation often results in guilt, as those who fall (or leap, as it may be) into its trap recognize that doing so is a wrong move. Advertising capitalizes on these common sentiments regarding temptation by promoting products that allow consumers to indulge without guilt. The "experience" sold is marketed as sinful (tasting delicious, feeling luxurious) yet guilt-free (being low in price, fat, calories, or, as the newest trend goes, carbohydrates). An awareness of and close attention to things deemed "irresistible" but too indulgent for a given demographic of the population can help companies maximize their sales by creating a product that allows the consumers to only *feel* like they are sinning.

Given the general pressure to avoid temptation or, as an alternative practice, to pseudo-indulge (that is, by consuming or partaking in things that are not *really* sinful), what are we to make of those who make staunch claims to abstain yet get very close to the things which they maintain they do not do? Why would abstainers put themselves near the fire or, to expand the metaphor, in the line of fire?[11] One answer is to focus on the psychology of these individuals and to assume they are somehow weak-minded or lacking in willpower or determination. Perhaps they simply *cannot* not-do, as temptation trumps their efforts. But this logic begins to crumble when we consider that these abstainers are not "falling" in some way; they are deliberately choosing to face temptation head-on. It is the difference between seeing them as victims of arson or as arsonists themselves.

Since these abstainers actively seek out temptation, a more likely interpretation of such behavior would be to dismiss them as "hypocrites." After all, so the thinking goes, would not any degree of participation in the behavior from which they abstain effectively nullify that abstinence? If such individuals believed in abstinence as a set point, an absolute zero, this criticism might have validity. Yet we must remember that those who fire walk conceive of abstinence as a zone, a range of appropriate behavior that counts as not-doing. They *do* draw a line at which abstinent behavior ends and doing begins, but that line may vary from person to person. While as outsiders we may disagree with its placement, when abstainers fire walk they remain rigid adherents to their personal lines, ensuring that they will not cross over regardless of how close they may get. In this sense, then, we might retract our charges against those who fire walk as lacking self-control. After all, willpower becomes a nonissue in spaces where temptation does not exist, as willpower entails an ultimate resistance in the presence of things that we desire.

Temptation as Identity Affirmer

Abstainers mention encounters with others who try to "taint" their abstinence, yet they too may intentionally put themselves dangerously close to the fire. Whereas the encouragement by others to participate in a behavior is sometimes malicious in its attempt to disprove one's not-doing, self-induced fire walking intends to accomplish the opposite goal of *affirming* one's identity. Most who adopt expanded definitions of abstinence (zones) often permit themselves to engage in acts that allow them to feel the heat of the flames. They welcome temptation, as such moments allow abstainers to see if they can approach the fire and escape without burns. It is a philosophy akin to "What doesn't kill us makes us stronger."[12]

Although I sat down with Amelia to discuss her lifelong vegetarianism, she mentions a recent time-out period from drinking. Worried about her nightly consumption in the context of a family with a history of alcoholism, Amelia made the decision to abstain from alcohol for a period of time. During this time, she had to deal with the death of her uncle, an experience she describes as "crushing" since he was like a father to her before his death. Rather than retreating from social situations where alcohol was present, Amelia found that her ability to face alcohol during this period of trauma verified for her that she would not follow the path of her family. Since that time, she has begun to drink again, reassured that she can do so in a healthy manner. Jayson, who is straight edge, also appreciates moments of temptation with cigarettes or alcohol precisely because, when they pass, they allow him to remember how thankful he is to be straight edge and "that it's really like the best thing in [his] life."

Again, we must be careful not to assume that the decision to walk near the fire with one's abstinence results from some risk-taking tendency in one's personality. For example, while Jayson welcomes the moments of temptation with cigarettes (as well as with other drugs and alcohol), he deliberately avoids situations in which sexual opportunities present themselves, as he feels the temptation would be more from physical desire than social pressure. In regard to sex, then, Jayson avoids the fire altogether: "But like sex, you know, there's all these people around, and you have a sex drive . . . and yeah, there's a lot of temptation. That's the type of thing where I just felt like if I put myself in like enough of that situation, I would just fold and wouldn't have the willpower."

Clearly, abstainers' ideas regarding what is an acceptable method of not-doing may vary across their abstinences, but this does not mean that they are without boundaries or limits in their fire walking practices. Sandy, a virgin who will engage in other types of sexual acts but will not have intercourse, says that she allows herself to be tempted, just "not so much that I can't stop myself." Nonetheless, she broadens the parameters of what does *not* count as sex, allowing her to engage in various noncoital sexual acts while maintaining her virginity and not feeling the need to bracket such behaviors. In outlining her definition of abstinence for me, she explains what counts as sex:

> I definitely consider like sex, when I mean I am abstinent I do not have intercourse, I do not engage in that. I do not do anything that I'm going to become

pregnant with or anything like that. Um, so I don't consider oral sex to be sex. Um, it's definitely something you just don't do with everybody, but, um, I don't consider it to be sex. I can't get pregnant from it—I could get an STD from it—but I can't get pregnant from it, so I don't consider that [sex].

Her seeming "anything but" definition of sex quickly fails as I choose to play devil's advocate with her and push her on the issue of anal sex (which she *does* consider sex), challenging her association between sex and those acts that may lead to pregnancy. Despite the problems with her definition, she holds fast to the line she has established between a variety of sexual acts and intercourse. She shares with me an interesting exchange at the dinner table between her parents and a former boyfriend as an example of just how rigid that line is.

We were sitting there eating our dinner and my dad just all of a sudden goes, "So Rick, do you like sex?" and Rick was like, "Excuse me, sir?" My dad was like, "Do you like sex?" Rick just looked at me, and I said, "You'd better tell the truth." And he's like, "Why yes, sir, I do." And my dad was like, "Well, good, you know what? Have fun, date my daughter . . . You will see [that] my daughter . . . she's harder to get into than Fort Knox." And I just cracked up laughing, and Rick just didn't think he was being serious. Rick found out about a month later that he was being very serious.

Marla, who is waiting until marriage to lose her virginity, also believes in the positive value of temptation, as she tells me that she would allow herself to get so close to the fire at times that she felt herself thinking "Give me a ring. Seriously, give me a ring. Get me to the altar." She describes a situation of nearing the fire with her past boyfriend: "It was like every time we would start making out it was just like it always got more and more intense." Eventually, Marla decided that she needed to move her line back a bit, as "it was too close." After these experiences, she believed that she could not "do this ever again" (i.e., getting that close to intercourse), especially since she regards her desire as "excessive" due to her "Latin hormones." Though she continues to brave the fire to a degree, she now implements more cautious limits. In her words, "I don't believe in trying to get so close to the fire that you get burned. You know, because the more you get involved [sexually], you're not supposed to stop. So it's like how close to the fire can you get without getting burned?"

It is important to note that some abstainers may avoid the fire themselves, yet remark that they are more impressed by others' abstinence when it occurs in the face of temptation. Georgia, herself a virgin who does not fire walk, thinks that not having sex outside of the context of a relationship is far less remarkable than remaining abstinent during an intimate relationship, the latter presumably amid greater and more persistent temptation. What those who fire walk and those who applaud their efforts are doing, then, is flipping commonsense notions of the dangers of temptation on their heads, arguing instead that temptation can be a positive energy force.

Historically, we are able to find examples that present temptation in a similar way, that is, as a tool for reaffirming one's commitment to not-doing. Stoics, for example, engaged in a practice called *askesis*, involving a series of "tests" in which the individual had to "verify whether he could confront events and use the discourses with which he is armed" (Foucault 1985, 35). These tests came in two forms: a philosophical meditation in which the individual imagines how he would act and react given certain circumstances (*melete*) and a form of training that takes place in "real" situations even if they are created by artificial means (*gymnasia*). Included in *gymnasia* were rituals of purification and various forms of abstinence, the ultimate goal being to "test the independence of the individual with regard to the external world" (37). Demonstrations of *gymnasia* included acts such as preparing lavish, tempting meals, giving them to one's slaves, and then eating the slaves' meals oneself.

This idea that one's ability to resist must be "tested" in order to prove its integrity is in no way unique to Stoics but persists throughout time. If we move centuries beyond the Stoics' practices of *gymnasia* to the Victorian era, we find a culture noted for its obsessive preoccupation with the purity of its women. As demonstrated repeatedly by the fiction[13] of this era, it was not enough for women to claim their purity; they had to demonstrate it through public battles with temptation. As a result, it was only subsequent to a woman's "facing the fire without getting burned," so to speak, that recognition of her capacity to resist became socially validated.[14] The point was to put oneself in situations that allowed one to demonstrate resolve in the face of the demon of temptation. A woman who avoided such a test often fared worse than one who accepted the challenge and failed. As William Thackeray warns in response to criticism of the behavior of Becky Sharp in *Vanity Fair*, others should not criticize those who go head-to-head with temptation, particularly when the only virtue of those casting judgment is a "deficiency of temptation" (Thackeray 1983, 725).

Nonetheless, just as socially sanctioned moments for proving one's abstinence through trials of temptation surface, there remain certain times and contexts where fire walking is frowned on or not recognized as a legitimate strategy of abstinence. In his work on the Catholic perspective on celibacy, Keane tries to debunk the myth that celibates are asexual or sexually neutral in some way. Instead, he argues that celibates serve God (and their fellow people) as *sexed* beings, illustrating a "simple anthropological truth" that we have many ways of being sexual in the world (1977, 150–51). Despite this acknowledgment of celibates as sexed, however, these individuals have moral and physical responsibilities to uphold. Keane offers the following unambiguous guidelines:

> For celibates the physical implication of their commitment to a certain style of freeing love is that they will abstain from genital sexual activity which includes not only sexual intercourse but also activities that are highly proximate to sexual intercourse. Sometimes today one hears the opinion suggested that as long as a celibate has the celibate mentality or attitude, he or she can engage in any physical sexual activities without violating the norm of celibate loving. It is true that celibate love has priorities that transcend the physical aspect of human life. Nonetheless, there remain certain physical sexual standards for celibates, and it would be a serious mistake to use our broader personal and communal approach to celibacy as a means of dismissing the physical aspects of celibacy. (156)

From this perspective, "technical virginity" may not suffice in declaring oneself celibate even if one participates in other sexual acts in the context of an exclusive relationship since such acts only gain legitimacy in the state of marriage itself (165).

While not attempting to declare technical virginity, former president Bill Clinton unsuccessfully attempted to present his case of "technical fidelity" through the utterance of one of his most notorious statements, "I did not have sexual relations with that woman." Though President Clinton initially used this phrase as an attempt to deny his affair with intern Monica Lewinsky, as evidence stacked up against him, he transformed it into a way of asserting that her performance of oral sex on him somehow did not "count" as sex. In another unrelated instance, Clinton similarly argued that, while he had smoked marijuana in the past, he "never inhaled." In both cases, then, Clinton presented his behaviors through the framework of fire walking by claiming that, while he had in fact gotten near the forbidden acts, he had somehow not engaged in "true" misconduct. Such instances show that individuals possess a degree of agency in deciding how they will "do" abstinence (by fire walking, for example), yet structural factors and institutional definitions limit or allow the legitimacy of these performances.

Feeling the Heat, Avoiding the Burn

Those who fire walk as a strategy of abstinence push the boundaries of both what it means to not-do and how it is actually performed. Fire walking implies that identity can take on an elastic quality, stretching the possibilities while having a clear but sometimes variable breaking point at which not-doing crosses into doing. When fire walking, individuals send the message that the degrees of doing in which one is participating are simply that: doings. Rather than having these doings "count" as attributions to their "beings," abstainers convince themselves and urge others to strip such behaviors of any symbolic meaning they typically carry. Abstainers who fire walk, then, may claim metaphorically that, while they may do as the Romans, Romans they are not.

Fire walking generally faces strong criticism as a strategy of abstinence not only from nonabstainers but from other abstainers as well. Their rejection of the premise that abstinence from a given behavior requires its total absence flies in the face of our dominant understanding of the concept. Furthermore, fire walking makes one an ambiguous character of sorts. As humans, we tend to obsess over classification schemes, feeling more secure in categories than in the spaces in between. Even in the rare moments when we revel and appreciate ambiguity,[15] identity still appears to be a category in which we appreciate clear definitions. While our tendency may be to condemn those who defy our established boundaries,[16] abstainers who fire walk offer a glimpse into how we might revise our division of people into "doers" and "not-doers" of a certain act, expanding the repertoire of possible behavior rather than dismissing these "deviants" as hypocrites of sorts.

With this said, many abstainers refuse to play with fire themselves. Believing that precarious and self-determined lines increase the potential to fall, slip, or otherwise totally negate abstinence, these individuals choose to adhere to an alternative, ultra identity-protective stance: fence building. As Ray expresses it, "I don't have this extreme amount of willpower. You know, I'm not—like in the words of this band Bane—I'm not a superhero." As the next chapter will show, while those who fire walk may have a superhero-like ability to walk near fire and escape without burns, most abstainers not only avoid the fire but surround themselves with an extra identity-protective layer.

CHAPTER SEVEN

Fence Building

In discussing how difficult it is to abstain, Ciara says that she thinks it might be really difficult were she "on the fence" about abstinence, but, because she is not, not-doing comes relatively easy to her. While she uses the analogy of sitting on a fence to describe the difference between uncertainty and steadfastness in conviction, the image of the fence aptly captures how some abstainers conceive of and perform abstinence. Fences in general create and define clear binary divisions, distinguish one side from another other, A from not-A. In this sense, then, the image of the fence resonates with the way many abstainers distinguish doing and not-doing as dichotomous, discrete, and mutually exclusive entities. "To define something is to mark its boundaries, to surround it with a mental fence that separates it from everything else" (Zerubavel 1991, 2), and fences serve to divide, set boundaries, and give life to and create difference where none may be apparent. Whether figurative or physical, fences create two distinct entities out of what would otherwise appear continuous (e.g., the grassy plot of land that becomes "your property" and "my property").

Fences function as an interesting visual tool for thinking about abstinence in other ways too. Although varying in the degree to which they keep out unwelcome eyes, bodies, and other unwanted guests, fences also provide a sense of insulation and protection from that which lies on the other side of the fence. The strategies some abstainers employ rely on both the principles of separation and safety. Furthermore, believing in the binary conceptualization of identity "sides" (here, doing or not-doing), abstainers often erect fences around their abstinence due to a concern that any association with the "other" side will expel them from abstinence. It is in this spirit of protection that fence building takes place.

We have seen that those who fire walk push the boundaries of abstinence and conceptualize it as an elastic form of sorts. From the outside, the practice of fire walking may appear to violate the integrity of abstinence, as it puts individuals dangerously close to doing the things from which they claim to abstain. Nonetheless, from the perspective of those who fire walk, abstinence remains intact since what one really avoids may not be the act itself but the symbolic meaning attached to that act. By contrast, when individuals fence build, they insist that abstainers cannot wish away or divorce the association of an act from its meaning. Instead, doing "counts" and threatens to contaminate abstinence. In this sense, the distinction between fire walking and fence building hinges on the difference between viewing abstinence through the framework of maximum capacity versus the one-drop rule, respectively. Fire walking implies that one can stuff abstinence to its near limit all the while maintaining its integrity. Fence building, on the contrary, operates in a manner similar to the historical one-drop rule regarding race. Just as "one drop" of "black blood" could designate a person as "Negro" and essentially override any other evidence of racial identity, any instance of doing threatens to contaminate and nullify one's abstinence if one proclaims to fence build.

At first glance, the measures taken to protect abstinence may appear quite diverse. A deeper look, however, reveals one common and important tactic: not only do some abstainers avoid the act on which their abstinence is based, they also refrain from engaging in acts tangentially connected to such behaviors. Since most abstainers believe that abstinence demands a real zero, that is, *never* engaging in the act at hand, one protective measure involves removing oneself one step farther away from *any* heat of the fire. Unlike the view from fire walking—where abstinence is flexible and zone-like—fence building implies that abstinence is a clearly defined set point of delicate glass, easily shattered by a wrong move. Operating by these principles of contagion and fragility, *those who fence build not only avoid an act itself; they simultaneously erect an extra protective layer around their abstinence that ensures its safety.* Whereas fire walking plays with heat and flames, we can think of fence building as using fences, firewalls, moats, cushions, and other structures of insulation and protection.[1]

Erecting Fences

I borrow the expression translated from Hebrew as the "fence around the law"[2] to illustrate this second performance strategy used by abstainers.

Before considering the fences specific to his own abstinence, I ask Benjamin, a Hillel director, to explain the origin of the phrase. He explains that

> there were oral things and then there were laws that the rabbis instituted in order to make sure that people kept the laws. So, for example, the Bible says that a man and woman shouldn't have sexual relations while she is during her time of menstruation, so the rabbis added, "Well, there should be seven days after to make sure that you really know when it ended," and that you shouldn't only not have sexual relationships, but you shouldn't do things that might lead to that. So those are called fences around the law. And they're regarded as law, you know, but in talking about how they became law, it's a fence around the law.

Other fences surrounding this period of sexual abstinence include prohibiting any touching between married couples and avoiding acts such as sitting on or sleeping in the same bed together. Benjamin also provides a food example that illustrates how fences may seem illogical to the outsider, as they do not appear to violate the "rules" of abstinence. Offering the example of chicken parmesan—a technically kosher dish—he tells me, "Well, it says in the Bible you shouldn't eat a kid and its mother's milk. So the question is why can't we . . . ? We don't eat chicken and cheese. So why isn't chicken parmesan kosher? Well, that's a fence around the law."

Fences indicate both a feeling that one cannot afford to err and that to do so would lead to a contamination of some sort. The history behind the Sabbath in Judaism serves as a clear instance where fear of desecration due to miscalculation leads to the institution of a protective measure. In response to debates about when the Sabbath should begin and end, ancient sages resorted to nature and determined that twilight should mark both sides of the Sabbath. Relying on nature alone, however, could be tricky, so the Talmud instructs Jews to extend the Sabbath as much as possible but within reasonable limits. In a very Durkheimian sense, the solution to the dilemma of clarifying the outer limits of the Sabbath involved extending the *sacred* time of the Sabbath rather than the *profane* time of the week surrounding it, since the sacred may enter the profane but not the reverse. In this sense, then, "hossafath Shabbath" ("addition to the Sabbath") serves as a fence that precludes any errors in religious observance (Zerubavel 1981, 126–28).

In addition to recognizing and adhering to institutionalized fences, abstainers erect fences of their own choosing as they deem necessary. It should not come as a surprise to hear that those recovering from drug and alcohol abuse build fences as they try to quit, since they may be dealing with physical consequences of addiction as well as cognitive, social, and behavioral ones. As examples of fences, recovering addicts mention practices that range from avoiding over-the-counter drugs to not dating individuals who use drugs or alcohol to refusing to enter bathrooms at clubs where they know they can easily obtain cocaine or other drugs. Still, the practice of erecting fences is by no means limited to those who vow to "never again" do something. Jehovah's Witnesses mention fences such as refusing to set up a gambling Web site for an employer (Lisa) and not working in places such as bomb-making factories (Emily), as such acts would put one closer to the prohibited acts of gambling and military involvement, respectively.

Fences may also have a more subtle quality. For example, when discussing her move to a "time-out" period of celibacy, Carol informs me of the explicit fence she put up by not allowing men to come back to her apartment. When I ask about other ways she guaranteed her celibacy to herself, she initially claims that she did little else. However, as our conversation progresses, she mentions how she cut her hair and stopped painting her nails and wearing make-up at this time, in essence erecting a fence by transforming herself in a way that she believed others could not interpret as sexual.

At several points in their interviews, the Witnesses capture the essence of fence building through their use of the phrase, "When in doubt, do without." Following the use of this phrase, Charles explains how it is impossible to know in advance if engaging in certain acts will violate one's abstinence, so the solution is to not take any chances. For example, while he does not abstain from music, movies, and other forms of pop culture, he finds certain types to be more dangerous to his abstinence than others. Discussing rap music in particular, he says, "The funny thing is that there might be one song that's a decent song to listen to, and you go and get the CD, and it's like that one song is the *only* song you can listen to on the CD (laughs). Everything else is like, 'Kill your mother.' And the way it refers to women . . . You know, it's like, 'Why did I get this CD to listen to one song?'" Such uncertainty and fear lead many abstainers to adopt the principle "When in doubt, do without" since, as the Witnesses proclaim, when it comes to abstinence, "You'd rather be safe than sorry."

Interestingly, some of the abstinences practiced appear to be fences themselves in that they are ways of avoiding something larger. This seems particularly true for those who abstain from some form of technology: cars, televisions, e-mail, cell phones. Contrary to what one might infer from such abstinences, these abstainers are not "technophobes"; instead, they refuse to own and/or engage in the use of such devices so as to not waste time or money, to avoid around-the-clock availability, and so on. When describing the things from which they abstain, the language of burden and even danger emerges: Craig refuses to e-mail, as he envisions it as an "encumbrance." Similarly, Rebecca will not own a cell phone, since she does not want "all of the other things that go along with a cell phone," including having both another phone to answer and others' expectation that she will call from the road when she is running behind schedule. Ruth, who owns neither a car nor a television, feels that owning either would lead to negative outcomes, particularly the latter, which she describes as a "trap." Listen to her repeated fear of the potential harm incurred by owning (and watching) a television:

> Television just seems like a trap. It just seems like danger because I know sometimes I'll be in a mood to turn on the television and then I turn it on and I'll just watch television all day. That's the one that I feel would be like probably the most dangerous to get. Actually that's the one that kind of I feel like needs to be actively avoided . . . getting a television.

The desire to avoid the spending involved with ownership of particular items also comes into play at times. Furthermore, abstainers seek not only to escape the expenses associated with owning such items but also what would appear to be unrelated expenses. Beth, struggling with the decision of whether to accept the gift of a car that carries sentimental value for her, worries about the consequences of owning a car. She associates car ownership with the status of adulthood and wonders if taking the car will lead her to embrace adult responsibilities or flee further from them. When I push her to think about how she would be affected by owning a car, at first she suggests the latter, as she says she will "be far out of control. I will find myself spending much more money than I have. I'm serious. It's going to take so much discipline . . . but I'm not good with that. I mean, I can't even have cookies around the house because I would eat them right away. I'm really not good with that." Immediately after this reflection on her inability to control herself, she reconsiders that "maybe now it's time to learn how to like have something and not use it all the time and, you know, just be more disciplined about it."

These statements regarding the need to "be more disciplined about it" or maintain self-control point to an important difference between the practice of fence building (including abstinence-as-fence building) and the traditional concept of "the fence around the law." Clearly, both strategies aim to define and keep something intact—to be, as the Witnesses like to say, safe rather than sorry—whether it be a holy day, dietary practice, or abstinent identity in general. However, those who fence build around their abstinence do so for an additional reason: they question their ability to engage in grace-ful self-control[3] and, consequently, believe in what I call a "slippery slope of doing," insisting that one act will send them spiraling out of control into a whirlwind of doing.

The Slippery Slope of Doing

Many may associate the use of the term "slip" with discourses regarding recovery from addiction, especially among those who adhere to a disease model of addiction. Though many programs posit that individuals are re-sponsible for stopping their own cycles of addiction, the language of "slip-ping" suggests, at least to a degree, that the disease contributes to such relapses. As the original "anonymous" group, Alcoholics Anonymous (AA) is largely responsible for the spread of the disease model of addiction, as well as the belief that one is always recover*ing* and never recover*ed*. Believing that one may never recover from addiction 100 percent, of course, implies the always-present possibility of relapse or slipping. From the perspective of AA groups, slipping does not involve a momentary loss of balance but a rapid slide down a steep incline. Captured in a popular saying of Alcoholics Anonymous, "one drink, one drunk," the common sentiment is that any use will lead to a total loss of control. One drink, then, is never one drink, but always a potential "drunk." For this reason, those who adhere to the AA model of recovery do not believe in the possibility of moderation.

A slippery slope notion of doing extends beyond those struggling with a recovery from addiction, but it nonetheless operates in a similar way. Re-gardless of their area of abstinence, those who believe in a slippery slope think that one act of doing will lead to an *excess* of doing. Some base this assumption on past experiences and fence build because of their previous failed attempts at moderation or temporary vacations from abstinence. Con-sider how Denis, who practices multiple forms of abstinence, must remove sweets from his environment to avoid the temptation: "My single . . . temp-tation is sweets, desserts, and if I'm in a place where there are lots of tempting desserts, I often have more than my share, but I normally have nothing like that in my house. So five or six days a week it isn't there, and I'm not going to the store to get it, so that's my measure of preservation in that regard." Since some of his past exits from abstinence entailed rapid slides down the slope, Ken builds such rigid fences around his addiction that he will not even allow himself to use over-the-counter medication. At one point in the past, Ken totally refrained from using any type of drug or alcohol for an eight- or nine-month period, yet, when he returned to doing, he soon found himself using drugs intravenously, something he had not done previously. Finding that he could not match the high through his old methods of snorting, he continued to shoot for a year and a half. Interestingly, some continue to believe in the extreme slipperiness of the slope even when their past slips were not slips at all. Carol, who is taking a time-out period from sex, tells me that, during the first months of abstaining, "It was very scary for me to think about going back to that loose promiscuity when I saw so many people infected [with HIV], so many people die." On saying this, however, she immediately realizes the oddity of this association between her behavior and a "loose promiscuity" since she "was pretty much monogamous" when she was having sex.

While we might not be surprised to see fence building among those who have had experience with moving in and out of abstinence, it may seem odd to find a similar type of thinking among those who have *never* engaged in the act. Interestingly, many people who have never participated in the act from which they abstain also conflate one instance of doing with multiple doings or assume that one time will lead to many instances. Consider the parallels between the fears of Shelley and Craig on their ideas about very different types of abstinence: alcohol/drugs and e-mail, respectively. In response to my question regarding why she is concerned with becoming addicted given that she has had no prior use of drugs or alcohol, Shelley replies, "I guess because I've heard so many horror stories of people who try drugs or alcohol one time and then they become alcoholics or drug addicts and how easily it can happen just by one time." While not using e-mail would pass unnoticed and be unremarkable in many occupations, for Craig, a scholar and professor of English, it becomes a quite identifiable aspect of who he is professionally. Claiming he is "not a Luddite," Craig says he simply wants to avoid what he sees as the pitfalls of opening oneself up to such a form of communication. Referring to the extra work created by junk mail and unsolicited messages, he worries that using e-mail would be a Pandora's box sort of move: "You can't turn it off.[4] It would be horrible." The dread of slipping into this or any form of promiscuity surfaces time and time again among those who currently fence build. In her discussion of fornication, Lisa, a married Jehovah's Witness, mentions her previous decision to wait until marriage to have sexual intercourse. Outlining the negative consequences of premarital sex, she repeatedly (and, I think, unknowingly) slips into the association of having sex one time and being "promiscuous." Sarah, who is still a virgin, echoes Lisa's assumption that one instance of premarital sex translates into multiple partners and sexual encounters. In revealing her reasons behind staying a virgin until this point in her life, she says that the main reason hinges on wanting to get "as close as you can to someone and not wanting to share it with five or ten people."

Despite their agreement on the dangers of the slippery slope, some abstainers who fence build are quick to note that not all slopes are equally slippery. Discussing her use of alcohol and cigarettes, Marta strongly believes the alcohol slope to be much more slick than that of cigarettes. Whereas "everything would change with alcohol," smoking a cigarette would produce less devastating effects. Nonetheless, Marta hopes she never smokes again, but says, "if I ever felt like I needed to lean on something like tobacco, I would definitely, it would be better than alcohol. . . . If I had to pick up a cigarette again to not drink, I would. But hopefully that won't happen."

Even those who feel certain that one doing will lead them to an unfortunate endpoint of excess may see that journey as one of downward stairs rather than slopes. Consider Todd's gradual return to full-blown using:

> I stayed clean for like eight months. I think it was my grandparents' anniversary party, some real big affair, maybe Christmas, that I decided to have a couple glasses of wine, and I didn't go back full force. In fact, it was real slow. After the couple glasses of wine, it was probably a couple of weeks, then I met up with people at work that smoked pot and started smoking pot occasionally on the weekends. It just progressively got back to the point where it used to be: where I was smoking pot all day long. Then I ended up back with [people around here] because of good drug connections, and I was out at the bar doing a little cocaine here, a little cocaine there. I ran into [an old acquaintance at a local bar] one night, and he was dealing heroin big time. I was drunk and then did heroin and was back on heroin for like three weeks.

In addition to his own example of a gradual but steady return, Todd offers a more generic analogy in explaining how the slippery slope operates in general. A musician, he draws parallels between the worlds of music performance and addiction performance, framing both as "skills."

> Six to seven months after playing [the tuba] serious again, going out to practice on a regular basis, you know, I found all these opportunities opening up for me. I could go out and take, you know, a San Francisco symphony audition playing just because I worked really hard to find a balance when I was younger with repetitions and doing the same studies over and over, breathing exercises, you know, all that stuff to build my foundations. And for most . . . for drug addicts, we do the same thing. We became really good addicts. We go in the same things over and over and over, and that repetition's built within us. So

seven years off of tuba playing, I can come back and I can gain those kinds of skills back. It's the same thing with that repetition you did in those behaviors [with addiction]. Eventually, you might have a glass of wine and then you'll abuse other substances—maybe not now, maybe not two years from now, but from what I've seen, a number of wise people get back to it.

From this perspective, even though the return may be gradual, those who fence build believe that it is in some ways inevitable once one decides to participate in doing to any degree.

Bracketing and the "Odometer" of Identity

Given the slippery slope notion of doing that often accompanies fence building, there remains a curious (and fairly common) practice among those who fence build: occasional, clear moments in which they undeniably and fully participate in the act from which they abstain. Again, this behavior is not simply engaging in a milder degree of the act or closely related alternatives, but absolute participation. What are we to make of such involvement? How do individuals negotiate such glaring contradictions to the ways in which they have defined abstinence?

In the minds of those who typically fence build, many such instances do not discredit their abstinence or make them hypocrites of any sort. For them, these decisions to engage in an act are not shifts to fire walking nor are they hypocritical whims motivated by a sudden desire to do their self-imposed forbidden acts. Instead, abstainers who generally fence build report moments when they feel obligated to do the things they normally resist (e.g., eating meat as a guest at someone's house) or when they do something unknowingly (e.g., accidentally consuming a beverage or food with alcohol in it). As engaging in these acts carries the risk of ruining the integrity of their not-doing, abstainers must find ways to account for these apparent breaches, to prevent their doings from tainting their abstinence.

Of her three central abstinences, Ruth believes that not owning a car provides her with the most "social mileage." While the term "mileage" resonates nicely with this particular transportation abstinence, it also aptly describes another type of identity work performed by the abstainers. Individuals often strive to control the mileage accumulated by their own identity "odometers" (Mullaney 1999). The analogy of an odometer serves as a useful way to think about strategies individuals use to prevent acts from counting. Using this analogy, we might better capture the difference between fire walking and fence building as follows: fire walking allows degrees of doing (tenths of

miles perhaps) without allowing a full mile to accumulate while fence building demands the mileage stay at absolute zero. Erecting fences usually allows
abstainers to keep their odometers set at zero, but this strategy falls through
when circumstances arise in which individuals elect to or must engage in
precisely the acts from which they abstain. In such moments, bracketing
serves as the most efficient identity maintenance strategy by implying that
what may have appeared inconsistent should not be taken as such, thereby
resetting one's odometer as a quick response to a potentially threatening
situation. This act of resetting one's behavioral odometer resembles the institutionalized practice of confession within some religions. Though serving a different function, confession similarly resets identity by effectively
erasing what has transpired from one's spiritual record.[5] Bracketing within
abstinence similarly allows for the opportunity to negotiate acts that are
dangerous to one's identity by preventing them from entering the official
record.

The concept of bracketing appears in many fields. In philosophy, bracketing serves as a means of putting something "out of action" (Husserl 1969,
108), suspending an entity in order to perceive that which remains (Welton 2000, 89, 102). In a similar vein, Schutz insists that we use bracketing
as a way of neutralizing larger slabs of our everyday world that cast doubt
on what we perceive to be true. What remains outside the brackets then becomes the constituent elements of our cognitive styles, in other words, where
we find meaning (Schutz 1962–66). Law, too, provides us with examples of
bracketing, as various practices in the legal system effectively relegate things
to brackets, in essence preventing them from counting. Consider how the
practice of striking something from the record brackets a piece of an ongoing
court transcript, erasing it from the memory of the jurors and other members
of the courtroom. While striking a statement from the record tells us to forget what we have heard, other tactics prevent certain facts from entering our
consciousness in the first place. The exclusionary rule, for example, prevents
the use of evidence obtained through illegal means in both federal and state
court cases. No matter how powerful such evidence might be, it must be
bracketed off from information obtained through legal measures.

History provides us with other instances of bracketing, especially in the
ways we bridge periods that have chronologically large gaps between them.
Through techniques such as numbering discontinuous periods consecu-
tively (e.g., as in the Second and Third Reich in Germany) and giving groups
the same names as predecessors, we bracket out and play down the inter-
mittent periods—ones that may be quite substantial in length. During other
historical moments, nations also reset their historical chronometers, that is,

by returning to year "zero" (Zerubavel 2003, 52, 91). Such strategies create for us a seamless, continuous, and uninterrupted image of time by drawing our attention away from what might be glaring gaps.

Goffman applies the use of brackets to the sociology of everyday life in his exploration of them as tools to frame and mark off a segment of activity "from the ongoing flow of surrounding events" (1974, 251). Bracketing becomes an important strategy when the events at hand are likely to cause tension in the overall performance (255). Bracketing, then, creates continuity by paradoxically removing a piece of activity while simultaneously allowing it to remain embedded in the thread of action. As a means of guaranteeing convincing performances, it redefines the situation for audience members by informing them not to interpret what they see at face value.

Studies document the use of bracketing in various social contexts. In their exploration of the practices of vegetarians, Beardsworth and Keil (1992) find that the individuals in their study *do* eat meat in particular circumstances. Often it is the case that hosts prepare a meat dish, unaware of their guests' vegetarianism. Such bracketing in relation to food abstinences may extend beyond individuals to social groups. Simoons discusses the variety of reasons groups may reject the flesh of particular animals or entire classes of animals and suggests that close contact with these creatures may lead to proscriptions from killing or eating them. Nonetheless, individuals do slaughter and/or ingest these animals from time to time, and they must find ways to assuage the guilt that results from such violations. Indians in the Quito area of Ecuador, for example, typically do not harm the fowl of which they are so fond. Yet, on occasion, a woman will kill a chicken for travelers who are guests in her home. Displays of tears, shrieks, and hand-wringing all serve to bracket the events as "inconsistent" despite the fact that not only does she kill and serve the birds, she accepts money for them as well (Simoons 1994, 314).

Abstainers commonly discuss such instances of inconsistent behavior, yet rather than allowing these acts to threaten the stability and coherence of their abstinence, they find ways to indicate to any audience (and to themselves) that such acts should not count. While I am less interested in the motivations for their abstinence (the "whys") and more concerned with the ways in which individuals practice abstinence (the "hows"), the whys are important in that they determine to a degree which acts individuals must attempt to bracket. So, for example, some vegetarians have no ethical opposition to the practice of eating meat in a general sense, but instead oppose the practices of the meat industry and, therefore, will not eat meat that gets processed in that way. For these individuals, then, eating hunted meat—in their eyes, "purer" meat—poses no threat to that type of vegetarianism. Those who abstain from meat coming from the animal rights motivation, however, could not easily write off such an act. Although we might logically suppose that those of the latter philosophy would never engage in such acts, inconsistent acts do arise from time to time.

So how do those who deliberately engage in what appear to be inconsistent acts make them appear less so? The answers seem to vary. Jayson, a straight edge kid who is a vegan for animal rights reasons, works in a sub shop, which entails cooking and serving meat. While he "[doesn't] really think that that's cool" because he profits from the death of animals, he feels a bit trapped in the job because it pays $8.50 an hour and he possesses no marketable skills. He prevents his employment from tainting his abstinent identity and the beliefs behind it by continually taking some of that money and putting it back into animal rights causes. Benjamin, despite becoming more stringent in observing the rules of *shomer negi'ah*, a prohibition against touching members of the opposite sex, refuses to stop a female from hugging him. In his mind, "no matter where [he's] been with shomer negi'ah," he believes "it's worse to embarrass somebody than to hug somebody." Nonetheless, his commitment to shomer negi'ah remains unharmed, as his doing merely served the best interests of the other party.

Appeals to intention seem to work beautifully as strategies to prevent acts from counting against abstinence.[6] Ray, a straight edge kid who opposes products whose creation involves any form of exploitation, says that, as much as he tries to be aware, "it's hard to know about that stuff." Lisa, a Witness, tries to avoid viewing R-rated movies due to their language and sex scenes, but admits that stumbling across an inappropriate movie while channel-flicking, for example, is less problematic than paying to see such a movie. Such consideration of intention allows Benjamin to think "that's weird" and move on subsequent to hitting a light switch during the Sabbath; and it permits Amelia, a lifelong vegetarian, not to reconsider her vegetarian identity after years of unknowingly eating french fries flavored with beef from a major food chain.

Generally, then, the abstainers feel that *doing without intent* bodes better in the counting game than *doing with intent*. Lisa shows the distinction in the following passage:

> When someone's doing something to the point where they're willingly and brazenly, like attitude and all, like, "Yeah, I did it. I know it's wrong and . . ."

That type of attitude, you know . . . We can't read hearts and judge; that's for Jehovah to do. But sometimes with people's actions, they show a spirit of disobedience and rebellion. And then you have others who just have habits that they're trying to break so hard, and they might just slip once in a while. And they pray, "Please help me, Jehovah; please help me to stop doing this." That's different, you know.

(Notice how her use of the term "slip" indicates the lack of intention, thereby removing any responsibility and blame from the individual.)

Yet, what happens when intention exists *without* a doing? Though not expressed by any other abstainer, Colin introduces this third and critical consideration. Speaking of the early stages of his clean period, he tells me of moments where he went as far as purchasing marijuana but never smoking it. Not being able to take the pot into his house (as his wife was also a recovering addict), his intent was

to smoke it in the car. And I would really want to do this and spend good money to do it, and then I would feel horrible that I did it. I'd feel like, "God, I screwed up here. This is so stupid." On two different occasions—it might have been more than that—I literally, driving down the highway, dumped the contents of a bag that I had just purchased out of the window of the car right after I got it.

It seems possible that such "almost doings" or "potential doings" (whatever the appropriate description may be) might also threaten the validity of one's abstinence even if no one else learns of the intent. The importance of one's cognitive state even in the absence of doing is captured in what came to be a very famous statement made by Jimmy Carter in his pre-presidential years. In a 1976 interview with *Playboy* magazine's Barry Golson and Robert Scheer, then Governor Carter iterated a phrase that would not only live through his run as president of the United States but for years after. During his response to a question on the role of religion in his life, Carter reflected on what he viewed as "almost impossible standards" set by Christ, as the latter likened looking at a woman with lust to engaging in adultery. As a follow-up, Carter offered this confession: "I've committed adultery in my heart many times."[7] Accepting the conflation of thinking and doing, Carter subsequently interpreted Christ's words loosely to mean, "Don't consider yourself better than someone else because one guy screws a whole bunch of women while the other guy is loyal to his wife."[8] Rather than defining an "adulterer" strictly on a behavioral level, Carter (invoking Christ's teachings) implies that, at times, the cognitive level can "count" more than—or, in a sense, override—one's (non)actions.

This acceptance that "lusting in one's heart" equates to following through on those desires raises interesting considerations not only for what counts as doing, but also for what counts as not-doing. Like the lust in Jimmy Carter's heart, the *thought* of getting high counted in Colin's mind. Both of these cases offer the possibility that intention trumps doing. It is precisely for this reason that bracketing becomes an identity tool among those who fence build and unintentionally engage in an act, but *not* for those who intend to commit an act but fail to do so. While we might perceive bracketing to be a moot point in instances of the latter (after all, no "doing" occurs), it is more likely the case that these individuals feel they cannot bracket because they have breached their abstinence with their thoughts.

The Decision to Fence Build

In thinking about the differences between the strategies of fire walking and fence building, the two seem in stark contrast to one another. Fire walking implies a flexible, elastic notion of abstinence. Fence building suggests the fragility of abstinence. Fire walking puts abstainers close to temptation. Fence building shields abstainers by moving them an extra degree away from the fire. Fire walking allows abstainers to engage in degrees of doing the act they have eliminated from their behavioral repertories or to do acts that are very closely related without violating the integrity of their abstinence. Fence building allows for neither of these options, as it demands an avoidance of the act itself and those behaviors tangentially associated with the act.

Yet, the fact remains that many of these abstainers end up participating in the acts they renounce in the first place. When such participation occurs, abstainers find that they must bracket the behavior after-the-fact as a way of affording them the possibility to reset an odometer that has already accumulated miles, so to speak, and as a means of upholding their original understanding of what it means to abstain. Regardless of when and how individuals bracket, the act allows individuals to reframe the structures of relevance for audiences of their identity performances and to convey the message that certain behaviors should not count or discredit one's abstinence. Does all this post-doing scrambling to reclaim abstinence suggest the futility and failure of fence building as a strategy of not-doing?

Since bracketing within fence building allows abstainers to essentially fire walk (in that it suspends the rules of counting and divorces the act from its symbolic meaning), we must ask why these individuals simply do not choose to fire walk in the first place. After all, the fire walking approach to abstinence avoids the need to bracket due to an expanded definition of abstinence. In attempting to answer this question, we need to return to the issue of intention. Admittedly, we may scoff at appeals to intention when attempting to bracket a given behavior and dismiss them as similar to childlike proclamations of "But I didn't *mean* it!" after engaging in a misbehavior of sorts. But, as with those who elect to fire walk, denouncing these abstainers as hypocrites misses the mark for two main reasons. First, those who gravitate toward fence building truly believe in the integrity of abstinence and the need to uphold the definition of abstinence as total not-doing. While this seems to fly in the face of the fact that they are engaging in the acts on occasion, they go the extra mile and attempt to bracket off this behavior precisely because they are so committed to their understanding of abstinence, *not* because they take it lightly. Arguably, if they perceived abstinence in broader, more flexible terms, they might opt to fire walk instead, but they steadfastly choose not to do so.

A second reason for validating appeals to the motivations behind doing when one claims to not-do is that, as a general principle, we think intention matters when it comes to the way we navigate through our social worlds. In our minds, intention is such a powerful force that it can lead us to reframe acts we normally perceive as absolutely transforming or irreparable, such as participation in sex or certain forms of criminal activity. For example, in their guidelines regarding celibacy in a Catholic context, Keane urges "pastoral sensitivity" when dealing with individuals who claim celibacy but may have experienced certain sexual acts due to circumstances "that are at least partly beyond their control."[9] As a more general example, criminal law has the principle of intention built into it. Consider Tappan's definition of crime as "an *intentional* act or omission in violation of criminal law, committed without defense or justification, and sanctioned by the state as a felony or a misdemeanor" (Inciardi 2002, 32). While civil law does not require mens rea[10] (criminal intent), criminal law does.[11] In fact, many factors—insanity, mistake of fact, mistake of law, self-defense (and defense of others), entrapment, or duress (Inciardi 2002, 36–39)—may mitigate a crime if the defense is able to show that no intention to commit a crime existed at the onset.

Regardless of whether we accept such explanations and reframing of events, the differences between fire walking and fence building feel real and meaningful for those practicing these strategies. Just as understanding fire walking allows us to better understand how virgins can engage in oral sex, knowing the generic features of fence building helps us to appreciate why

Jews who keep kosher will not eat chicken parmesan or why some Mormons will not drink herbal tea—despite its lack of caffeine—due to its association with coffee (a hot beverage *with* caffeine).[12] Coming to terms with these diverse ways of performing abstinence also sheds some light on why, paradoxically, the escapades of *Temptation Island* do not constitute cheating while "lusting in one's heart" just may.

CHAPTER EIGHT

Negotiating Abstinence Strategies

In the past three chapters, we have seen how abstainers differ in their definitions and reported strategies of how to perform abstinence. On the one hand, some abstainers adhere to an absolute zero conceptualization of abstinence. Despite their self-confessed violations of abstinence at times, in principle these individuals remain committed to the idea that not-doing must be just that: not-doing. By removing themselves one additional degree from the thing from which they abstain, these individuals erect metaphorical fences of protection and insulation. As an alternative approach to this somewhat literal and rigid framework, other abstainers adopt an expanded definition of not-doing that allows them some freedom of movement away from an absolute zero in behavior, stretching the boundaries to range from 0 to .9999. . . . In pushing the limits of abstinence, they get dangerously close to the thing they have identified as capable of burning them. Appropriately, I have dubbed these two diverse (and, admittedly, ideal-typical) approaches to conceptualizing and practicing abstinence as "fire walking" and "fence building."

I have opted for the active characterizations of these strategies (i.e., walk*ing* and build*ing*) as opposed to terms that would risk essentializing those performing the abstinence (as would the terms "fire walk*ers*" and "fence build*ers*"). Using nouns to mark the ways in which individuals not-do runs the risk of tracing the roots of abstinence to some innate trait or tendency within individuals and ignores the other factors that contribute to the ways in which individuals abstain at a given moment. Abstainers themselves implicitly urge us not to overlook this distinction between viewing abstinence strategies as an inherent part of who one is and appreciating them as ways of practicing not-doing that are subject to change. The most persuasive evidence regarding why we must not relegate abstainers to essentialist categories lies in the fact that many individuals claim to practice *both* strate-gies—that of fire walking and fence building. The performance of both fire walking and fence building may occur in one of two ways. First, polygamous abstainers (i.e., individuals who practice multiple abstinences simultane-ously) may show signs of the coexistence of both strategies, as they might elect to fire walk on one abstinence and fence build on another. Second, abstainers may vary their strategies not across different abstinences (e.g., sex and alcohol) but within a single type of abstinence (e.g., dietary practices) over the course of time.

Returning to the variation in Marta's practicing of her abstinence trio—sugar, alcohol, and cigarettes—allows us to see an example of this first type of flexibility across multiple abstinences within a person at one point in time. Though she tries to avoid moderation in her sugar intake, she realizes that her "way of being moderate" is through "the fact that sugar is in ev-erything." In this sense, then, Marta appears to fire walk in her abstinence from sugar. She is unlike others who choose to fire walk in that she does not actively seek out encounters with the thing from which she abstains, yet her way of abstaining from sugar does in fact appear to be fire walking in that she does not view a small intake of sugar as invalidating her gen-eral claim to abstain from it. In contrast, she allows for no moderation in alcohol, as she feels she must "absolutely abstain" from it and take other protective measures as well (fence building). Finally, while she describes rituals around smoking that sound very much like fence building, she ad-mits that she would suspend this strategy and smoke a cigarette if it kept her from taking a drink of alcohol. Such differences in strategies mentioned by polygamous abstainers serve as a reminder that one may not be predis-posed to fire walk or fence build, but that the type of abstinence itself may determine how individuals implement strategies.

As mentioned above, in addition to varying their approaches across dif-ferent not-doings, some abstainers also change their strategies within the same not-doing. Though most abstainers believe in adhering to one strategy at a time, they find that they must change over time for a variety of reasons. This shift from one strategy to the next is not whimsical. Instead, abstainers tend to adhere strictly to and take seriously one strategy at a given time. But their choice of strategy may change over time, that is, by moving from fire walking to fence building or from fence building to fire walking. Typically, abstainers move through the former progression, that is, from fire walking to fence building and not vice versa.

The transition from a more flexible practice of abstinence to a more rigid one often occurs as individuals are "learning" to abstain or testing their own level of seriousness and commitment to not-doing. In detailing his switch to a more orthodox practice of Judaism, Benjamin says,

> It was a gradual process for me. I took on Shabbat first, but I still didn't keep kosher and I didn't keep Shabbat in the way that I do now. And then I started doing both of those around the same time. I still wasn't sold on the idea of sexual abstinence though. I know I wasn't actively having sexual relationships, but I hadn't ruled it out. And that was something I struggled with a while before I finally decided that that was part of my belief system.

Marla, too, talks about her changing attitude toward sexual abstinence. The difference for her was that she was already committed to the idea; what changed was her conceptualization of what qualified as abstinence. In discussing her relationship with an ex-boyfriend, she says, "I did everything else I thought I could do." Over time, however, she began (and continues) to feel guilty over what she now deems as inappropriate behavior for someone claiming sexual abstinence.

Still, others find that their definitions of what counts as abstinence and their notions of acceptable ways of performing it shift as their reasons for abstaining change. Jada, for one, began experimenting with vegetarianism initially because she felt a strong opposition to the practices of the meat industry. As a result, in her early stages of vegetarianism, she would eat meat obtained through hunting, such as venison her father's friend would provide, because it did not violate the principles of vegetarianism she established. While she never fully decided that eating meat in general was problematic, she eventually got to the point where she believed that it was wrong for her. As she gradually became more committed to the idea of not eating any form of meat, she moved away from making any exceptions and implemented more restrictions, such as not buying products made from leather.

Though the move between strategies appears to be largely one of shifting from fire walking to fence building, the opposite course does arise, especially among those who see abstinence as a necessity. Believing that they must quit whatever has become problematic for them, these abstainers initially erect many fences so as to not-do at all costs. In speaking of his abstinence from drugs and alcohol, Ken describes the start of this trajectory as a time of rigid fence building. For example, in addition to abstaining from the drugs to which he was addicted, Ken says that he had to also watch anything that might "trigger" a slip, such as coffee and over-the-counter medications. Though perhaps not yet performing a strong illustration of fire walking, Ken has gradually become more confident in his ability to abstain and, as a result, has safely eliminated some of these fences. Still, he clearly expresses reservations toward embracing fire walking, as he believes "your ass is in trouble if you think you are recovered."

While many abstainers outline unidirectional moves away from one of the strategies and toward the other, the movement may also be a somewhat less predictable and more erratic course. Benjamin, who describes his move from fire walking to fence building above, admits that, in addition to figuring out his own commitment to Judaism, he also once thought some of the "fences" within the faith were both "outdated" and "overdone." Despite the fact that he now adheres to many of them, he nonetheless uses the analogies of waves and cycles to describe his shifting strategies of abstinence, suggesting that the tendency to fire walk or fence build may wax or wane over time.

Why might individuals change strategies across different abstinences or even within the same abstinence? Clearly, we might expect to see some variation in the early stages of abstinence when one may be attempting to iron out commitment issues or experimenting with abstinence in order to determine whether it fits into one's identity repertoire. Yet deciding for oneself whether one will keep abstinence or simply test drive it cannot fully account for shifting strategies. After all, individuals who have abstained for years may continue to oscillate between fire walking and fence building at points long past any trial period. Interestingly, although the factors that shape whether one fire walks or fence builds seem disconnected from one another, they all largely hinge on temporal issues in both one's own biography and that of the surrounding culture.

Who I Am: Present Thoughts Regarding What Is "Characteristic"

While insisting that they are not necessarily fire walk*ers* or fence build*ers*, some make claims to the essence of their identity in other ways. Whereas a psychological interpretation of whether one fire walks or fence builds might frame the differences between these strategies as ones of risk taking (fire walking) versus phobic avoidance (fence building), abstainers insist that what drives their tendency to engage in a given strategy has less to do with these types of personality characteristics and more with their perceived relationship to the things they choose to do and not do. By framing the tendency to abstain or not to abstain from certain things as "characteristic" of who they are, abstainers set up a scenario in which they feel either comfortable enough to fire walk or obligated to fence build (although it is usually the latter).

Some clearly believe that abstaining falls in line with their personalities; therefore, abstaining comes almost "naturally" to them. Craig, for example, tells me that most people who know him well are not surprised by his abstinence from e-mail because it is very consistent with who he is. (Interestingly, however, this is Craig's only abstinence. At the end of our conversation, he informs me that he participates in every other "vice.") For Denis, who tries to live simply, eat simply, and avoid substances such as drugs and alcohol, these abstinences, too, are in line with how he views himself. He says,

> Health has always been a very important concern for me. I started being a long distance runner when I was about fourteen, so, you know, if you want to keep yourself in pretty good shape and keep improving, then you take care of your body. Now I'm also lucky in that none of the standard attractions is pleasant to me. I have no taste at all for alcohol or smoking or drugs or anything. It's just completely uninteresting to me. I don't have to exercise any restraint.

In contrast to such "logical" abstainers, some find that they must continually erect fences in order to avoid violating their abstinence because participating in the act, not abstaining from it, serves as the default mode for them. Raven frames her desire to drink as consistent with her "personality traits," the primary characteristic being obsessive-compulsiveness. For her, abstinence is a full-time career rather than a part-time job since it requires continual monitoring and protection from her "natural" inclination to drink. When discussing this high level of identity maintenance, she says,

> I believe that if I stop going to meetings and stop talking to other alcoholics and don't treat my disease, I do believe I will get drunk. For me, I can feel the disease not in compulsions or obsessions with alcohol, but in my personality traits. When I don't go to a lot of meetings, I start acting in ways similar to the way I acted when I was drinking.

Todd also presents abstinence as a "constant struggle" since "it's just a natural reaction for me to be like a mother fucker," part of which for him means using substances in an uncontrollable way. He recounts a particular moment in the past as a prototypical example of what happens when he chooses to ignore or too easily dismisses what he sees as the driving tendencies in his personality. An extremely talented musician with a variety of options in terms of geographic location, he decided to move away from his home on the east coast not only to attend an outstanding music school but also to move away from his addiction. He describes why the plan ultimately failed:

I just started taking auditions for schools and got a bunch of scholarships and decided to take off to Michigan, and I thought that was going to fix me. Take me out of the environment. It's not me; it's the environment. I found out real quick that it wasn't the case either because when I got to Michigan, for a couple years I was getting high on a daily basis.

Ken, also a recovering addict, echoes the sentiments of Raven and Todd. While he is not telling me about his own struggles with addiction and abstinence in this instance (in fact, he's telling me about why his brother did not become an addict), he nonetheless argues that the tendency to either do or not-do is somehow programmed into one's body. In Ken's mind, what prevented his brother from becoming an addict had nothing to do with the amount of drugs and alcohol he ingested or consumed. (He apparently used heavily.) Instead, Ken believes that his brother did not become addicted when Ken did because those addictive tendencies present in Ken simply were "just not in [his brother's] disposition."

Among cases of multiple abstinence, individuals may feel predisposed to participate in one behavior while, for another, the perceived natural reaction may be to abstain. Again, abstainers often frame such inclinations in the language of personality, traits, characteristics, or a combination thereof. Yet such appeals to "natural" parts of the self need not indicate rigid beliefs in some form of essentialism. Instead, an individual's own understanding of his or her personality may change over time. In the context of a history of addiction and a present struggle with abstinence, for example, an individual may frame doing rather than not-doing as a consistent part of who he or she is. This is not to say that this will not and cannot change and that, in thirty years' time, sobriety may be the reference point of any discussion on "who I am."[1] When listening to any discourse regarding the nature of the self, then, we should keep in mind this desire to create a narrative consistent with one's current intentions concerning the temporality of abstinence.

Who I Once Was and Who I Will Become: Considerations of Past and Future

Beliefs about one's present self certainly may lead one to fall into a given category (if I think I'm an addict with no hope of full recovery, I might convince myself that "never again" is the only option for me). Yet, the decision to fire walk or fence build may be independent of beliefs about what lies at one's "core" and have more to do with one's views on the perceived duration of abstinence and the connections between past, present, and future selves.

Returning to the matrix presented in chapter 4, we can imagine the implications of abstinence on identity based on whether one perceives oneself to be a waiter, a never, a time-outer, or a quitter. As the abstainers show, these implications do in fact vary, albeit not always in predictable ways.

When identity implications are strong, abstainers can't be "fuzzy" and fire walk. Instead, the distinction between those who do and those who do not relies on the establishment of clear and unambiguous boundaries, as the strategy of fence building affords. Of course, individuals may perceive their abstinence as carrying strong identity implications regardless of whether they are waiters, nevers, time-outers, or quitters, but these categories themselves also bear implicit messages regarding the centrality of abstinence. In thinking about the groups for whom abstaining might carry the strongest identity consequences, the quitters and nevers seem the logical candidates. Among the quitters, an intense contrast surfaces between who one is currently and who one appeared to be in the past. Not only must this contrast be performed in a cogent way; it must become a permanent piece of one's self in order to remain convincing. On the other hand, while the nevers need not build up this contrast between past and present selves, one would imagine the struggle to create a consistent, stable, and unchanging self over time to be an exhausting task. A commonsense view of the waiters might suggest that abstinence carries few consequences for identity since abstaining is simply a progression or stop along the way toward a state of doing. Finally, among the time-outers, abstaining would seem relatively inconsequential to identity in that the potentially cyclical nature of the narrative allows individuals to oscillate between doing and not-doing in fairly convincing ways.

Interestingly enough, only two of the four of these commonsense predictions hold up. Whereas there appear to be relatively strong identity implications of abstaining among quitters and relatively weak ones among the time-outers, the nevers and waiters defy expectations in that the narratives of the nevers imply few consequences of abstaining on identity while those of the waiters suggest strong ones. Consequently, we see more instances of fence building among quitters and waiters and a penchant for fire walking among the time-outers and the nevers. Why might this be?

To start to answer this question, we can compare the similarities and differences among the groups that tend to either fire walk or fence build. If we consider the relationship between the quitters and waiters, we see that they have neither of the matrix's two dimensions in common (whether one has participated in the act in the past and perceived permanence of abstinence). What they do share, however, is a reliance on narratives that are unilinear (unlike the time-outers) and discontinuous in some way (unlike the nevers). In her discussion of how individuals edit their lives via the con-struction of narratives, Andrea Hood (2001) suggests that reframing serves both instrumental and social roles in that it allows for a smoothing out of an otherwise jarring cross between two seemingly inconsistent identities. Re-framing measures, then, "adjust the meaning of the behavior, cognition, and values associated with the pre-transformation identity," thereby precluding or resolving any autobiographical inconsistencies that may arise (5). Hood argues that, in contrast to narratives that demand no reframing (i.e., those that are multilinear, cyclical, or continuous), unilinear and discontinuous narratives must rely heavily on reframing, presumably due to their severe implications for identity (10, 7).

Who Others Think I Am: External Definitions

A third factor that may affect how individuals do abstinence concerns the au-dience for whom they are performing. Interestingly, many individuals claim that the presence of fellow abstainers makes abstaining an easier accom-plishment, yet they simultaneously feel that they must adhere to more rigid definitions of abstinence (and, thus, erect more fences) in the company of other abstainers. Lisa tells me that, while "you're not encouraged to take a vacation from Jehovah," some Witnesses become more lax with particular abstinences when they are not in the presence of other Witnesses. Using the example of dress, she tells me that she would wear a bikini on vacation with her husband, yet, around other Witnesses, she would consider no less than a one-piece bathing suit with a t-shirt over it. Charles, Lisa's husband, makes similar remarks about facial hair, claiming that he might grow a beard on vacation, but he always remains clean-shaven when in the presence of other Witnesses.[2]

Clearly, individual definitions of abstinence strongly affect whether one will fire walk or fence build, and personal definitions may change over time and circumstance. Yet, the factors affecting whether one gravitates toward fire walking or fence building extend beyond the individual. While individ-uals may negotiate within them, systems of classification shape understand-ings of what counts as abstinence (or nullifies it) and, as a result, influence whether one needs to bracket off a given behavior. Asia Friedman's fascinat-ing analysis of the classification of sex acts illustrates how a changing des-ignation of what qualifies as sex allows teens to engage in sexual activities while not compromising their virginity. Specifically, the traditional system of "bases" (modeled after the sport of baseball) entailed a linear progression from first base (kissing) to second base ("feeling up" a woman) to third base (petting or what Friedman calls "feeling down") to the eventual crossing of home plate (intercourse). Alternatively, the new teen model not only introduces acts omitted from the traditional base system (such as oral sex); it reclassifies acts in a perplexing way. What distinguishes those acts that count as sex from those that do not, Friedman argues, is whether one can get pregnant from the behavior. Consequently, penis-vagina sex remains "real" sex, and oral sex, anal sex, and a variety of other acts become "not a big deal" and part of the realm of "abstinence." Friedman argues that such a scheme may be, "at least in part, the unintended offspring of 'abstinence only' education" (2002, 12).

While it is difficult to substantiate this intriguing idea, it nonetheless remains the case that the revised system of classifying sex acts may currently allow teens to fire walk and perform certain acts with relatively few (if any) threats to their virginity. Interestingly, if teens were to practice such acts under the previous base system, they would need to engage in some form of bracketing so as to not "count." Obviously, not all teens subscribe to this revised model of classification. The important point, however, is that, while etically these acts are the same, emically they may be very different depending on the larger models of classification. It is precisely this common emic understanding of certain acts that contributes to the need to fire walk or fence build.

Fires, Fences, and Shifting Strategies

As ways of performing abstinence, fire walking and fence building seem worlds apart. In its daring nature, fire walking revolves around testing the limits of abstinence, while fence building ensures an additional degree of protection from the thing or act avoided. Despite the clear differences between these strategies, we cannot neatly separate those performing these strategies into categories of daredevils and those more disposed to "play it safe." Abstainers themselves make it quite clear that their decisions to engage in a particular style of abstaining hinge on a host of factors that cannot be reduced to psychological predispositions.

As a result, abstainers' performances of not-doing take on a complicated scheme: fence building and fire walking simultaneously on different abstinences, fence building at one point in time and later fire walking on the same abstinence, or fire walking on an abstinence only to fence build later. Sometimes the shifts between strategies take on a complicated and unpredictable pattern, as seen below in Ciara's discussion of her substance and dietary abstinences:

I will take it so far as to not have a dessert or a dinner that has been cooked with alcohol. That is obviously not about like getting drunk or whatever. It's this whole thing of oh, well, I don't want anything that's touched alcohol or that is like associated with it or whatever, and it's . . . There probably have been times when I haven't been as strict like that, but you know if something's been cooked in wine . . . and I've kind of let it go. I've been like, oh, okay, well that's all right. Or if there's been a dessert that has some alcohol in it, and I've been like, "Oh, I shouldn't eat that," and somebody's like, "Come on. You're not going to get drunk." So I definitely think in terms of that there have been shifts in terms of how like hard-core I am. That probably mirrors what's going on in my life in terms of how controlling I'm being in general. Like I don't eat red meat, and so the same thing would happen. Like sometimes I'll be so extreme that it's like I wouldn't eat something off of somebody's fork that had touched red meat or I won't even take cold cuts off a platter that's included ham, as well as turkey or whatever. Other times, I'm not as, you know, pure.

While her shifts seem somewhat whimsical at first glance, she acknowledges that her decisions to fire walk or fence build ultimately depend on "what's going on in [her] life" and do not reflect a lackadaisical attitude toward abstinence. Unlike the frequent shifts seen in Ciara's account above, however, most abstainers who change strategies do so slowly over time, yet their decisions remain deliberate and purposeful.

Some may argue that practicing both strategies simultaneously or moving from one to the next reflects a lack of commitment or seriousness in abstinence. Yet, these shifts more likely highlight the limitations of fire walking and fence building as analytic categories. In real life, of course, abstainers do not think in terms of whether they are fire walking or fence building at a given moment; they are instead focused on the ways in which they can not-do that are acceptable to the standards set by themselves and, at times, others. Rather than being a purely individual decision, an abstinence-tied relationship to others either contingently (needing to not-do in order to qualify for group membership) or conjointly (choosing to not-do in conjunction with others) may shape how one abstains in a given instance or even as a general practice.

Furthermore, while the strategies of fire walking and fence building as categories of analysis appear in complete opposition to one another, they may occasionally overlap and blur into one another in practice. In an article detailing his status as a "professional ex," J. David Brown argues that he is among the many who "trade on their past to re-enter society." A former alcoholic, Brown found that taking a position as a primary therapist at a substance abuse treatment center facilitated his own move into and through sobriety. Taking a role as counselor, Brown argues, compels individuals "to abandon previous work they increasingly view as mundane and polluting" (2003, 501–2). Following this logic, Brown's abstinence strategy appears to be one of fence building, a move of protection. Yet, he chooses to use as a fence that which he precisely tries to avoid: alcoholism. Fence building? Fire walking? Brown's career and identity move reminds us that other possibilities exist. In fact, one might argue that Brown in essence *fire builds*, surrounding himself with that which he strives to avoid, the constant reminder of his past serving as his protection in the present.[3] These examples remind us that, in the end, these conceptual tools may be just that. Nonetheless, the strategy individuals choose to employ shapes and gives meaning to their experiences of not-doing.

CHAPTER NINE

Verbal Performances of Abstinence

Toward the end of his writing career, Herman Melville created "Bartleby the Scrivener," a character who would frustrate and perplex readers through the polite repetition of four simple words: I prefer not to. Hired as the third copyist for a lawyer, Bartleby initially engages in his writing voraciously, the narrator describing Bartleby as "gorging" on documents with "no pause for digestion." On the third day, however, when asked to examine some of the completed work, Bartleby replies in a "singularly mild, firm voice" that he would prefer not to. While Bartleby's language and tone convey politeness, the lawyer-narrator quickly realizes that courtesy need not involve flexibility and that "preferring not to" was Bartleby's way of saying that "he would refuse point-blank" (Melville 1982, 752, 755).

Bartleby's preference "not to" not only remains steadfast but intensifies as he refuses to engage in various tasks such as examining copies, checking mail, and running errands. Yet Bartleby's refusals are not limited to his duties as copyist, as he excludes all food from his diet save for ginger-nuts and never engages in activities such as reading the newspaper, going for walks, disclosing personal information, or complaining. These "preferences not to" cause turmoil in the office, as the other two office workers, Turkey and Nippers, fluctuate in their willingness to tolerate Bartleby by time of day. As Turkey's paroxysms begin at noon (just as Nippers' fits are ending), there is a constant strain of intolerance toward Bartleby, often accompanied by the wish to "black his eyes for him." The lawyer, however, finds himself intrigued by Bartleby's eccentricities and begins making excuses for maintaining this "perverse" and "unreasonable" fellow. Ultimately, Bartleby neglects to perform any of the duties for which he was employed, and the lawyer feels that he must fire this troublemaker. Bartleby, though, *prefers not to leave.* The lawyer, completely under the spell of Bartleby at this point, responds to the latter's resolve by removing himself from Bartleby, that is, relocating his business entirely. Left behind for the new inhabitants of the office, Bartleby is soon taken to jail for vagrancy, where he then *prefers not to eat* and, as a result, dies of starvation.[1]

Though polite in its tone, Bartleby's reiterated phrase "I prefer not to" does more than simply state his distaste for certain foods, tasks, and hobbies: it *rejects* these things upon its utterance. J. L. Austin terms moments like these "performatives," sites where doing and its verbalization collapse. Performatives, Austin argues, "do not 'describe' or 'report.'" Instead, "the uttering of the sentence is, or is a part of, the doing of an action, which . . . would not *normally* be described as . . . 'just' saying something" (Austin 1975, 5). As illustrations of performatives—statements that produce that to which they refer (Diamond 1986)—Austin uses examples from diverse areas of social life. Performative statements range from declaratory ones, such as "I name this ship," to contractual ones, such as "I bet" and "I promise" (Austin 1975, 5, 7). In many instances, Austin insists, the same act could occur in the absence of verbal expression and through alternative means. Nonetheless, "the uttering of the words is, indeed, usually a, or even *the*, leading incident in the performance of the act (of betting or what not), the performance of which is also the object of the utterance, but it is far from being usually, even if it is ever, the *sole* thing necessary if the act is to be deemed to have been performed" (8). For example, in order for the performative to succeed, I cannot already be married to another person when I say "I do" during a wedding ceremony, nor is my statement of gift-giving complete if I never give the gift to its recipient (8–9).

The strategies of abstinence described in the previous chapters show that, while abstinence is a largely personal act in terms of whether one gravitates toward fire walking or fence building, the performance of abstinence does not occur in a vacuum. Although individuals exercise a degree of control regarding *how* they perform, the initial impetuses behind these performances often come from the outside, from interactions with others. If individuals are not engaging in particular behaviors, often such abstinence must be verbally communicated in order to become visible in the first place. Performances of abstinence, then, do not end at the behavioral level. Abstainers often find themselves called on to engage in abstinence performatives during which they must verbally announce (and simultaneously reject) an activity at hand. While the burden to disclose one's abstinence may feel cumbersome at times to abstainers, these self-revelatory acts to others paradoxically facilitate the strengthening of an identity—one based on personal choices—through the reactions of others.

In the case of abstinence, the utterance "I don't X" is the most typical performative. This statement does not merely serve as a claim about one's penchant for participating in certain not-doings. Instead, when the expectation to engage in the behavior presents itself and individuals must disclose their abstinence, "I don't X" actually performs something simultaneously—in this case, resistance or refusal. The performance, however, usually does not end with the performative. Someone, of course, is on the other end of the performative, reacting to this disclosure in any of a variety of ways, perhaps initiating further conversation or demanding an explanation of the abstinence. The intention of abstainers during these exchanges is to convince others (and perhaps themselves) of the legitimacy of their personal choice to abstain. Nonetheless this insistence on recognition of one's individual agency in shaping one's own identity largely relies on recognition by others.[2] Abstinence, then, may not only be about not-doing, but in part about the verbalization of and response to that not-doing as well. The reactions to abstinence vary from total acceptance to extreme hostility. Interestingly, those who do not react negatively or simply regard the abstinence of others as "unmarked" may actually weaken the importance of not-doing by causing it to fade into the background. Somewhat paradoxically, the strongest reactions to abstinence may play the most important role in helping to establish and legitimate one's identity based on not-doing.

Initial Performative Performances

Some abstainers choose to reveal and draw attention to their abstinence unsolicited. For example, Beth tells me that she likes people to know that she does not own a car and feels that she "probably [winds] up explaining it to people who haven't necessarily [an] interest in knowing." Yet, sentiments similar to Beth's appear to be the minority, as most choose not to, in Asia's words, "advertise it." In talking about his variety of abstinences, Denis sums up what many others say about self-revelation. He says, "I don't usually do a lot of blatant publicity. The people around me know something of my lifestyle and that maybe kind of spreads indirectly. That's fine. You know, I don't try to throw it in people's faces." Inevitably, however, situations arise in which others must become aware of one's abstinence. Often these situations involve moments where an immediate expectation to participate in the behavior exists (e.g., at a bar where alcohol is served or at someone's home where meat is being offered for a meal). Even though abstainers may not feel compelled to announce, "Attention, everybody!" (Ciara's words) in social situations, frequently some level of disclosure must take place.

It is not surprising, then, that when abstainers generalize about the re-actions of others, most focus on moments of *first* disclosure in social situations, that is, when others initially become aware of their abstinence. Initial disclosures can be vulnerable moments for abstainers, as possible reactions constitute a vast and unpredictable range. When I ask Ray what kinds of reactions he has received when discussing being straight edge with others for the first time, he says,

> Oh, I've gotten anywhere from like awesome reactions to like the biggest jerk-offs in the world, you know. I almost got in a fight with this fucking guy at this tattoo shop about like animal rights and shit, uh, and like other guys are completely cool with it. You know they're really interested in it. It differs with the person. Some people it almost seems like I offend them or something.

Bewilderment is a common reaction of others to abstainers' "I don't X" performative. In these responses of confusion, others do not necessarily express hostility or rejection of one's abstinence but instead appear curious about why or how one chooses to not-do. At times, abstainers feel reactions of bewilderment imply that the decision to not-do is extreme, excessive, crazy, or rare. Perhaps not intended to offend, such reactions put abstainers on the defensive. Ciara tells me that a common reaction she receives when she informs people of her abstinence is, "Whoa, I've *never* met anyone who doesn't drink before." Not interpreting this emphasis on her uniqueness as a compliment, Ciara often thinks, "Okay, that's nice. I'm glad I'm a freak. Let's bring me to the circus."

A reaction of bewilderment may have its origins in one of two sources. In one sense, others may claim to understand the reasons behind abstinence and think the individuals practice it in the "right" way (or at least an accept-able fashion), yet they may still experience difficulty imagining the *how* or the logistics of abstinence. Ruth, who owns neither a television nor a car, finds that people react more strongly to the latter abstinence. She describes a typical reaction: "'Boy, that's really fun not having to have a television.' But with the car it's more like, 'How can you get by? How can you do it? That's really hard in [this state] to live without a car.'" Beth, who also does not own a car, reinforces Ruth's point when she tells me that she thinks "the idea . . . that someone might not own a car, I think they get. Fathoming how someone actually manages that, they don't get." What may continue to bewilder others is how individuals can abstain for extensive durations. So while they may be receptive to the idea of not engaging in a particular act, abstainers claim that the thought of *never* doing something eludes and perplexes others.

On another level, others may express bewilderment because they simply do not understand the logic of the category itself. There appear to be three main reasons others may not understand entire abstinence categories: (1) they are so invested in *doing* that they do not "see" abstinence as a possibility; (2) they simply lack familiarity with the abstinence; and (3) they feel that the abstainers violate the "normal" way of practicing a given form of abstinence. In regard to the first reason, at times, certain social encounters and relationships are so saturated with expectations and assumptions of doing that others cannot imagine alternate possibilities. When discussing her past relationships, Lineya tells me that problems inevitably arose surrounding the issue of intercourse: "Some of the guys that I've dated were sexually active when they were younger, so they don't, you know, that's the only thing they've been used to. They started dating, and *it's been automatic sex, so they don't see it any other way*" (emphasis added). Some abstainers interpret such responses of bewilderment as stemming from another source, namely others' lack of experience with and knowledge of the form of abstinence at hand. For example, Benjamin recalls giving a guest lecture in a course on Jewish and Christian feminism in which he referred to the concept of shomer negi'ah, which prohibits touching between men and women. He says that when he

> mentioned the fact of this shomer negi'ah concept, somebody said, "Wait, wait. You're just not allowed to have sex with members of the opposite sex [aside from one's spouse], right?" And I said, "No. No touching." And they said, "Well, that means no like hugging and kissing?" And I said, "No, it means no touching." Like it was inconceivable and it was also oppressive to the student that, you know, she couldn't . . . She was very bothered by it.

Finally, there are times when others cannot comprehend the abstinence category because individuals are not performing it in ways that correspond with conventional assumptions. As an example, Ciara abstains from alcohol because she considers herself an alcoholic; yet, her "alcoholism" looks unlike that of many others. When I ask her why she abstains, she surprises me with the following response:

> I think the major reason is honestly I don't trust myself. I feel like I could very easily have an alcohol problem. . . . I can say that even though I've never been

drunk and I've never been dependent on alcohol, I would consider myself an alcoholic just because of my personality, and um, that I mean I'm just very compulsive and excessive. I self-medicate in other ways, like with food and sleep and, um, caffeine . . . same thing with exercise.

Due to her unique take on addiction, she believes that "people don't understand" or they think that she's "overreacting in some way."

Another reaction to the performative "I don't X" is to challenge that not-doing and attempt to convince the abstainer to participate in the act. Sometimes abstainers claim the language is strong and direct, as Shelley says that one man claimed he was "going to change that" (i.e., her virginity) by the time they graduated from college. In a similar way, Kia elaborates on a common exchange with men regarding her virginity:

> KIA: I've got responses like "Well, we'll talk about it when we get there" or "Okay, um, yeah" with this notion that they will change me, some way they would break me down, after twenty years of being a virgin I'm going to just break down.
>
> JM: Do they say that or do you think that's the implication when they say "It's okay"?
>
> KIA: They say, um, they laugh or they do a little smirk like, "Okay, we'll see later on." Um hmm.
>
> JM: "We'll see"? What's your reaction to that?
>
> KIA: I have been told by a Christian guy, "Oh, we'll cross that road when we get there." What's my reaction?
>
> JM: Yeah, what's your reaction when they say, "We'll see"?
>
> KIA: I usually laugh like, "Okay, *we will*." (laughs)

Repeat Performative Performances

While performatives such as "I don't X" usually occur during moments of first disclosure, they may resurface in encounters with individuals who already know of one's abstinence. During an informal conversation with a vegetarian friend, it became clear how others may prompt performances of performatives subsequent to initial disclosure. Telling me how others—who know him very well—"forget" on occasion that he is a vegetarian, he feels prompted to *re*announce his vegetarianism despite his reluctance to do so. He interprets this "amnesia" (as he refers to it) as a refusal on some level to fully accept and embrace his vegetarianism.

Since I do not talk directly to those who react or respond to abstinence performatives, I must rely on abstainers' perceptions of these encounters. As a result, I am not able to substantiate whether "forgetting" one's abstinence is truly a refusal to accept not-doing or if the response is more benign in nature. Abstainers themselves vary in their interpretations of these amnesic responses. Marta perceives others' forgetting her nonsmoking to be genuine, as many of her friends continue to smoke. However, Bruce, also an ex-smoker, seems more skeptical of these moments of amnesia. Todd alternates between these two explanations, as he at times thinks people simply forget that he is recovering from addiction when they go to hand him a beer in a social situation, while in other instances he feels that they are trying to "taint" him.

Perhaps others may genuinely forget that a person abstains because they may identify him or her more in terms of other doings or not-doings and not the particular abstinence at hand. The degree of sincerity in forgetting seems the less relevant point in these situations. Instead, the significance of forgetting is that it implicitly promises that future performances will occur, especially when forgetting becomes instituted as a routine event in certain relationships and not just a one-time occurrence. For example, Jake, who has been a vegetarian for seventeen years (half of his life), tells me that every time he goes home to see his mother, she asks him if he will eat—"not even just a little?"—meatloaf.

Reactions of others, of course, occur beyond initial points of discovery and those instances where abstainers must remind others of their not-doing. For example, those who are aware of an individual's abstinence and have continued interaction with him or her may react in supportive ways, in essence aiding the performance of abstinence. When becoming a vegetarian, Rebecca tells me that, while cutting out meat was somewhat difficult, her mother helped to make the process much easier by coming up with meals that were vegetarian for her to eat. Jake, also a vegetarian, feels flattered by the efforts made by others to respect his eating practices, as friends will often cook meatless meals or check to see if the menu of a restaurant they are planning to patronize includes vegetarian options. Sarah's abstinence affected eating practices in a different way, and she worried that her parents would be opposed to her move toward what she calls the "opposite direction," that is, becoming more observant in Judaism. To her surprise, her family would do things to make the transition for her as easy as possible, such as waiting until nine-thirty in the evening to make dinner reservations if the Sabbath was ending near nine o'clock.

Such gestures of accommodation are common among various food practices but are not limited to this area. As mentioned earlier, Benjamin, who tries to abide by the principles of shomer negi'ah as much as possible, finds that he would prefer not to embarrass someone than to tell the person that he cannot hug or shake hands with them. Despite his flexibility, he finds that those who are aware of his practices often assist his performance by "warning" others in advance. Speaking of students on campus, he says,

> I think that they probably prepare people before they come to Hillel, you know, that you shouldn't touch the Hillel director. . . . Yeah, yesterday . . . so two [of our college] students got married—Orthodox students—and I was at the wedding, and there were a lot of their friends from [the college] who weren't Jewish at the wedding. And they had been prepped that, you know, they shouldn't touch anybody. . . . It was very funny (laughs).

Abstainers' Responses to Not-Doing

In discussing the responses of others above, I do not mean to set up an us–them distinction between those who abstain and those who do not. Abstainers, too, may be the "others" in any performance of not-doing. While we might assume responses to abstinence from fellow abstainers to be generally favorable, this may not be the case. In fact, other abstainers may be a *less* receptive audience at times since they have their own highly invested ideas about what may pass as acceptable ways of abstaining. Jake offers insight into such a situation when he tells me of a strong negative reaction from other vegans at a vegan bed-and-breakfast in Vermont when he put honey on his oatmeal, as they deemed it "inconsistent" behavior. While it is impossible to predict with great certainty the reaction of a particular group of others, this incident suggests that responses may vary depending on who is on the receiving end.

While I am not able to observe abstainers' direct responses to other abstainers, I ask them to tell me if there are any behaviors that would seem strange, odd, or inappropriate from which to abstain. Some express a general acceptance toward any abstinence regardless of type. Denis offers one of the most unconditional and tolerant views on others' abstinences:

> I'm pretty strongly convinced that individuals are very different creatures. They have a wide range of desires and fears and insecurities and so on, so what persons choose to do or not to is, should be expected to be very diverse, and I

think we should support and tolerate that. There are things that are others-destructive and self-destructive, which all of us should work to minimize, but, um, in view of the tremendous diversity of persons—you know, their backgrounds, their ideals, their conditions, and so on—you know, we need to have tolerance for the very different things that people pursue and fear and avoid.

Even if they express a proclivity to be more open-minded in evaluating others' abstinences, most abstainers find some forms of abstinence unacceptable or incomprehensible in some way. In addition to behaviors in which abstaining would impede basic survival (e.g., breathing, eating), break a law (e.g., wearing clothes), or be the result of a phobia or involuntary condition, the list of "strange, odd, or unacceptable" abstinences included the following responses:

- not watching television: "seems elitist and ridiculous, implies that there's absolutely nothing on television worth watching" (Jake)
- not masturbating
- staying single (or at least uncoupled)
- not riding in automobiles or not driving
- avoiding particular words or not cursing
- not reading: "I think it's really weird and disappointing when people say that they don't read. I don't mean stop signs and stuff; I mean books." (Bruce)
- not eating chocolate
- not using technology
- not having sex: "would seem pretty extreme" (Craig)
- abstaining for religious reasons

Not only are some of these not-doings common forms of abstinence, some of the "unacceptable" abstinences are precisely the ones they practice. More specifically, while abstainers perceive their own abstinence as appropriate for themselves at this point in their lives, they may feel less willing to accept the same abstinence in a different form or in a different context for others. For example, though Marla justifies her abstinence from sex as a virgin who wants to wait for the "right" moment, she thinks that everyone *should* have sex at some point. Those who do not, she says, are "crazy": "Why would anyone not want to have sex?!" Todd, who has struggled deeply with drug and alcohol addition, curiously maintains that those who *never* experiment with one or the other might be more secure with themselves but nonetheless a bit "square." Similarly, Craig, who resists using e-mail in a profession that relies heavily on it, says that he thinks "it's cranky" when people avoid technology in general. When I ask him to clarify, he elaborates:

> Just getting their cranks. I think, you know, questions of the relation between technological innovation and culture are enormously important. Um, but, you know, along the end of the spectrum, interesting questions about that relation is that since those that think technology means progress and progress is a bad thing and that we need to stay with the old ways. . . . I mean, it just seems so obviously a simplistic attitude.

It appears that, with the exception of those who have never engaged in the thing from which they abstain, most abstainers express that others should "try" the act at some point in their lives—precisely the attitude they resent on occasion when it comes from others regarding their own abstinence.

The reactions of abstainers to other abstainers highlight the difficulty of not-doing in the context of expected doing. It may seem surprising that those who abstain are reluctant to embrace abstinence as a generic social practice. But since there is no anticipatory socialization for abstinence, we can assume that abstainers, like nonabstainers, grew up with the implicit or explicit message that "doing" is somehow "normal." Despite the moments of intolerance mentioned above, based on what the abstainers report on the reactions of others and their own opinions toward abstinence, Jada offers what appears to be a fairly accurate conclusion: "I think that our culture does a really, really shabby job of preparing us for like people having different ideas . . . and that any time that something of that realm enters into our daily mundane life, people don't know what to do with it." Nonetheless, the reactions of others—whether these individuals are nonabstainers or fellow abstainers—become critical moments in identity performances for both parties involved.

The Tacit Functions of Performatives

The role of witnesses to identity performances is a recurrent theme in the research. Attribution theory—labeled by Fiske and Taylor as the "leading theoretical concern and dominant empirical topic of the field [of social psychology]"—elevates these observers to the center of its analysis. Regarding social perceivers as naive (but somewhat good) scientists, attribution theorists strive to unveil the processes through which individuals gather information and draw conclusions about what causes things to happen. Fiske and Taylor further imply that, while attribution is an everyday, common-place event, we notice the process of determining causality best in moments "when people are surprised or threatened by events that undermine their beliefs and expectations" (1984, 137, 21).

Other theorists, particularly those identified with the symbolic interac-tionist school of thought, shift the focus away from the "whys" and more toward the "hows" of others in identity performances. Mead recognizes the central role others play and suggests that these individuals serve as social measuring rods for actors even if they are not physically present. Specif-ically, individuals learn how to regulate and modify their behavior only subsequent to internalizing the attitudes and responses of what he calls the "generalized other." It is this understanding of the perspective of society at large that marks the development of the "me," "the organized set of atti-tudes of others which one himself assumes" (Mead 1934, 175). Using a dra-maturgical analogy to discuss the performances of everyday life, Goffman, too, highlights relationships between "actors" and their "audiences." Here he explores the struggles of the former to manage the impressions and to control the definition of the situation by the latter. The presentation of self, then, Goffman warns, may be precarious work, as audiences may ultimately discredit or reject offered performances through various tactics.[3]

Of course, the power of others may not stop at their ability to discredit one's projected identity. While one strand of labeling theory[4] focuses on the institutional creation of deviance and its functional utility, one theme that runs throughout the theory concerns the notion that actors may behave in deviant ways only subsequent to having labels thrust upon them (Jenkins 1996). Collectively, then, such research on labeling elucidates the brawn others bear in the formation of personal identity. Though somewhat diverse in their approach to the role of others in identity performances, these theo-rists together support the idea that individuals continually define themselves in the context of interaction even if, as Jenkins suggests, their internal self-definitions are a direct resistance to others' external definitions (1996, 27).

That others play such an instrumental role in the construction of per-sonal identity appears to contradict what some theorists say about the self in contemporary times. Specifically, theorists argue, individuals are currently more detached from others than at any previous point in history. Giddens explains this separation as a result of the loss of tradition's hold on daily life, leaving individuals the ability to exercise more agency in terms of how they construct themselves (1991, 5). Such freedom to design one's self would, at first glance, appear to *decrease* a reliance on others for any sense of self. Yet the evidence suggests otherwise. In his historical analysis of etiquette books, Arditi argues that individuals initially practiced politeness because to do so was the morally right choice for a virtuous *person*. Gradually, however, a keener sense of individuation and the normalization of detachment from others paradoxically led to a need to practice etiquette for and in front of others. In a seemingly contradictory way, then, individuation and a need to perform for others developed a strong positive relationship over time (Arditi 1998).

Interestingly, while abstainers need recognition from others in shaping their identities, interactions between abstainers and those who do not abstain may inadvertently help affirm the identities of the latter as well. The need for performatives often arises in situations where others are engaging in the act from which the abstainer abstains. The performative "I don't X," then, not only directs the attention to what the abstainer does not do but to what nonabstainers are *doing*. Abstainers believe that this unsolicited attention to doing sometimes takes nonabstainers out of "their comfort zone" (Benjamin).

While many abstainers feel that others "can't handle it" (Sandy) when they learn of one's abstinence, this reaction heightens in immediate contexts of doing more than in other situations. Although Jada tells me that some people "just don't know what to do with" her vegetarianism, she senses that people become "a lot more defensive during food time rather than like sitting over coffee or whatever. I mean, honestly, that's understandable because they probably have meat on their plate while we're talking about it." These defensive moments usually manifest themselves in one of two (though not mutually exclusive) ways: fear of judgment of one's own doing or expressed hostility toward the abstainer's not-doing.

In the first case, abstainers often mention that others fear that they will be judged on their nonabstinence. Kia, who abstains from sex and alcohol, tells me that others continue to probe after she initially discloses her abstinence. When I ask her why she thinks this might be the case, she says, "I don't know. I really think they try to find some way to justify their actions, but like I say, you don't really need to justify them to me. And that's when I really realize people are truly not in sync with me and they don't know who I am because they would know that it's more of a personal decision. That's the way I feel." Not only do abstainers believe that others feel that they must justify their nonabstinence at times; they sometimes sense that others fear conversion attempts. Georgia, who also abstains from sex and alcohol, tells me that she definitely perceives a fear among nonabstainers in their interactions with her, specifically, a concern that she will try to "change" them in some way despite the fact that she has no interest in trying to "convert" others.

For whatever reasons abstainers believe others respond to them in a negative way, these situations appear to create uncomfortable situations for all involved parties. Jayson, who does not smoke as part of being straight edge, finds that even when he tries not to draw attention to this particular abstinence,

> it's other people that give *me* a problem about it. I'm hanging out in a room with people that are smoking and secondhand smoke is all over the place, and I'm like, "What do I care?" because I used to purposely put it in my lungs. Now it's not like a big deal for smoke to be in the air really. I personally don't mind secondhand smoke or whatever, but I never say anything about it. They're the ones that go to me and say, "Oh, does this bother you?" and make a big deal about it. So yeah, I mean, it puts other people off.

One way to prevent tensions of this sort is to offer an alternative form of account: the ambiguous performative. In contrast to a strong performative—such as "I don't X"—ambiguous performatives soften the exchange between abstainer and audience. The result is that the abstainer effectively declines to participate in the activity while leaving space for interpretation in a way that prevents the listener from definitive conclusions about whether one abstains in general or simply prefers not to at that moment. For example, although Ciara claims that a lot of times she'll actually volunteer the fact that she does not drink alcohol, at other times, she "might just say 'no thanks.'" Similarly, Maya remembers the early stages of her pregnancy in which she did not want to drink but also did not feel ready to disclose her pregnancy to everyone. As someone who drank a lot socially, she felt that her friends were "tiptoeing around asking" her direct questions. Rather than supplying unsolicited information, she would simply state, "I just don't feel like having a drink."

Ambiguous performatives such as "No, thanks," "I'll pass," "None for me," and "I don't want any," serve as ways of refusing to participate in the activity in a way that can preclude the possibility of having others take offense. In this sense, then, such performatives lubricate the relations between doers and not-doers, as they clearly locate the abstinence in the moment while leaving conclusions about abstinence as a general practice more open-ended and subject to multiple interpretations.

Ambiguous performatives also serve to protect abstainers as well as doers, as ambiguity allows abstainers to be honest without full disclosure. When pushed to participate in conversations about sexual experiences, Sarah simply replies that she "[doesn't] discuss that kind of stuff" without volunteering the information that she is a virgin. When asked if she has ever denied her abstinence or has downplayed it to any degree, Raven responds: "I've never denied it, but, um, I have, you know, I have on occasion . . . someone will offer me a drink and I'll decline but not say that I'm an alcoholic. I don't know if that's playing it down or not. I mean to me it's not playing it down. It's just saying, 'No, I don't want a drink.' I don't feel any need to go into my life story because I don't want to drink." Nonetheless, as Raven acknowledges, ambiguous performatives sometimes fail. Though she feels she can safely tell someone she does not know well that she "[doesn't] drink anymore" or that she "used to but had enough," she finds it more difficult not to reveal the full story to someone she knows on a more intimate level. She illustrates this in her account of an incident with her boss, a bookseller, whom she also considered a friend:

> We would talk about a lot of things, but we never like socialized outside of work, and the subject never really came up. Once or twice he would talk about someone who was an alcoholic, [but] I never told him. Then about two months ago we were working the book fair and he brought a bottle of wine. When we close down each night, the dealers usually drink wine as they're packing up their stuff, and he brought this bottle for the two of us. And I said, "No, I don't want any." He seemed sort of offended and confused, and so I told him. He was like stunned. It was really weird, but, um, I mean, yeah, I suppose when I meet people I just don't announce it, but eventually if I have any sort of relationship, it comes up.

The Importance of Verbalizing Abstinence

As previous chapters show, the visibility of abstinence depends on a variety of factors ranging from where one abstains, in whose presence, at what time in the life course, the manner in which one elects to not-do, and so on. Like most identity markers, then, abstinence can be easier or more difficult to "see" given the context. As Amelia comments when referring to her school days, "If I walked into school and wore glasses, [the kids would say] 'four eyes,' but they don't say 'vegetarian.'"

Verbal performances of abstinence make not-doing visible in ways that might not occur in the absence of such statements. While some abstainers freely choose to verbally state their practices to others, it is more often the case that audiences to abstinence demand both disclosure and explanations of not-doing. As a result, these revelations—frequently met with bewilderment, confusion, and even hostility—rarely take the form of boastful self praise but instead allow abstainers to manage the situation at hand. Disclosing one's decision to not-do, however, need not leave abstainers feeling fully exposed, as they can choose to tell only part of the story through the use of ambiguous performatives. Rather than announcing abstinence as a master status of sorts, vague responses, such as "No thanks" or "I won't have any" allow individuals to safely not-do without revealing whether they always abstain or are just deciding to do so during that particular instance.

Beyond moments of first disclosure, repeat verbal performances of abstinence become necessary when others conveniently "forget" or ask abstainers to defend their decisions to not-do. Though such statements sometimes stem from nonabstainers' perceptions that abstainers judge their decisions to eat, drink, smoke, or whatever the act may be, asking abstainers to verbalize their not-doing serves to uphold and make visible those differences. The distinction between doers and not-doers, of course, cannot be a complete separation, as even abstainers express that certain forms of not doing are, in a word, puzzling. In the end, performative moments—whether they are direct or ambiguous, are met with scorn or curiosity—allow both abstainers and nonabstainers to engage in forms of identity work that ultimately make their sense of self very "real" and defensible.

CONCLUSION

Virgins. Born-again virgins. Recovering addicts. No-carbohydrate dieters. Vegetarians. Simple livers. Straight edge hardcore punks. At first glance, the only thing such seemingly diverse abstainers appear to have in common is simply the fact that they do not do something. After all, some who abstain have never participated in the act they choose not to do while others enjoy an extensive history with doing. Some see abstinence as temporary, some as a lifelong choice. And when it comes to reasons behind the decision to abstain, the list is lengthy. This analysis has taken to its center the question of what—despite the apparent endless differences—abstainers have in common with one another. Specifically, how does not-doing operate as an important organizational piece of identity regardless of whether the abstinence is from food, sex, driving, technology, or substances?

Throughout the book, I have argued that what often gets lost in the politics and morality debates that frequently accompany the subject of abstinence is what a *Newsweek* article quite shrewdly identifies as the continued and "real issue" of abstinence: personal choice (Ali and Scelfo 2002). While I stand by my position that abstinence hinges on choice, it is, of course, necessary to qualify this statement by thinking through some of the ways in which even the decision to not-do depends on a certain degree of privilege, power, and access to resources in order for it to have any sort of meaning. In this final section, I will return to the relationship between abstinence and personal choice, focusing on the ways in which abstinence may be a luxury of sorts both in terms of who can practice it and at what point. I will conclude the analysis with some thoughts about how the study of not-doing may inform our understanding of doings as well as our understanding of identity as a whole.

The "Choice" of Abstinence

In chapter 3 on modern abstainers, I argued that, although abstinence as a practice enjoys a long history, both the forms it takes and the conditions under which it now operates as a basis for identity formation may be unprecedented. Based on resistance of some kind, abstinence always has roots in individual agency, but this choice has a unique quality today. Theorists of identity rightly note individuals' increasing freedom from external labeling and the resultant discretion they enjoy in determining for themselves "who they are" more so than at any other point in history. In her well-known work on ethnicity, for example, Mary Waters argues that, although ethnicity may not play a significant role in individuals' daily lives, people nonetheless "cling tenaciously to their ethnic identities" and use them in voluntary ways of their own choosing depending on the situation at hand (1990, 147). Ethnic identities become convenient tools of identity, as they afford individuals the elements of choice and individuality. Somewhat paradoxically, however, the choice to identify with an ethnicity aligns individuals with a particular ethnicity as it simultaneously embraces individuality (150–51). Waters ultimately resolves this paradox by arguing that communities of ethnicity operate in more benign ways than other communities, as they do not undermine or interfere with one's individuality. Instead, ethnic identification offers identity rewards in the absence of the "stifling and constricting" components that often accompany community (154).

So what of community? If, as we have seen, abstainers do not uniformly respond to other abstainers in favorable ways, can we insist, as Waters does regarding ethnicity, that abstinence allows individuals the rewards of community without the costs? The fact that some abstainers express hostility to others who engage in not-doing suggests that abstinence is largely about the self, existing on a microlevel. Still, abstainers may reap the benefits of a community of not-doers even though the parameters of that community change from context to context. Abstainers identify with other abstainers with varying degrees of openness: at times only with those who abstain in ways identical to their own circumstances, at other times by group (Jehovah's Witnesses, virgins, etc.), and still at other times with abstainers at large. Less important than how one defines community remains the critical point that one's abstinence is a basis for self-identity more so than group membership.

Like ethnicity, abstinence is a relatively high-control, low-cost identity option. Waters suggests that one of the predominant messages reiterated in

American culture is that "you have to have something you can identify with" (1990, 155). The decision to abstain takes on a significant meaning in a context where individuals arguably possess a greater ability to create themselves than in any other point in history yet still need to identify with something. Unlike other identities, which may require financial capital, prestige, and so on, identifying with abstinence becomes a tool for identity building that is accessible to many. In this sense, abstinence is a relatively cost-free means to the end of gaining some control over the self.

In all this talk of choice, however, it is important to remember not to "exaggerate the opportunities for personal expressiveness" (May and Cooper 1995, 77). Even during times when abstinence is thought to signal one's worth or goodness, abstaining simply does not exist as an option among those who cannot take the existence of a given resource for granted. Turner reminds us of this somewhat obvious but easily overlooked point when he says in his discussion of the previous marriage between capitalism and Protestant values of asceticism, "the notion of diet was irrelevant to a working class periodically subjected to starvation. Since the eighteenth-century worker depended on cereals, abstinence from meat was not a relevant issue."[1] For sure, time has brought about change, and concepts that once applied exclusively to members of the upper classes (as in the case of "diets") now exist among other classes as well. As a result of expansions of this sort, some rightly argue that the possibility of a negotiating, performing self is no longer a middle- or upper-class privilege but has become a reality among the lower classes of society as well.[2]

To point to the spread of concepts and options of abstinence to those for whom abstaining made little sense in the past, of course, does not mean to imply *equal* access to these ideas and practices among social actors. Individuals continue to develop preferences (or what we commonly refer to as "taste") for the things that are readily available to them.[3] Abstinence from something—the "preference" not to do something—can only make sense if one has the ability to "prefer" that thing in the first place. On this point, May and Cooper warn that we not confuse the increasing *visibility* of options with their *availability*. In this discourse of choice, then, we have a responsibility not to ignore the "forces at work in contemporary society that restrict life chances and constrain social behaviours." In order to be meaningful to those individuals it seeks to represent,

> any sociological account must involve an appeal to the subjective experience and resources of actors. It must equally involve recognizing the constraints that are placed on actors that are experienced in an immediate and concrete

form. Self-authoring, then, must take place in social contexts in which there are both obstacles to, and opportunities for, sovereign self-authorship. Here, things get in the way of self-authorship differentially according to actors' locations within the social structure and according to their access to cultural and material resources. (May and Cooper 1995, 79)

So while abstinence may not *require* financial status, for example, it fails to make sense in a context where such resources are absent or minimal. To speak of a severely impoverished person who can barely meet his or her basic needs of food and shelter as an abstainer or "simple liver"[4] is not only inaccurate but irresponsible.

This luxury component of abstinence need not apply only to one's financial situation. While admitting that his secure income allows him to "decide" to eat organic and locally grown food as part of his vegetarian diet, Denis notes how other abstinences hinge on contingencies not necessarily related to income. Preferring to live simply, Denis nonetheless found that particular periods of his life would not accommodate such choices. Though claiming he has always preferred a simple lifestyle, Denis felt unable to follow through with some of his wishes (e.g., not owning a television) in the past due to the presence of his three children in the home. Now, as a sixty-five-year-old retired professor who lives alone, he is better able to engage in some of the abstinences he associates with simplicity. For him, this shift has been a luxury of time and age, not money.

It is important to note that the informants for this research are those who have the luxury of abstaining. Even among those who deny feelings of desire or temptation and claim, as Bob does, that they "just don't prefer 'em" (whatever "they" may be), the ability to effectively make this statement relies on the possibility of access—whether one wants it or not—in the first place. This book, then, is made up of the experiences of those who have the means to own a car but do not; can ingest certain foods, drinks, and substances without ill effect but do not; can bear children but do not.

Abstinence and the Identity Story

So what does not-doing tell us about the workings of identity in general? One of the basic principles of gestalt psychology is that one must understand the parts in order to understand the whole (and vice versa).[5] Extending this idea to our thinking about how individuals build identity, we cannot treat what individuals do not do as dormant, noninfluential, and uninteresting pieces of the identity puzzle. Though it may appear that I have focused on those who identify abstinence as a more central part of identity than others, this assumption needs a degree of qualification. The method of snowball sampling[6] at times led me to individuals whom *others* perceived as "abstainers." While these individuals certainly abstained from a given behavior, the fact that they did not identify it as a master status of sorts does not weaken (and may, in fact, strengthen) the utility of the conclusions regarding not-doing.

In addressing the larger issue of how the study of not-doings informs the study of identity as a whole, a logical first step is to see the similarities between those identities based on not-doings and those based on doings. As I will show below, most of the issues discussed in this book—parameters of identity, how one arrives at a given identity, strategies of maintaining a "pure" identity, issues of relations with and opinions of others, and the constraints of language—are ones used by everyone at some point in regard to both not-doings *and* doings. An example from the work of fiction *Life of Pi* begins to make this point. In *Pi*, the narrator, struggling with his personal beliefs in regard to religion, reaches a conclusion that might initially arouse suspicion in others. Comparing atheists to religious fanatics—two groups that are typically set up as strict opposites of one another—Pi insists that, even though the content of their (dis)belief differs, the form of their practice remains the same in that both "go as far as the legs of reason will carry them—and then they leap" (Martel 2001, 28). Whether or not we accept Pi's ideas, such logic challenges us to think across firmly established lines and to imagine the similarities between practices such as compulsive eating and drinking with their "opposites" of dieting or teetotaling. In fact, along the continuum of behavior, the strongest and most interesting comparisons surround the poles, that is, the realms of total not-doing and doing in excess.

When thinking about how doing and not-doing may fare similarly in terms of how individuals perform identity, it is useful to return to the strategies I identified as "fire walking" and "fence building" earlier in the book. Fire walking relies on an expanded notion of not-doing and allows individuals to "play with fire" without fully discrediting their claims to abstinence. When fence building, however, individuals hold their abstinence to the highest standard of purity and, consequently, erect a protective "fence" around their abstinence, in essence removing themselves one additional degree from the fire.

In terms of frequency, most of us, most of the time, choose to fire walk with our doings and not-doings. Among our *doings*, fire walking draws little attention as it basically means that, for the most part, we participate in an act, but sometimes we prefer not to. We may smoke, but sometimes we may not in certain company. We might drink alcohol, but at some parties we opt for a soda instead. We have sex, but some nights we say "no." Rather than bringing the charge of hypocrisy, most of this behavior likely passes with little notice on the part of others. An occasional not-doing in someone who typically engages in the behavior appears to be little cause for alarm. Yet fire walking on our not-doings commands significantly more attention than does fire walking on our doings. This is in large part due to the fact that we appear to hold abstinence to higher standards of purity than doing. For example, while we may question the validity of someone's virginity after engaging in oral sex (fire walking a *not-doing*), we are unlikely to question someone's identity as a carnivore if he or she orders eggplant one night at dinner (fire walking a *doing*). While the difference may hinge in part on the varying degrees to which our culture dictates sex and food affect the body, it also reflects the unequal standards to which we hold doing and not-doing. Unlike doings, where we allow room for flexibility and "breaks," we often hold abstinence to a literal meaning, expecting those who violate to account for such "slips" or deliberate breaches of their not-doing in some way.

This difference in the need for accountability might lead us to conclude that not-doings are much more fragile pieces of identity than are doings since it seems that doing can easily ruin not-doing, but that the reverse appears to be less true. While this reasoning may hold true for the "middle ground" of fire walking, it falls through when we move outward to the poles of extreme doing and not-doing. Just as we sometimes "fence build" around our abstinences, we do the same with our doings when we engage in any behavior to excess. It may seem difficult to imagine how an individual might fence build when he or she does something to excess, especially if we get caught up in the right-or-wrong, moral approach to abstinence. After all, fence building aims to keep out the impurities, and are not the doings of excess precisely about impurities (smoking, drinking, sex, etc.)? As we move away from a moralistic framework and toward a strictly behavioral interpretation of identity, we can rethink impurities as those things that harm a desired identity and not things that bear inherent negative connotations. Making this shift in perspective, we can see that those who fence build with their not-doings quite remarkably resemble those who fence build with their doings. Regardless of which side seems more admirable or enjoyable, they ultimately boil down to having the same aim, that is, keeping out anything that would tarnish the reputation of living at the extreme.

The informants who have a past of excess offer some insight into how fence building on a doing might work. Raven very candidly talks about her

previous excessive ways when talking about the shift to abstinence. Referring to her days of drinking and using drugs, she tells me that she "was
constantly high and drunk," and insists that she "had never done anything
sober: never dated sober, never worked sober." As someone who gravitated
toward fence building among her doings, she found quitting especially difficult, not necessarily due to the physical dimension of the addiction, but
because not drinking or using required a complete change in the way she
approached alcohol and drugs. Sober for some time now, she thinks back
to what she initially thought about the prospect of abstaining: "I hear in AA
a lot of people talking about trying to quit and not being able to. And, you
know, as far as I remember *I never really tried not drinking*" (emphasis added).
It was a friend who first introduced the possibility to her:

> He looked at me and said, "Why don't you just stop drinking?" I'm like, "Why?
> I don't need to." He said, "Just stop for a year." This was so beyond my com-
> prehension. I just couldn't image being able to do it or wanting to do it. I
> didn't want to stop drinking. I wanted my life to change. I wanted to stop
> waking up in bizarre places. But I didn't want to stop drinking.

Joining Alcoholics Anonymous, then, was a momentous occasion for her, as
the organization would essentially require her to practice the same strategy
of fence building, only this time with abstinence rather than excess. Many
other former addicts recount similar practices of doing to excess with little
or no reprieve. As Todd tells me, "When others would drink maybe three or
four beers, I would drink five, six, seven, eight, nine, ten, eleven, or twelve
beers or until I was throwing up. It was the same thing with smoking pot.
It was never okay just to smoke a joint for me. It was smoke until the bag
was gone."

We can more clearly see the similarity between fence building in abstinence and the same strategy in excess when we consider how one instance
of not-doing threatens to "taint" one's identity based around obsessive doing in a way that a doing would call into question one's total abstinence.
Just I may challenge the validity of someone who claims to be 100 percent
abstinent but has a drink at a wedding, I may also doubt the credibility
of someone's reputation for being a "partier" if he or she refuses to drink
one night. Martin and Hummer's study on fraternities—sites many associate
with excess as the norm—shows how fence building around excess can protect the reputation of both the fraternity and its members as "all masculine."
Specifically, Martin and Hummer find that fraternities "work hard to create a
macho image and context and try to avoid any suggestion of 'wimpishness,'

effeminacy, and homosexuality." In recruiting for the organization, members deny "'geeks,' nerds, and men said to give the fraternity a 'wimpy' or 'gay' reputation. Art, music, and humanities majors, majors in traditional women's fields (nursing, home economics, social work, education), men with long hair, and those whose appearance or dress violate current norms are rejected" (Martin and Hummer 1989, 460). Once the "purity" of the fraternity is in place, daily rituals of excess then ensure the security of this reputation of hypermasculinity.[7]

In thinking about how these two different strategies of fence building and fire walking would apply to the entire continuum of identity, ranging from the ideal typical poles of absolute not-doing to absolute doing, we arrive at the following visual representation of behavior:

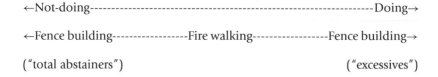

←Not-doing---Doing→

←Fence building-----------------Fire walking-----------------Fence building→

("total abstainers")   ("excessives")

Both "total abstainers" and "excessives" fence build in the spirit of maintaining the integrity of their identities by not allowing any impurities (whether they be doings or not-doings) to enter. Fire walking (among both doers and not-doers), then, occupies the space in between these poles and allows for a more negotiable conceptualization of identity. Again, since most individuals fall somewhere in the middle of the continuum whether they identify more as a "doer" or "not-doer," we find ourselves increasingly aware of the behavior of those individuals who move toward the poles. Perhaps this explains why the sampling for this book led to a disproportionate amount of abstainers with a tendency to fence build: they become the most visible due to their more extreme practices of abstinence.

The observation that not-doing and doing lie on a continuum rather than in discrete and disconnected pockets of identity suggests that rigid treatments of the two may be ineffective when dealing with real-life situations. Current efforts to enforce strict abstinence-only programs, for example, may benefit from allowing for a more flexible interpretation of what it means to abstain. In their study of virginity pledges, Bearman and Bruckner (2001) found that pledging only works in moderation in that pledges succeed precisely when everyone is *not* pledging. In short, the somewhat nonnormative character of pledging leads to its effectiveness. According to the *Oxford English Dictionary*, definitions of "abstemious," too, reflect this flexibility, as they have changed over time to include moderation and temperance (Simpson and Weiner 1989, 53). The recognition that doing and not-doing are more complex and come with more nuance than moral debates over right and wrong permit could open the door for a better understanding of the identity decisions people make.

There is still a great way to go, however. Even in my own efforts to bring attention to the workings of not-doings in identity, I have reinforced the status quo of how we think about identity by always framing abstinence in reference to doing. From one of the most frequently used terms in the book (*"not*-doing") to the terms chosen to identify abstainers temporally ("waiters," "nevers," "time-outers," and "quitters"), these terms all embrace doing as the default practice of identity, the starting point from which we understand ourselves. Are those I have identified as "quitters" those who have stopped doing or are they "starters" of new identities based on abstinence? Even among terms that seem to carry no judgment about whether the doing or not-doing should be the reference point, the question of how we perceive such identities remains. Are vegetarians, for example, those who do not eat meat or those who have a plant-based diet? The challenge for us is to begin to imagine and rethink how we are accustomed to understanding identity.

The abstainers' voices we have heard here allow us to begin this journey. They offer us a glimpse into what it means to abstain, the ways one might go about it, the obstacles faced, and the changes in perceptions of self that all of us face over time. Clearly, while these interviews provide glimpses into the past and future, they ultimately only teach us about individuals' perspectives on abstinence at that moment. Had I captured them during another period in time, at a past or future point in their life trajectories, the meaningful *not-doing* they currently practice easily could have been just another noninfluential "not doing" among many others. Often by chance, I continue to receive updates on several of my informants; while many continue to maintain an outlook similar to when we met, others have radically changed. Craig has given in to the demands of his profession and has started to use e-mail. Todd had a few months of relapse following the need to take prescription medication for kidney stones. Two years after our interview, Eve and her husband welcomed a baby boy. And I have heard that Jayson, who opened chapter 4 with the coffee shop exchange in which he spoke of the lifelong quality of abstinence within straight edge, entered law school and "broke edge." Rather than assuming such changes of heart—whether temporary or permanent—discredit the conclusions made in this book, I see these examples as reminders that interview conversations serve as still shots in the longer film of individuals' lives. Nonetheless, these snapshots ask us to reconsider what we know in a new light.

By treating abstinence in a generic sense, I do not mean to discredit the important work being carried out in any given field on a particular form of abstinence. Recent research has been quick to respond to the questions of what counts as abstinence,[8] how we define it, and what the implications are for individuals' everyday lives. Nonetheless, in focusing on the specific manifestations of abstinence, it is important not to regard abstinence as an abnormal form of identity work. We cannot pretend that abstinence belongs to the realm of extremists, whether it be religious zealots or, as was suggested to me, animal rights activists throwing orange paint on fur coats. Not only is everyone not "doing it," but, to some degree, everyone is also *not-doing*.

APPENDIX A

A Note on Methodology

Abstinence as a Generic Category

In the earliest musings about this project, I knew that I wanted to explore the formation of abstinent identities as a generic social process rather than to focus on one particular identity "type." It was not hard to anticipate the justified criticism that a study of the latter sort would tell us something only about recovering alcoholics, virgins, vegetarians, nondrivers, or whatever the chosen topic might have been.

At one point, I considered selecting two abstinent identities in order to avoid (to some degree, at least) the limitation of findings resulting from the methodology mentioned above. I found myself drawn to virginity and recovering alcoholism as abstinent identities and thought they would serve as strong candidates for analysis for two reasons. First, when talking to others earlier about my interest in abstinence, it appeared that people associate the term with resistance to sexual intercourse or an avoidance of drugs and alcohol. Second, I anticipated individuals practicing these forms of absti-nence to be both accessible and largely willing to participate, alleviating a bit of the stress sometimes associated with the recruitment of interview in-formants. Observing the rise in and growing popularity of groups in which individuals pledge their abstinence to others initially intensified the logic of selecting these groups. In terms of virginity, I began to hear more about the Christian-based virginity pledge system of True Love Waits, in which in-dividuals vow—in front of parents, friends, and God—to abstain from sex until marriage. Of course, recovery organizations such as Alcoholics Anony-mous (AA) and Narcotics Anonymous (NA) have enjoyed a long history in promoting abstinence from alcohol and other drugs. I found recovery from addiction attractive as an abstinent identity for another reason, that is, the recent rise of alternative approaches to the AA/NA model. Newer models, such as Moderation Management (MM)[1] and Rational Recovery (RR)[2] challenge former assumptions of the most effective path to recovery.[3]

In the back of my mind, I still anticipated the criticism that such an analysis would tell a nice story about how abstinent identities operate but perhaps only in the areas of sexuality and recovery. As I thought more about these two categories, I realized that, in some ways, drawing from these two areas would be an exercise in comparing apples and oranges. Not only are the two substantively different, they are different in another very significant way. Whereas virginity typically involves not doing an act in which one has *not yet* engaged, recovery often mandates *never again* performing an act. Furthermore, in most instances, virginity serves as a *temporary* state of not-doing, whereas most recovering addicts envision abstinence to be a *permanent* part of their future.

At this point, I began to think further about the temporal components of abstinence and created the 2×2 matrix (introduced in chapter 4) along the dimensions of whether one has engaged in the act in the past and whether one anticipates doing the act in the future, in other words, if the abstinence is a temporary or permanent part of identity. This revised design appealed to me, as it allowed me to flesh out the temporal possibilities while also opening up the research to abstinence in many substantive areas, moving the analysis toward a more generic level.

Narrative Events

The method I chose for this project entailed interviewing the individuals at a time when they were abstaining and asking them to produce not merely an account of their current practices but a more detailed narrative that included a consideration of both the past and the future. While I believe this to be a useful approach to understanding abstinence, clearly there are issues surrounding narrative as a means of tracking pathways in identity, and it is imperative to explore some of the strengths and limitations of this approach.

Though their terminology may differ, those interested in the topic of narrative increasingly distinguish between the *narrated event* and the *narrative event*, the former referring to the content of the story, the latter to its telling. While this distinction between what Langellier calls "what happened to me" (narrated event) and "let me tell you" (narrative event) may be analytically useful, it is difficult to separate out these highly interdependent pieces (2001, 151). Narrative events, then, do not recount the "facts" per se but instead become the vehicles for creating meaning within one's life. In this quest for meaning, Freeman (2001) argues that there appear to be four dimensions of this relationship between narrative and identity: experiential, rhetorical, cultural, and historical.

In terms of the experiential, Freeman insists that we move beyond the idea that narrative constitutes a fictive imposition, a story that becomes a strategy forced on our lives rather than something lived (2001, 294). As an alternative, Freeman offers the possibility that the source of one's identity might, in fact, be narrative itself, reflected in the unique way we compose our stories. Narrative clearly falls short of full disclosure of "real events" and introduces issues of both presentation of self and impression management (Goffman 1959), as well as a picking and choosing from an array of events. As Bateson suggests, "composing a life involves a continual reimagining of the future and reinterpretation of the past to give meaning to the present, remembering best those events that prefigured what followed, forgetting those that proved to have no meaning within the narrative" (1989, 29–30). Despite this retrospective bias, the narrative event carries the advantage of allowing individuals to serve as experts on their own experience (Langellier 2001).

The narrative presented, of course, depends on several aspects related to the rhetorical dimension. If identity is relational, intersubjective, produced and reproduced through communication as teller and listener attempt to agree on a definition of the situation, then the conditions under which this production occurs will undoubtedly affect the narrative (Freeman 2001). Throughout the interviews, I felt the awareness of my various positions heighten and diminish: at times, as a researcher, as a young, white woman, as a nonabstainer, or as a stranger. In addition to my appearance and relationship to the people I interviewed, I also felt the influence of time constraints on the story told. While I tried to be thorough, there were times when I was sure details of the narratives were a bit incomplete. These factors, combined with my desire to hear the "whole journey," clearly affected the stories I heard regarding the informants' pathways to abstinence.

While the narratives of their journeys to (and at times from) abstinence are of their own telling, cultural and historical dimensions also present themselves in the narratives. If the production of narrative in this context is a relational one, between an informant and typically (but not always) a stranger (myself), then the informant must situate his or her story in narrative structures that are familiar cultural models. Such models do not strip the storyteller of agency but rather guide the process of "making sense of his or her own unique past" as the individual "tries to discern how it may have culminated in what exists now" (Freeman 2001, 286). Asking these individuals to describe their pathways to abstinence produces autobiographical narratives, stories that are broad in scope and cover a range of perhaps otherwise seemingly discrete episodes (Zussman 2000, 5). Clearly, there are limitations to the narrative model used here, yet, as Spence argues, examining the ways in which individuals strive to create coherent accounts of the self may be more significant than trying to establish some form of personal or historical "truth" (Pillemer 1998, 10).

The way in which the informants create these narratives, of course, may change. One's narrative regarding the pathways of abstinence could look starkly different depending not only on the experiential, rhetorical, cultural, and historical dimensions mentioned above but also on when one is engaging in the narrative event in terms of one's life course. Still, my ability to understand individuals' paths to their current abstinence hinges entirely on their own assessment of this path *at the time we sat down together for the interview*. This snapshot of abstinence not only limits the possibility of seeing how stories change through retellings but also prevents my ability to verify the accuracy of my own interpretations of their narratives. What remains significant, however, is the ability to see how individuals make sense of their current positions based on their understanding of past events, as well as a yet-to-be-seen future.

Sampling Issues

Having four overarching categories of abstainers (waiters, nevers, time-outers, quitters), forty informants (ten individuals in each cell) seemed a practical and manageable number, as I would be conducting in-depth qualitative interviews. I anticipated and welcomed the possibility that individuals abstaining from the same behavior (sexual intercourse, e.g.) might fall into different cells of the matrix. As we often change the term used to refer to abstinence as it moves between cells (consider the "virgin" versus the "celibate"), I believed it would become important to see if and how abstinence "looks" different within the same substantive area but in a different temporal location (for example, as a waiter versus a never). I planned to use snowball sampling,[4] and I worried about the difficulty of relying on referrals to obtain an equal number of abstainers within each cell. I initially regarded this as a "cross-that-bridge-when-I-get-to-it" issue. I quickly realized that I would never get to that "bridge" for a reason I did not foresee.

I began the sampling process by contacting individuals I knew to be abstainers (one virgin, one childless, one recovering addict). Interestingly, while I knew all of these individuals on a somewhat personal level, I had never discussed their abstinence with them. Despite our acquaintance with each other, the stories of abstinence in the interviews felt as new as those told by individuals with whom I had no prior contact. The snowball approach put me into contact with additional interviewees at a rate much faster than I anticipated. Although the interviewing spanned the course of a year, I completed the bulk of the interviews in the course of a summer.

Despite its limitations, snowball sampling appeared the best method available, as no registry of abstainers exists. Also, I did not want to limit or predetermine the forms of abstinences in the study; therefore, I chose to avoid contacting groups or organizations that center around issues of abstinence, such as vegetarian clubs or recovery groups. Snowball sampling eventually bore another fruit, one I initially mistook as a setback. On occasion, when I contacted some of the individuals others identified as abstainers, they often thought they were somehow less than qualified to participate. Acknowledging their abstinence, they often did not regard it as their master status but instead viewed it as one piece of who they are. Eventually, I came to realize that this sampling "dilemma" reinforced another observation: the reactions of others are, at times, critical in one's identity formation. Furthermore, not limiting myself to a group of what Brekhus calls "lifestylers"— that is, those who perform at high density (e.g., 100 percent abstinent or never doing to any degree) and high duration (e.g., 100 percent of the time; Brekhus 2003)—brought me one step closer to understanding abstinence as an *everyday* process of identity performed in part by all of us.

With that said, problems did arise. Very early in the process of collecting data, I became aware of a factor that would affect and hinder the original plan to interview ten individuals from each cell. One of my final questions in all of the interviews was "Do you abstain from any other behaviors?" In most cases, the answer was "yes," and, in many instances, individuals practiced other abstinences that they considered equally, if not more, important than the abstinence on which the interview was based. In one case in particular, we started the interview discussing an informant's refusal to own a cell phone, but when she introduced her vegetarianism, we agreed to redo the interview with vegetarianism as the focus. In this instance, we did what amounted to a complete interview on each of the two topics. Typically, however, if an informant mentioned other abstinences, we would briefly discuss them, keeping the focus on the original abstinence.

Due to the realization that the interviews would take many unpredictable turns and that individuals may give equal or more weight to other abstinences, sampling on the basis of these categories no longer seemed appropriate. While I had hoped that these categories would be salient in the analysis, I eliminated the goal of selecting ten individuals per cell, as individuals often fell into several cells at once. Also, this sampling goal was faulty in relation to snowball sampling. Specifically, those giving referrals were sometimes mistaken about which category a potential interviewee fell in. For example, someone may have suggested a contact as a "never" when, in fact, this person identified him- or herself as a time-outer. Though errors in categorization were less frequent than the surprise of multiple abstinences, they nonetheless made the task of finding exactly ten interviewees per category problematic.

The ultimate selection criteria, then, simply became the following:

The not-doing must be voluntary. From the study I excluded individuals who must not do something for involuntary reasons, for example, health issues. As I mention in the introduction to the book, involuntary "not doing" does not count or qualify as abstinence (not-doing). In fact, the first formal question of every interview (see appendix B) ensured that the abstinence was a deliberate choice of the individual. (In all cases it was.)

Individuals must be currently abstaining. I was not interested in retrospective accounts of abstinence (although several informants discussed past periods of abstinence in the context of their current not-doings). In order to understand more fully how individuals construct and maintain abstinent identities and to avoid bias introduced into retrospective accounts, it was imperative for the abstinence to be in the present.[5]

The Informants

There were twenty-four women and fourteen men in the study, ranging in age from seventeen to sixty-five (mean age thirty-two, median twenty-eight). In terms of race and ethnicity, twenty-eight identified as white and five as black/African American. Each of the remaining five classified themselves in one of the following categories: White and Middle Eastern, Asian, White and Asian, Hispanic, and "Pink" (a rejection of standard racial categories).

Occupations were fairly diverse and included (but were not limited to): student, professor, professional dancer, jewelry maker, account executive, publisher, rare book seller, interior designer, cashier, office clerk, social worker, childcare provider, and graphic designer. The final sample together abstained from one or more of the following: sex, substances (illegal drugs, alcohol, some over-the-counter and prescription drugs), driving (or owning a car), particular foods (sugar, meat, dairy) or foods in specific combinations (e.g., bread and cheese), e-mail, cell phones, and television. Four of the informants were also interviewed regarding their decisions not to take the expected rites of passage (Van Gennep 1960) of having children and getting married. Again, many of the informants abstained on multiple dimensions.

All names have been changed to protect the informants. Informants were given the chance to choose their pseudonyms subsequent to the interviews, and I honored these requests. For those who did not express a preference, I selected the pseudonym.

The Interviews

In designing the interview questions, I chose to vary the questions by the four general categories presented in the matrix. As the goal of the project entailed drawing conclusions on abstinence as a generic social process, it seemed counterintuitive and counterproductive to vary the questions according to substantive area. I did, however, find it imperative to vary the questions somewhat according to matrix cell, particularly due to the goal of tracing one's abstinent career. For example, I needed to ask different questions of someone who had previously participated in the act from someone who had never engaged in it. If we discussed multiple abstinences that spanned different cells of the matrix in the course of the interview, I would change lists as appropriate.

I carried out the interviews in locations that were convenient for the informant. The sites included my home, their homes, coffee shops, restaurants, my office, and their workplaces. I conducted interviews in two different states on the east coast. The Institutional Review Board of Rutgers University (where I was a graduate student at the time) approved the research project, and all informants signed informed consent forms.

The interviews lasted anywhere from forty-five minutes to three hours. All interviews were tape-recorded and transcribed with the consent of the informants. I, along with three other individuals, transcribed the interviews. In the event that I did not do the transcribing, I checked major spots of the interviews for accuracy by listening to portions of the tapes again.

In one instance, the tape recorder failed to record, so the entire interview had to be reconstructed from my notes. In attempting to be as true to the interview as possible, I sent my typed notes to the informant, and he revised, corrected, and added to what we had discussed. While this limited my ability to quote him directly, I feel that I was able to accurately represent the interview given the circumstances.

I did not pay informants for their participation. All willingly volunteered their time.

Toward Analysis and Theory

The approach taken in this study is one of grounded theory (Glaser and Strauss 1967), an inductive process of moving from data to theory rather than working deductively, that is, starting with theory. Recognizing that nowhere in the literature had anyone attempted to address how abstinence operated as a generic category of identity organization, I made it my goal to begin to fill this lacuna. Not having a clear sense of how such identities operate, I took a chance and hoped that there would be commonalities among the various types. While I knew the general areas I wanted to explore, I allowed the data to drive the final categories of analysis. I used the qualitative data analysis program QSR NUD*IST to assist in the process of creating the categories. The software was also useful in attempting to organize and manage the vast amount of data.

Strauss and Corbin argue that solid grounded theory should remain "faithful to the everyday reality of the substantive area and [be] carefully induced from diverse data." Strong grounded theory should also "be abstract enough and include sufficient variation to make it applicable to a variety of contexts related to that phenomenon" (Strauss and Corbin 1990, 22). As I discuss in the book's conclusion, I believe the parameters of this study allow me to generalize to any identity based on a voluntary decision to not-do and to imagine the commonalities between identities centered around the things we both do and choose not to do.

Interview Guide

General

1. To what degree is your abstinence voluntary?
2. How central is abstinence in this area to your overall identity?
3. How often do you feel aware of your abstinence? Are there moments when it becomes more of an issue?
4. What are your reasons for not engaging in this behavior?
5. How difficult is it for you to abstain?

Background: Quitters and Time-Outers

1. What are your earliest memories of learning about [relevant area]? What were your reactions to this information? Do you think this information played a role in your decision to engage in this behavior?[6]
2. Could you talk about your experiences engaging in this behavior (amount, duration, etc.)?
3. At what point did abstinence become an issue for you?
4. Have you made any prior efforts to abstain from this behavior at any other point in the past? What were your goals? What happened? Do you think this attempt is different? Why/not?
5. At what point did you decide to abstain? Why did you decide against moderation/cutting back? Do you think moderation works for others?
6. Was there a defining moment at which you decided deliberately to abstain? Could you talk about this process?
7. How did the prospect of not engaging in this behavior (either temporarily or permanently) make you feel?

8. How do you compare your abstinence to the period before you engaged in the behavior for the first time?

Exiting

1. Have there been shifts in intensity in your desire to abstain? Have you ever been tempted to give in? Have you ever outright doubted your decision?
2. Have you witnessed others exit abstinence in this area? What was the process like for them? Did this affect your decision to abstain?

(*#3 and #4 for waiters and time-outers only*):

3. Do you have a sense of when you will engage in this behavior?
    Definite: Why at this point?
    Indefinite: How do you anticipate knowing when you will be ready?
4. Do you expect exiting this abstinence to be a major event?

Changes to Identity

1. In what ways do you think you would be affected by engaging in the act (either for the first time or again)?
2. Is it possible to engage in the behavior and still make valid claims that one is generally abstinent?
3. In your mind, what would disqualify someone from claiming he or she is abstinent?

Experiences with Others

1. How aware are others of your abstinence?
2. What have been some of the various reactions you have received?
3. Do you feel obligated to explain your decision to abstain to others? Do you feel that others often expect some form of explanation?
4. Are there times (intentional or unintentional) when your abstinence becomes more visible? Could you give me an example of when you feel it's appropriate or necessary to inform others of your abstinence?
5. Do/have you ever denied or downplayed your abstinence? If so, what were the circumstances?
6. Do you form friendships/connections with others based on your abstinence?

Concluding Questions

1. What do you think the general attitude of others is toward those practicing this form of abstinence?

2. Are you aware of anyone else who also abstains from [X] that has had a different experience than you have?

3. How remarkable do you think it is to abstain from [X] at this point in history? At this point in your life?

4. (*for all categories except nevers*) What are your opinions of those who will never engage in [X]?

5. Are there any behaviors in which you feel abstaining would be strange/inappropriate/unacceptable?

6. Do you abstain from any other behaviors? Are these temporary/permanent? Have you engaged in the behavior before?

NOTES

INTRODUCTION

1. Thanks to Matt Buckley for this observation during a seminar at the Center for
    the Critical Analysis of Contemporary Culture (CCACC), Rutgers University,
    January 2002.

2. See appendix A for a thorough discussion of methodology as well as an explana-
    tion of how the sampling technique influenced the degree to which abstinence
    was a central component of each informant's identity.

3. It will soon become clear that an "expected social behavior" is contingent on
    one's social location. So while not e-mailing may not seem a form of abstinence,
    in an environment where it is one of the primary modes of communication, this
    not-doing becomes a salient identity marker.

4. Brekhus 1996, 500. Using sexual behavior as his model, Brekhus then pushes
    the original binary conception of marked and unmarked to a *trinary* model,
    arguing that, among any continuum of behavior, we tend to mark the poles—
    e.g., the "virgin" and the "stud"—while ignoring the vast space in between, in
    his terms, the "averagely experienced" (501).

5. An exception would be the category of "crimes of omission," marked non-acts
    that we are legally obligated to perform but fail to do so (Albanese 2002, 155–
    56).

6. Brekhus also notes how who performs an act may influence what is perceived as
    marked or unmarked. In many countercultures, the marking system is reversed.
    For example, among those who engage in sadomasochism (s&m), "vanilla" (or
    "normal") sex gets established as a marked practice (1996, 513).

7. See also Brekhus 1996 and Mullaney 1999 for discussions on the perceived
    mental gap between doing something zero versus one time.

8. It is possible, of course, to acquire other labels, such as "slut," "nymphomaniac,"
    or "sex fiend" if one has "too much" sex. The crossing of this line, however,
    seems much more arbitrary and debatable than the line between virgin and
    nonvirgin.

9. Mary Douglas makes a similar point in her discussion of the concepts of dirt
    and pollution. Insisting that we typically view dirt as "a residual category," it
    takes some effort for us to move it from the periphery to the center of analysis
    (1966, 37).

10. On this note, a colleague of mine once told me that, while he appreciated what I was doing, he thought I needed to invent an alternative term to "abstinence," as it is such a weighty and emotionally charged term.

11. I had a similar experience about a month later when it was my turn in rotation to present my work in the interdisciplinary seminar of which I was a part. Walking up the stairs to the seminar room that morning, a colleague grabbed my shoulder from behind and said, "I just read your paper. Wow, what a bunch of narcissists!"

12. Thanks to Wayne Brekhus for this smart phrase.

13. See Edgley and Brissett's (1999) fascinating analysis of the phenomenon of meddling and, in particular, chapter 2 of their book for the history behind the rise of the professional meddler.

14. It is probably no coincidence that this brief and sardonic reaction to the president's quote and decision in general appeared with a briefing on the arrest of Noelle Bush (daughter of Florida Governor Jeb Bush and niece of President Bush) for prescription drug fraud earlier in the week.

15. Of course, the relationship between abstinence and morality need not be a positive one (that is, to abstain is "good"), and in some instances the association is deemed negative. As mentioned, our laws mandate that we *not* abstain from certain behaviors and that abstinence can incur criminal liability. Presumably we are subject to such mandatory doings for moral and ethical reasons. It is "right" to pay taxes, protect children, and obey traffic laws, and failure to do so qualifies as an "omission," legally recognized as a sufficient characteristic of a criminal act (Albanese 2002, 155–56). Nonetheless, the link between abstinence and morality appears to be a close one.

16. See, e.g., Abramson 1987 and Bahn and Jaquez 1997.

17. See Cindoglu 1997 for a discussion of such operations in Turkish society. These procedures result directly from the practice of virginity testing found in many parts of the world.

18. Virginity pledging receives increasing attention, the most popular group perhaps being True Love Waits, run through local churches. See Bearman and Bruckner 2001 for an analysis of the effectiveness of pledging among teens.

19. While Keller (1999) and True Love Waits (TLW) both suggest that a return to "secondary virginity" is possible and convincing, they target different audiences, as Keller gears her book toward adults waiting to find "Mr./Ms. Right" whereas TLW targets teens.

20. For two popular examples, see Wendy Keller's aforementioned *The Cult of the Born-Again Virgin: How Single Women Can Reclaim Their Sexual Power* (1999) and Donna Marie Williams's *Sensual Celibacy: The Sexy Woman's Guide to Using Abstinence for Recharging Your Spirit, Discovering Your Passions, and Achieving Greater Intimacy in Your Next Relationship* (1999). Also see Cutrer 2002; Rajani 2002; Sather and Zinn 2002; Toups and Holmes 2002.

21. For some examples, see Ahluwalia et al. 2002; Cutrer 2002; Rajani 2002; Sather and Zinn 2002; Shiffman et al. 2002; Toups and Holmes 2002.

22. While a quick look at the long lists of examples of abstinence offered in the *Oxford English Dictionary* reveals some obscure forms (such as not writing epigrams!), food, drink, and sex make up the majority.

23. See Ferentzy 2001 for a discussion of the changing frames of alcoholism, namely from one of sin to addiction.

24. Thanks to Don Korobkin (CCACC) for pointing me to Debtors' Anonymous as another incarnation of the "anonymous" organizations.

25. It is important to note, however, that alternative models of recovery arise from time to time, challenging the position taken by Alcoholics Anonymous that one must always be recovering. For example, Rational Recovery posits that an addict can, in fact, reach a point where he or she is recovered, and that addiction need not continue to be a permanent part of the self when one no longer abuses substances. See Trimpey's studies (1992, 1996) for a description of the philosophy behind Rational Recovery.

26. While it may appear that the emphasis on abstinence from such substances stems from the potential harm they cause to individuals, those who study the history of drugs offer another possibility. Often, our rejection of particular drugs—socially or legally—depends on factors independent of their physiological effects, typically their association with specific social groups. This connection between drugs and groups perceived as somehow threatening or undesirable explains radical changes in both law and attitudes regarding drugs such as opium (associated with Chinese immigrants in the 1800s), marijuana (associated with Mexican workers who competed for scarce jobs during the Great Depression of the 1930s), and cocaine and its derivative, crack (linked to African Americans). For an interesting history of our changing attitudes toward drugs, see Henslin 2000. For arguments specific to the crack "epidemic," see Humphries 1999 and Reinarman and Levine 2000.

CHAPTER ONE

1. See Brekhus 1996.

2. See chapter 4 for a discussion of pathways to abstinence.

3. For a discussion of the changing notions of the concept of "childhood," e.g., see Postman 1994 and Kincaid 1998. Also, see Kurz's (1997) argument regarding the terminology surrounding wife abuse, as she argues that the semantic differences in describing the same phenomenon ("family violence" versus "violence against women") serve as mirrors for our attitudes toward these topics.

4. This assumption of abstinence as an outdated and old-fashioned practice surfaces from time to time. In her book of dating rules for black women, Millner claims that while abstinence "is a beautiful thing, indeed" her "survey of [her] girls" indicates that the last time a woman waited until marriage to have sex "was sometime in the early fifties" (1997, 69).

5. Gumbel also suspected this trend to be a "female thing," suggestive of both stereotypes and norms of gender and abstinence.

6. Leach 1964, 34. Of course, variation exists between social groups as well. Simon and Burns's (1997) account of life in inner-city Baltimore shows how distinctions recognized by law, for example, may bear little importance on the classification systems of certain groups. So while they are aware of the difference between "misdemeanor" and "felony," those interviewed by Simon and Burns relied more on the distinction between "caper" and "crime," the former referring to a crafty (but still illegal) act in which no one is harmed or runs the risk of being harmed (11). To use an example specific to abstinence, "vegetarians" may see meaningful distinctions between lacto-vegetarians, lacto-ovo vegetarians, etc.

7. For a discussion of color as a metaphor for markedness, see Brekhus 1996.

8. Many thanks to Tom DeGloma for pointing out the positive connotations of "fake" food among vegetarian and vegan products.

9. Watson in Stepaniak 1998, 2.

10. Not only did many vegetarians resist the label; many regarded such practices themselves as nonsensical.

11. While food-combining may not initially appear to be a form of abstinence, I believe it qualifies if we push our notion of abstinence one step further. Specifically, abstinence need not refer to sole acts that individuals resist doing, but also those that individuals resist doing in combination.

12. Colin connects this language of self-talk to his own situation later in the interview when he insists that "if you describe yourself as being an addict or an alcoholic or whatever, then I think that that's who and what you are, and that's not who and what I am. I am someone who has chosen not to be that."

13. See E. Abbott for a discussion of how celibacy and chastity are interchangeable today, as both refer to "abstaining from sexual relations, intentionally or under duress, temporarily or for indefinite periods" (2000, 17).

14. See Letherby 1994 for a discussion regarding the different language used to characterize voluntary and involuntary decisions surrounding motherhood. Also see Morell 1994 and Bartlett 1995.

15. See Murray Davis's (1983) discussion of "normal sex" and the common perception that sex transforms individuals in fundamental ways.

16. Thanks to Jenna Howard for this example.

17. Of course, some individuals (and even recovery groups) insist that individuals can fully recover from addiction. Raven, however, expresses the position of groups such as Alcoholics Anonymous when she explains to me why she won't say that she's recovered, but instead says that she is always recovering. In part, her decision to think of herself in this way stems from the fact that she is "a very superstitious person" and that attitude "would be like jinxing [herself]." More important, though, she feels "that would be too arrogant, and I don't feel recovered. If I felt recovered I wouldn't go back to Alcoholics Anonymous."

CHAPTER TWO

1. Becker describes moral crusaders as those who tackle a social issue with "an absolute ethic," see "evil with no qualification," and believe "any means is justified to do away with it." He further charges them with being "fervent and righteous, often self-righteous" (1963, 148).

2. Luther Martin describes the Stoics as teaching "the taming of human passions by self-examination in order to effect a harmonious relation with the external order of things. True freedom was the moral freedom of a philosophical self-knowledge which recognized and conformed to an assumed orderly principle of the cosmos" (1988, 51).

3. Kosnik et al. 1977, 24–25. Kosnik et al. suggest that Stoic morality may not have been the only influence on Saint Paul's views regarding abstinence. The "new ascetic movements at Corinth, which required complete sexual abstinence even for the married," may have contributed to the valuing of celibacy (26).

4. It is important to note that even Saint Paul recognized the value of sex in the proper context. While he himself preferred the practice of celibacy, he was opposed to demonstrations of "exaggerated asceticism" (Kosnik et al. 1977, 31).

5. See, e.g., Brumberg 1988; Bynum 1987; and Frost 2001.

6. Bynum 1987, 31, 33. Bynum also insists that fasting as a general practice pervades many preindustrial societies "where resources are limited," and "men and women frequently respond to the rhythm of plenty and scarcity, harvest and famine, by deciding to control it through voluntary fasting" (34).

7. Mellor 1991, 57–58. See this article also for an interesting comparison of the different approaches to the body and suffering in the contexts of Buddhism and Christianity.

8. Goffman introduces the concepts of "front region" and "backstage" when drawing parallels between dramaturgical performance and the everyday presentation of self. While the front region refers to the more public aspects of performance, the backstage is "where the suppressed facts make an appearance," a region, "relative to a given performance, where the impression fostered by the performance is knowingly contradicted as a matter of course" (1959, 112).

9. According to Bailey (1998), some controversy over the origin of the term "Luddite" exists. Some attribute the term to Ned Ludd, a youth who smashed the needles of a stocking frame as an angry response to punishment received from his employer. Others, however, believe the group adopted the name from King Lud, a British king of the first century BCE, whose name resurfaces in various English counties such as Luddenham in Kent and Ludham in Norfolk.

10. The entire passage reads: "There was only one catch and that was Catch-22, which specified that a concern for one's own safety in the face of dangers that were real and immediate was the process of a rational mind. Orr was crazy and could be grounded. All he had to do was ask; and as soon as he did, he would no longer be crazy and would have to fly more missions. Orr would be crazy to fly more missions and sane if he didn't, but if he was sane he had to fly them. If he flew them he was crazy and didn't have to; but if he didn't want to he was sane and had to" (Heller 1961, 47).

11. Gandhi 1996, 9. Gandhi himself attributes the origin of the term "civil disobedience" to Thoreau, who used the phrase "to signify his own resistance to the laws of a slave state" (51).

12. In fact, Gandhi (1996, 51) adopted the term precisely as a deliberate attempt to distinguish his methods from those of the Suffragettes.

13. See Turner 1982b.

14. Graham in Sokolow 1983, 100.

15. In his piece on Cassian, the late fourth- and early fifth-century monk who devised the causal chain of the vices, Michel Foucault argues that, while later centuries tended to be obsessed with the issue of masturbation, the concern (albeit in a different form) dates back much earlier than most historical accounts assume (1985, 14).

16. See Moran 2000 for a discussion of both G. Stanley Hall's contribution to the "invention" of adolescence and the various other factors that influenced the shape sex education courses would take.

17. For this reason, the emergence of anorexia nervosa as an eating disorder only makes sense in the context of societies and social groups where food is both plentiful and available.

18. "I'd Like to Go as Far as I Can," CNN interview with David Blaine, 2003.

CHAPTER THREE

1. Bell claims that the way in which we experience the world in modern times is

shaped by the following four factors: number, interaction, self-consciousness, and time-orientation. The discussion in this section pertains to the third element, self-consciousness (1978, 88–91).

2. Sennett 1978, 324. Lasch echoes Sennett's sentiments, as he identifies narcissism as a struggle to put meaning into one's life and to gain control over a tenuous self. He ties a rise in narcissism to structural changes, namely the increasing control of bureaucracies over individuals' lives and the mechanical reproduction of culture (Lasch 1979, xvi, 8, 47).

3. Giddens 1991, 80. See also May and Cooper 1995, 77.

4. As I write this chapter, however, the "more is better" logic is becoming increasingly scrutinized. In part a response to high rates of obesity in America, more companies are beginning to emphasize "cutting" of sorts: carbohydrates, calories, etc. In fact, when all eyes turned to McDonalds following the release of the documentary *Supersize Me*—in which one man ate all of his meals from the fast-food restaurant for one month, tacking on twenty-five pounds and a host of health problems—the company responded by promptly discontinuing the option to "supersize" any part of one's meal.

5. See Mullaney 2001, 3.

6. Jacoby makes a similar point about the psychological treatment of "narcissism." He states, "as a social category, narcissism . . . suffers from the danger of personalizing the impersonal. Political and economic power is sublimated into individual pathology, as if the traits of a character and not the economy were the evil" (1980, 59).

7. See Grigsby 2004.

8. Hillel is a college student organization designed to connect Jewish students to their heritage and to other Jewish organizations.

9. While phrases such as "one day at a time" are specific to the "anonymous" recovery groups, abstainers not associated with these programs often use similar language.

10. Here Charles uses the term "disfellowshipping" to refer to the termination of one's membership in the congregation.

11. Straight edge is referred to as a philosophy. Thought to have been coined in the 1980s by Ian Mackaye, then a member of the band Minor Threat, straight edge promotes a drug-free way of life. Those who are straight edge often abstain from other things as well. Mackaye summed up his philosophy simply: "Don't drink/don't smoke/don't fuck" (http://www.straightedge.com).

12. See Mullaney 2001 for a further discussion of the distinction between purity and innocence.

13. With that said, Denis, a proponent and practitioner of simple living, raises the possibility that abstinence may in fact be *harder* in such a context, precisely because we are "overwhelmed with clutter and distractions."

14. Gooldin makes this point referring to the specific abstinence of fasting (2003, 30).

15. See Brekhus 2003, esp. 28, 30, 35–47.

CHAPTER FOUR

1. Hankiss 1981, 203. See also Giddens's argument that "autobiography is a corrective intervention into the past, not merely a chronicle of elapsed events" (1991, 72).

2. A. Abbott 1997, 89. After reviewing several hundred biographies, Hankiss (1981) concludes that narratives fall into four main categories, defined exclusively by the perceived relationship between one's past and present (simplified down to either generally "good" or "bad"). Specifically, she identifies a narrative typology that includes dynastic (good past and present), antithetical (bad past, good present), compensatory (good past, bad present), and self-absolutory (bad past and present).

3. Giddens makes the point that the "reconstruction of the past goes along with the anticipation of the likely life trajectory of the future" (1991, 72).

4. See, e.g., Bearman and Bruckner's (2001) study on what factors contribute to successful virginity pledging.

5. The title of this section is quoted from James.

6. The title of this section is quoted from Emily.

7. The title of this section is quoted from Marta.

8. As another example of this gradual process of cutting out, see Gandhi's description of his practices of fasting and restriction in diet in which he experimented with increasingly fewer types and amounts of food (1983, 286–87).

9. The title of this section is quoted from Carol.

10. Thanks to Robin Wagner-Pacifici for referring me to Svevo's book and Zeno's ritualizing of the last cigarette.

CHAPTER FIVE

1. Many sociologists frequently tease out the "near poor" as an economic category so as to not overlook those who are not deemed poor by official poverty lines but who nonetheless cannot meet their basic needs.

2. For a discussion of how such differences are made to seem more comparable, see Purcell 1996 on the process of mental leveling.

3. See also Brekhus 1996; Mullaney 1999.

4. For a fascinating discussion regarding the sociology of "firsts," see Robinson 1992.

5. Recall, for example, the fall of Ann Moore as a fasting girl when others discovered that she had taken in small amounts of food from time to time. Rather than being impressed with her ability to survive on what little amount she consumed, others dismissed her as a fraud because she did not remain at absolute zero (Brumberg 1988, 58).

6. On February 24, 2004, National Public Radio (NPR) reported results from the NPR/Kaiser/Kennedy School of Government's "Sex Education in America" survey. Subsequent to asking respondents whether they agree with the statement "Abstinence from sexual activity outside marriage is the expected standard for all school-age children," researchers had respondents define what they mean by abstinence. While 95 percent agree that abstinence entails no sexual intercourse, the numbers start to drop when considering other sexual acts. Eighty-nine percent think abstinence means no oral sex, 63 percent no intimate touching, 44 percent no masturbation, and 40 percent no passionate kissing. See "Sex Education in America" 2004.

7. Gandhi offers an example of this variation among abstainers of the same type in his discussion of fasting. While Hindus would allow themselves milk and fruit on fasting days, Gandhi drew his own line at a point that permitted water only (1983, 295).

8. Zerubavel 1991, 121. While some may argue that this approach rings more of what Zerubavel calls the "fuzzy mind," a mindset "made up of vague essences fading gradually into one another" (115), I believe the flexible mind is more apt. In particular, as I will show below, despite the grayness of the abstinence-as-zone approach, lines and boundaries still exist. Where the line is drawn, of course, remains an individual decision, but the existence of the line in the first place convinces me that this perspective is ultimately about the flexible, not fuzzy, mindset.

9. See Douglas's discussion of Van Gennep and thresholds (1966, 114).

10. Rachel Askew, pers. comm., August 17, 2003.

CHAPTER SIX

1. For anyone who has watched any amount of *American Idol*, it is obvious that I am referring specifically to the notoriously uncensored comments of Simon Cowell, one of the show's three judges.

2. I am grateful to Wayne Brekhus for pointing out this ideal popular representation of the concept of fire walking.

3. Taken from the website to the original version of *Temptation Island*, Fox Broadcasting Company.

4. While four couples started on the show, the producers chose to disqualify one couple as they had a child, sending the message that it is only appropriate to subject childless individuals to such extreme forms of temptation.

5. Apparently, this was not the case for some of the contestants on later shows, as the temptation was too much for them and their relationships to handle.

6. As I myself did not succumb to the temptation to watch this series, I retrieved this information from Fox Broadcasting Company.

7. A somewhat optimistic consequence of Pandora's act was that one positive thing, Hope, was also in the box. See Hamilton 1942, 71–72.

8. Special thanks to Lydia Senter for helping me locate specific biblical passages.

9. The actual line in the Rush song is "I can learn to resist anything but temptation."

10. I am grateful to Rich Roisman and his impressive musical knowledge for the songs in this section.

11. Thanks to Alexys Vaastrom for suggesting this alternate use of the term "fire."

12. Thanks to Sybil Turk for reminding me of this very apt expression.

13. While these accounts are fictional, they nonetheless serve as cultural artifacts that capture the social dynamics of the time.

14. See Mullaney 2001.

15. See Mary Douglas (1966, 38) for some examples of pleasurable ambiguity (e.g., poetry, art).

16. Douglas suggests several common ways in which we deal with anomalies: "Negatively, we can ignore, just not perceive them, or perceiving we can condemn. Positively, we can deliberately confront the anomaly and try to create a new pattern of reality in which it has a place. It is not impossible for an individual to revise his own personal scheme of classifications. But no individual lives in isolation and his scheme will have been partly received from others" (1966, 39).

CHAPTER SEVEN

1. Thanks to Julia Kunin for the example of cushions.

2. Zerubavel, in fact, notes that the Hebrew words for "fence" (*gader*) and "definition" (*hagdara*) share the same root (1991, 129). Many thanks to Barbara Roswell for introducing me to this very fitting expression and concept.

3. I am grateful to Dan Chambliss for the suggestion that a fundamental difference between the strategies of fire walking and fence building can be seen when regarding them as statements about self-control.

4. Here Craig is referring to the unwanted messages, not e-mail itself, which obviously can be turned off.

5. See Mullaney 2001, 9–10.

6. This is a clear example of how the workings of abstinence differ from those of taboo. Whereas individuals may make appeals to intention when violating abstinence, this is not the case in taboo. In taboo, it matters not "that any breach of the prohibition was unintentional or well-intentioned . . . no allowance is made for either the ignorance or the praiseworthy purpose of the taboo-breaker" (Webster 1942, 17).

7. Thanks to Brian Walsh at the CCACC, Rutgers University, for reminding me of this example.

8. The full quote was as follows: "Because I'm just human and I'm tempted and Christ set some almost impossible standards for us. The Bible says, 'Thou shalt not commit adultery.' Christ said, 'I tell you that anyone who looks on a woman with lust has in his heart already committed adultery.' I've looked on a lot of women with lust. I've committed adultery in my heart many times. . . . This is something that God recognizes, that I will do and have done, and God forgives me for it. But that doesn't mean that I condemn someone who not only looks on a woman with lust but who leaves his wife and shacks up with somebody out of wedlock. Christ says, don't consider yourself better than someone else because one guy screws a whole bunch of women while the other guy is loyal to his wife. The guy who's loyal to his wife ought not to be condescending or proud because of the relative degree of sinfulness" (*Playboy*, November 1976).

9. In the same vein, Keane goes on to discuss how individuals cannot bracket certain acts, "especially if the intercourse and heavy petting go on for a long time" (1977, 163).

10. The term is derived from Latin for "guilty mind."

11. Interestingly, all intent does not fare similarly under criminal law, as there is a distinction between "specific" and "general" intent. Whereas specific intent refers to situations in which an individual commits the crime he or she originally intended to commit, general intent refers to cases where an individual attempts to commit one crime and ends up committing another, unanticipated one. Even if an individual does not intend to commit the ultimate crime, the intent to commit *a* crime in general nonetheless existed (Inciardi 2002, 34–35).

12. Thanks to Tom DeGloma for this example.

CHAPTER EIGHT

1. In one sense, this may be a poor example since most recovery groups instill in addicts the understanding that they have always been and will always be "addicts," regardless of whether they still drink or use drugs. On the other hand, I offer the example as an alternative to this perspective and as recognition of those individuals who truly believe they have fully recovered and no longer need to identify as "addicts."

2. The apparent need to publicly signal to other abstainers may explain these practices. Thanks to Jeffrey Shandler at the CCACC, Rutgers University, for pointing
   out how reminding oneself and others of one's abstinence may be intrinsic to
   the process itself.
3. Thanks to Ian McHarg, a student in my Deviance and Social Control class,
   for this outstanding observation regarding the possibility of framing J. David
   Brown's strategy as one of "fire building."

CHAPTER NINE
1. Thanks to Mary Marchand for her insights on Bartleby.
2. Turner suggests that the new personality type of the "performing self" is one
   that requires validation from an external source (1996, 195).
3. Goffman 1959. The ability of audiences to spoil identity performances has been
   further explored on a more general level by Goffman (1963) in *Stigma* and by
   other theorists on a more site-specific level, such as Vinitzky-Seroussi's (1998)
   work on high school reunions.
4. See Becker 1963; Matza 1969; Scheff 1975.

CONCLUSION
1. Turner 1982b, 27. See Turner also for a discussion of the connection between
   anorexia and privilege. Anorexia, Turner argues, is a disease of location in that
   "only a social system based on mass consumption can afford the luxury of slim-
   ming" (1996, 109).
2. See, e.g., Featherstone 1982, 29.
3. See Shilling's discussion of Pierre Bourdieu's ideas on the relationship between
   the body, social class, and personal taste (2003, esp. 111–16).
4. Simple livers "say that there is no built-in or culturally established concept of
   'enough' in the dominant culture" and "maintain that a voluntary simplicity
   lifestyle is more fulfilling for the individual, creates a stronger community, and
   decreases environmental damage" (Grigsby 2004, 1).
5. See Eshleman 2003.
6. See appendix A for a discussion of methodology and this issue in particular.
7. I do not mean, of course, to stereotype all fraternities as operating in this fashion. The practices among the particular groups studied by Martin and Hummer
   (1989), however, lend themselves to such an analysis of how fence building
   may operate around the norms of excess.
8. See, e.g., Bogart et al. 2000; Remez 2000; and Sanders and Reinisch 1999.

APPENDIXES
1. See Kishline 1994.
2. See Trimpey 1992, 1996.
3. Moderation Management went beyond both Rational Recovery and Alcoholics
   Anonymous in that it proposed the possibility of returning to moderation rather
   than complete abstinence. The program lost much of its momentum and credibility when its founder, Audrey Kishline, was charged with driving under the
   influence.
4. See, e.g., Biernack and Waldorf 1981.
5. Of course, the informants must give retrospective accounts to some extent in
   that one part of the interview asks them to trace their abstinent "careers." In or-

der to develop an understanding of *how* individuals abstain, however, I thought it best to keep the focus in the present. Nonetheless, since I am not observing the abstinence firsthand, the interviews technically capture the informants' *representations* of how they abstain.

6. I also asked this first set of questions of nevers and waiters with the difference in wording being in the last question: Do you think this information played a role in your decision to *abstain*?

Abbott, Andrew. 1997. "On the Concept of Turning Point." In *Comparative Social Research: Methodological Issues in Comparative Social Science,* vol. 16, ed. Lars Mjoset, Fredrik Engelstad, Grete Brochmann, Ragnvald Kalleberg, and Arnlaug Leira, 85–105. Greenwich, CT: Jai Press.

Abbott, Elizabeth. 2000. *A History of Celibacy.* New York: Scribner.

Abramson, Arthur S. 1987. "Beyond the Samoan Controversy in Anthropology: A History of Sexuality in the Eastern Interior of Fiji." In *The Cultural Construction of Sexuality,* ed. Patricia Caplan, 193–216. New York: Tavistock Publications.

Ahluwalia, Jasjit S., Kari Jo Harris, Delwyn Catley, Kolawole S. Okuyemi, and Matthew S. Mayo. 2002. "Sustained-Release Bupropion for Smoking Cessation in African Americans: A Randomized Controlled Trial." *Journal of the American Medical Association* 228 (4): 468–74.

Albanese, Jay. 2002. *Criminal Justice,* 2nd ed. Boston: Allyn and Bacon.

Alcoholics Anonymous. 1976. *Alcoholics Anonymous: The Story of How Many Thousands of Men and Women Have Recovered From Alcoholism,* 3rd ed. New York: Alcoholics Anonymous World Services, Inc.

Ali, Lorraine, and Julie Scelfo. 2002. "Choosing Virginity." *Newsweek,* December 9.

American Psychiatric Association. 1994. *Diagnostic and Statistical Manual of Mental Disorders,* 4th ed. Washington, DC: American Psychiatric Association.

Andrews, Charles F. 1930. *Mahatma Gandhi's Ideas.* New York: Macmillan.

Arditi, Jorge. 1998. *A Genealogy of Manners: Transformations of Social Relations in France and England from the Fourteenth to the Eighteenth Century.* Chicago: University of Chicago Press.

Armesto, Felipe Fernandez. 2003. "Blaine Isn't New, Even Buddha Warned Us against Publicity-hungry Fasters." *London Times,* October 21.

Austin, J. L. 1975. *How to Do Things with Words,* 2nd ed. Cambridge, MA: Harvard University Press.

Bahn, Adele, and Angela Jaquez. 1997. "One Style of Dominican Bridal Shower." In *The Family Experience: A Reader in Cultural Diversity,* 2nd ed., ed. Mark Hutter, 194–204. Needham Heights, MA: Allyn and Bacon.

Bailey, Brian. 1998. *The Luddite Rebellion.* Phoenix Mill, UK: Sutton Publishing.

Bartlett, Jane. 1995. *Will You Be Mother? Women Who Choose to Say No.* New York: New York University Press.

Bateson, Mary Catherine. 1989. *Composing a Life*. New York: Plume.

Beardsworth, Alan, and Teresa Keil. 1992. "The Vegetarian Option: Varieties, Conversions, Motives, and Careers." *Sociological Review* 40:253–93.

Bearman, Peter S., and Hannah Bruckner. 2001. "Promising the Future: Virginity Pledges and First Intercourse." *American Journal of Sociology* 106 (4): 859–912.

Becker, Howard S. 1963. *Outsiders: Studies in the Sociology of Deviance*. New York: Free Press.

Bell, Daniel. 1978. *The Cultural Contradictions of Capitalism*. New York: Basic Books.

Bellah, Robert N., Richard Madsen, William M. Sullivan, Ann Swidler, and Steven M. Tippen. 1991. *The Good Society*. New York: Alfred A. Knopf.

Berger, Peter L., and Thomas Luckmann. 1966. *The Social Construction of Reality: A Treatise in the Sociology of Knowledge*. New York: Anchor Books.

Biernacki, Patrick, and Dan Waldorf. 1981. "Snowball Sampling: Problems and Techniques of Chain Referral Sampling." *Sociological Methods and Research* 10:141–63.

Bogart, Laura M., Heather Cecil, David A. Wagstaff, Steven Pinkerton, and Paul R. Abramson. 2000. "Is It 'Sex'? College Students' Interpretations of Sexual Behavior Terminology." *Journal of Sex Research* 37:108–16.

Brekhus, Wayne. 1996. "Social Marking and the Mental Coloring of Identity: Sexual Identity Construction and Maintenance in the United States." *Sociological Forum* 11:497–522.

———. 2003. *Peacocks, Chameleons, and Centaurs: Gay Suburbia and the Grammar of Social Identity*. Chicago: University of Chicago Press.

Brown, J. David. 2003. "The Professional Ex-: An Alternative for Exiting the Deviant Career." In *Constructions of Deviance: Social Power, Context, and Interaction*, 4th ed., ed. Patricia A. Adler and Peter Adler, 494–506. Belmont, CA: Wadsworth/Thomson Learning.

Brown, Peter. 1999. "The Earliest Christian Ascetics." In *Sexuality*, ed. Robert A. Nye, 35–37. New York: Oxford University Press.

Browne, Ray B. 1984. "Don't Touch, Don't Do, Don't Question—Don't Progress." In *Forbidden Fruits: Taboos and Tabooism in Culture*, ed. Ray B. Browne. Bowling Green, OH: Bowling Green University Popular Press.

Brubaker, Rogers, and Frederick Cooper. 2000. "Beyond 'Identity.'" *Theory and Society* 29:1–47.

Brumberg, Joan Jacobs. 1988. *Fasting Girls: The Emergence of Anorexia Nervosa as a Modern Disease*. Cambridge, MA: Harvard University Press.

Butler, Judith. 1990. *Gender Trouble: Feminism and the Subversion of Identity*. New York: Routledge.

Byman, Seymour. 1978. "Ritualistic Acts and Compulsive Behavior: The Pattern of Tudor Martyrdom." *American Historical Review* 83:625–43.

Bynum, Caroline Walker. 1987. *Holy Feast and Holy Fast: The Religious Significance of Food to Medieval Women*. Berkeley: University of California Press.

Cindoglu, Dilek. 1997. "Virginity Tests and Artificial Virginity in Modern Turkish Medicine." *Women's Studies International Forum* 20:253–61.

Cutrer, Corrie. 2002. "How Effective?" *Christianity Today* 46 (8): 14.

Davis, Lloyd. 1993. "The Virgin Body as Victorian Text: An Introduction." In *Virginal Sexuality and Textuality in Victorian Literature*, ed. Lloyd Davis, 3–24. New York: State University of New York Press.

Davis, Murray S. 1983. *Smut: Erotic Reality/Obscene Ideology*. Chicago: University of Chicago Press.

Diamond, Elin. 1986. "Introduction." In *Performance and Cultural Politics*, ed. Elin Diamond, 1–12. New York: Routledge.

Douglas, Mary. 1966. *Purity and Danger: An Analysis of the Concepts of Pollution and Taboo*. Boston: Ark Paperbacks.

Ebaugh, Helen. 1988. *Becoming an Ex: The Process of Role Exit*. Chicago: University of Chicago Press.

Edge, Simon. 2003. "As Headline-grabbing Illusionist David Blaine Begins a Risky Survival Stunt in London, We Look at His Troubled Childhood, His Tortured Obsessions and Ask . . . : Just How Far Will This Man Go?" *Express*, September 5.

Edgley, Charles, and Dennis Brissett. 1999. *A Nation of Meddlers*. Boulder, CO: Westview Press.

Eshleman, J. Ross. 2003. *The Family*, 10th ed. Boston: Allyn and Bacon.

Featherstone, Mike. 1982. "The Body in Consumer Culture." *Theory, Culture, and Society* 1:18–33.

Ferentzy, Peter. 2001. "From Sin to Disease: Differences and Similarities between Past and Current Conceptions of Chronic Drunkenness." *Contemporary Drug Problems* 28:363–90.

Fischer, Louis. 1956. "The Last Fast." In *The Gandhi Reader: A Source Book of His Life and Writings*, ed. Homer A. Jack, 451–57. Bloomington: Indiana University Press.

Fiske, Susan T., and Shelley E. Taylor. 1984. *Social Cognition*. New York: Random House.

Fleck, Ludwik. 1979. *Genesis and Development of a Scientific Fact*. Trans. Fred Bradley and Thaddeus J. Trenn. Chicago: University of Chicago Press.

Foston, Nikitta A. 2004. "Is Celibacy the New Virginity? Living the Single Life without Sex." *Ebony*, January.

Foucault, Michel. 1985. "The Battle for Chastity." In *Western Sexuality: Practice and Precept in Past and Present Times*, ed. Philippe Ariès and André Béjin and trans. Anthony Forster, 14–25. New York: Basil Blackwell.

Fox Broadcasting Company. *Temptation Island*. http://www.fox.com/temptation.

Frankel, Loren. 2003. "Hands Off! The Taboo Surrounding Males' First Ejaculation." In *Sexual Lives: A Reader on the Theories and Realities of Human Sexualities*, ed. Robert Heasley and Betsy Crane, 307–17. New York: McGraw Hill.

Freeman, Mark. 2001. "From Substance to Story: Narrative, Identity, and the Reconstruction of the Self." In *Narrative and Identity: Studies in Autobiography, Self, and Culture*, ed. Jens Brockmeier and Donal Carbaugh, 283–98. Philadelphia: John Benjamins Publishing Company.

Freud, Sigmund. 1966. *The Complete Introductory Lectures on Psychoanalysis*. New York: W. W. Norton.

———. 1999. "Between Abstinence and Masturbation." In *Sexuality*, ed. Robert A. Nye, 141–42. New York: Oxford University Press.

Friedman, Asia. 2002. "The 'Real' and the 'Safe': A Sociological Perspective on the Classification of Sex Acts." Unpublished manuscript, Department of Sociology, Rutgers University. New Brunswick, NJ.

Frost, Liz. 2001. *Young Women and the Body: A Feminist Sociology*. New York: Palgrave.

Fuss, Diana. 1989. *Essentially Speaking: Feminism, Nature, and Difference*. New York: Routledge.

Gandhi, Mahatma. 1983. *Autobiography: Or, The Story of My Experiments with Truth.* Trans. Mahadev Desai. New York: Dover Publications.

———. 1996. *Selected Political Writings,* ed. Dennis Dalton. Indianapolis, IN: Hackett.

Gell, Alfred. 1979. "Reflections on a Cut Finger: Taboo in the Umeda Conception of Self." In *Fantasy and Symbol,* ed. R. H. Hook, 133–48. New York: Academic Press.

Giddens, Anthony. 1991. *Modernity and Self-Identity: Self and Society in the Late Modern Age.* Stanford, CA: Stanford University Press.

Glaser, Barney, and Anselm Strauss. 1967. *The Discovery of Grounded Theory.* Chicago: Adeline.

Goffman, Erving. 1959. *The Presentation of Self in Everyday Life.* New York: Doubleday.

———. 1963. *Stigma: Notes on the Management of Spoiled Identity.* New York: Simon and Schuster.

———. 1974. *Frame Analysis: An Essay on the Organization of Experience.* Boston: Northeastern University Press.

Gooldin, Sigal. 2003. "Fasting Women, Living Skeletons, and Hunger Artists: Spectacles of Body and Miracles at the Turn of a Century." *Body and Society* 9:27–53.

Gottlieb, Roger S. 2003. *A Spirituality of Resistance: Finding a Peaceful Heart and Protecting the Earth.* Lanham, MD: Rowman and Littlefield.

Grigsby, Mary. 2004. *Buying Time and Getting By: The Voluntary Simplicity Movement.* New York: SUNY Press.

Gusfield, Joseph R. 1963. *Symbolic Crusade: Status Politics and the American Temperance Movement.* Chicago: University of Illinois Press.

Hamilton, Edith. 1942. *Mythology: Timeless Tales of Gods and Heroes.* New York: Mentor Books.

Hankiss, Agnes. 1981. "Ontologies of the Self: On the Mythological Rearranging of One's Life History." In *Biography and Society,* ed. Daniel Bertaux, 203–9. Beverly Hills, CA: Sage.

Hareven, Tamara K., and Kanji Masaoka. 1988. "Turning Points and Transitions: Perceptions of the Life Course." *Journal of Family History* 13 (3): 271–89.

Heller, Joseph. 1961. *Catch-22.* New York: Dell.

Henslin, James. 2000. *Social Problems,* 5th ed. Upper Saddle River, NJ: Prentice Hall.

Hood, Andrea. 2001. "Editing the Life Course: Autobiographical Narratives, Identity Transformations, and Retrospective Framing." Unpublished manuscript, Department of Sociology, Rutgers University. New Brunswick, NJ.

Humphries, Drew. 1999. *Crack Mothers: Pregnancy, Drugs, and the Media.* Columbus: Ohio State University Press.

Hunt, Morton. 1994. *The Natural History of Love.* New York: Anchor Books.

Husserl, Edmund. 1969. *Ideas: General Introduction to Pure Phenomenology.* New York: Humanities Press.

"I'd Like to Go as Far as I Can." 2003. CNN Interview with David Blaine, August 30. http://www.cnn.com/2003/SHOWBIZ/08/30/cnna.david.blaine/.

Inciardi, James. 2002. *Criminal Justice,* 7th ed. New York: Harcourt College Publishers.

Jacoby, Russell. 1980. "Narcissism and the Crisis of Capitalism." *Telos* 44:58–65.

Jenkins, Richard. 1996. *Social Identity.* New York: Routledge.

Journal of Studies on Alcohol. Guidance for Authors on the Policy of the *Journal of Studies on Alcohol* Regarding the Appropriate Use of the Term "Binge." http://www.rci.rutgers.edu/ cas2/journal/Binge.html.

Kaczynski, Ted. "Industrial Society and Its Future." 1995. *Washington Post*, September 19, SS1.

Kafka, Franz. 1977. "The Hunger Artist." In *Twelve German Novellas*, ed. and trans. Harry Steinhauer, 573–81. Berkeley: University of California Press.

Keane, Philip. 1977. *Sexual Morality: A Catholic Perspective*. New York: Paulist Press.

Keller, Wendy. 1999. *The Cult of the Born-Again Virgin: How Single Women Can Reclaim Their Sexual Power*. Deerfield Beach, FL: Health Communications, Inc.

Kessler, Suzanne J., and Wendy McKenna. 1978. *Gender: An Ethnomethodological Approach*. Chicago: University of Chicago Press.

Kincaid, James R. 1998. *Erotic Innocence: The Culture of Child Molesting*. Durham, NC: Duke University Press.

Kishline, Audrey. 1994. *Moderate Drinking: The Moderation Management Guide for People Who Want to Reduce Their Drinking*. New York: Three Rivers Press.

Koffka, Kurt. 1935. *Principles of Gestalt Psychology*. New York: Harcourt and Brace.

Kosnik, Anthony, William Carroll, Agnes Cunningham, Ronald Modras, and James Schulte. 1977. *Human Sexuality: New Directions in American Catholic Thought*. New York: Paulist Press.

Kubler, George. 1962. *The Shape of Time: Remarks on the History of Things*. New Haven, CT: Yale University Press.

Kurz, Demie. 1997. "Violence against Women or Family Violence? Current Debates and Future Directions." In *Gender Violence: Interdisciplinary Perspectives*, ed. Laura L. O'Toole and Jessica R. Schiffman, 443–53. New York: New York University Press.

Lambek, Michael. 1992. "Taboo as Cultural Practice among Malagasy Speakers." *Man* 27:245–66.

Langellier, Kristin M. 2001. "'You're Marked': Breast Cancer, Tattoo, and the Narrative Performance of Identity." In *Narrative and Identity: Studies in Autobiography, Self, and Culture*, ed. Jens Brockmeier and Donal Carbaugh, 145–84. Philadelphia: John Benjamins Publishing Company.

Lasch, Christopher. 1979. *The Culture of Narcissism: American Life in an Age of Diminishing Expectations*. New York: W. W. Norton and Company, Inc.

Leach, Edmund. 1964. "Anthropological Aspects of Language: Animal Categories and Verbal Abuse." In *New Directions in the Study of Language*, ed. Eric H. Lenneberg, 23–63. Cambridge, MA: MIT Press.

Letherby, Gayle. 1994. "Mother or Not, Mother or What? Problems of Definition and Identity." *Women's Studies International Forum* 5:525–32.

Lyman, Stanford, and Marvin Scott. 1989. *A Sociology of the Absurd*, 2nd ed. Dix Hills, NY: General Hall, Inc.

Mackenzie, Midge. 1975. *Shoulder to Shoulder: A Documentary*. New York: Alfred A. Knopf.

Mackenzie, Midge, Verity Lambert, and Georgia Brown. 1988. *Shoulder to Shoulder* [videorecording]. Alexandria, VA: PBS Video.

Martel, Yann. 2001. *Life of Pi*. New York: Harcourt.

Martin, Emily. 1992. *The Woman in the Body: A Cultural Analysis of Reproduction*. Boston: Beacon Press.

Martin, Luther H. 1988. "Technologies of the Self and Self-Knowledge in the Syrian Thomas Tradition." In *Technologies of the Self: A Seminar with Michel Foucault*, ed. Luther H. Martin, Huck Gutman, and Patrick H. Hutton, 50–63. Amherst: University of Massachusetts Press.

Martin, Patricia Yancey, and Robert A. Hummer. 1989. "Fraternities and Rape on Campus." *Gender and Society* 3:457–73.

Marx, Patricia. 2002. "My So-Called Drinking Problem." *Glamour*, December.

Matza, David. 1969. *Becoming Deviant*. Englewood Cliffs, NJ: Prentice Hall.

May, Carl, and Andrew Cooper. 1995. "Personal Identity and Social Change: Some Theoretical Considerations." *Acta Sociologica* 38:75–85.

Mead, George Herbert. 1934. *Mind, Self, and Society*. Chicago: University of Chicago Press.

Mellor, Philip A. 1991. "Self and Suffering: Deconstruction and Reflexive Definition in Buddhism and Christianity." *Religious Studies* 27:49–63.

Melville, Herman. 1982. "Bartleby the Scrivener." In *Fiction 100: An Anthology of Short Stories*, 3rd ed., ed. James H. Pickering, 748–68. New York: Macmillan.

Merton, Robert. 1976. *Sociological Ambivalence and Other Essays*. New York: Free Press.

Merton, Thomas. 1999. *The Intimate Merton: His Life from His Journals*, ed. Patrick Hart and Jonathan Montaldo. San Francisco: Harper.

Millner, Denene. 1997. *The Sistahs' Rules: Secrets for Meeting, Getting, and Keeping a Good Black Man*. New York: Quill.

Moran, Jeffrey P. 2000. *Teaching Sex: The Shaping of Adolescence in the Twentieth Century*. Cambridge, MA: Harvard University Press.

Morell, Carolyn M. 1994. *Unwomanly Conduct: The Challenges of Intentional Childlessness*. New York: Routledge.

Mullaney, Jamie L. 1999. "Making It 'Count': Mental Weighing and Identity Attribution." *Symbolic Interaction* 22:269–83.

———. 2001. "Like a Virgin: Temptation, Resistance, and the Construction of Identities Based on 'Not Doings.'" *Qualitative Sociology* 24:3–24.

Newman, David M. 2000. *Sociology: Exploring the Architecture of Everyday Life*, 3rd ed. Thousand Oaks, CA: Pine Forge Press.

Paden, William E. 1988. "Theaters of Humility and Suspicion: Desert Saints and New England Puritans." In *Technologies of the Self: A Seminar with Michel Foucault*, ed. Luther H. Martin, Huck Gutman, and Patrick H. Hutton, 64–79. Amherst: University of Massachusetts Press.

Pankhurst, Christabel. 1999. "The Need for Chastity in Males." In *Sexuality*, ed. Robert A. Nye, 134–36. New York: Oxford University Press.

Pillemer, David P. 1998. *Momentous Events, Vivid Memories*. Cambridge, MA: Harvard University Press.

Playboy Interviews: Jimmy Carter. 1976. *Playboy*, November. http://www.playboy.com/worldofplayboy/interviews/.

Porphyry. 2000. *On Abstinence from Killing Animals*. Trans. Gillian Clark. Ithaca, New York: Cornell University Press.

Postman, Neil. 1994. *The Disappearance of Childhood*. New York: Vintage Books.

Powney, Janet, and Mike Watts. 1987. *Interviewing in Educational Research*. London: Routledge and Kegan Paul.

Prus, Robert. 1987. "Generic Social Processes: Maximizing Conceptual Development in Ethnographic Research." *Journal of Contemporary Ethnography* 16:250–93.

Purcell, Kristen. 1996. "In a League of Their Own: Mental Leveling and the Creation of Social Comparability in Sport." *Sociological Forum* 11:435–55.

Pyarelal (Nayyar). 1956a. "Gandhi Fasts in Prison." In *The Gandhi Reader: A Source Book of His Life and Writings*, ed. Homer A. Jack, 281–87. Bloomington: Indiana University Press.

————. 1956b. "The Fast is Broken." In *The Gandhi Reader: A Source Book of His Life and Writings*, ed. Homer A. Jack, 290 93. Bloomington: Indiana University Press.

Rajani, Nicole. 2002. "The Case for Comprehensive Sex Education." *AIDS Patient Care and STDs* 16 (7): 313–18.

Reinarman, Craig, and Harry G. Levine. 2000. "The Crack Attack: Politics and Media in the Crack Scare." In *Sociology: Exploring the Architecture of Everyday Life*, 3rd ed. readings, ed. David M. Newman, 51–68. Thousand Oaks, CA: Pine Forge Press.

Remez, Lisa. 2000. "Oral Sex among Adolescents: Is It Sex or Is It Abstinence?" *Family Planning Perspectives* 32:298–304.

Robinson, John A. 1992. "First Experience Memories: Contexts and Functions in Personal Histories." In *Theoretical Perspectives on Autobiographical Memory*, ed. Martin A. Conway, David C. Rubin, Hans Spinnler, and Willem A. Wagenaar, 223–39. Boston: Kluwer Academic Press.

Rosario, Vernon A. 1999. "Masturbation and Degeneracy." In *Sexuality*, ed. Robert A. Nye, 139–41. New York: Oxford University Press.

Sanders, Stephanie A., and June Machover Reinisch. 1999. "Would You Say You 'Had Sex' If . . . ?" *Journal of the American Medical Association* 281:275–77.

Sather, Linda, and Kelly Zinn. 2002. "Effects of Abstinence-Only Education on Adolescent Attitudes and Values concerning Premarital Sexual Intercourse." *Family and Community Health* 25 (2): 1–14.

Saussure, Ferdinand de. 1959. *Course in General Linguistics*. New York: Philosophical Library.

Savage, Dan. 2002. *Skipping towards Gomorrah: The Seven Deadly Sins and the Pursuit of Happiness in America*. New York: Dutton.

Scheff, Thomas J. 1975. "Labeling, Emotion, and Individual Change." In *Labeling Madness*, ed. Thomas J. Scheff, 75–89. Englewood Cliffs, NJ: Prentice Hall.

Schutz, Alfred. 1962–66. *Collected Papers*, ed. and intro. by Maurice Natanson. The Hague: M. Nijhoff.

Schutz, Alfred, and Thomas Luckmann. 1973. *The Structures of the Life-World*. Evanston, Ill.: Northwestern University Press.

Sennett, Richard. 1978. *The Fall of Public Man: On the Social Psychology of Capitalism*. New York: Vintage.

"Sex Education in America." 2004. National Public Radio, February 24. http://www.npr.org/templates/story/story.php?storyId=1622610.

Sherman, Allan. 1973. *The Rape of the A*P*E* (American Puritan Ethic): The Official History of the Sex Revolution, 1945–1973*. Chicago: Playboy.

Shiffman, Saul, Carolyn M. Dresler, Peter Hajek, Simon J. A. Gilburt, Darren A. Targett, and Kenneth R. Strahs. 2002. "Efficacy of a Nicotine Lozenge for Smoking Cessation." *Archives of Internal Medicine* 162 (11): 1267–76.

Shilling, Chris. 2003. *The Body and Social Theory*, 2nd ed. Thousand Oaks, CA: Sage.

Simmel, Georg. 1950. "Sociability: An Example of Pure, or Formal Sociology." In *The Sociology of Georg Simmel*, ed. and trans. Kurt H. Wolff, 40–57. New York: Free Press.

Simon, David, and Edward Burns. 1997. *The Corner: A Year in the Life of an Inner-City Neighborhood*. New York: Broadway Books.

Simoons, Frederick J. 1994. *Eat Not This Flesh: Food Avoidances from Prehistory to the Present*, 2nd ed. Madison: Wisconsin University Press.

Simpson, J. A. and E. S. C. Weiner, eds. 1989. *Oxford English Dictionary*, 2nd ed., vol. 1. New York: Oxford University Press.

Sokolow, Jayme A. 1983. *Eros and Modernization: Sylvester Graham, Health Reform, and the Origins of Victorian Sexuality in America.* Cranbury, NJ: Associated University Presses.

Stepaniak, Joanne. 1998. *The Vegan Sourcebook.* Los Angeles: Lowell House.

Strauss, Anselm, and Juliet Corbin. 1990. *Basics of Qualitative Research: Grounded Theory Procedures and Techniques.* Newbury Park, CA: Sage.

Svevo, Italo. 1930. *Confessions of Zeno,* trans. Beryl de Zoete. New York: New Directions.

Thackeray, William. 1983. *Vanity Fair.* New York: Oxford University Press.

Thody, Philip. 1997. *Don't Do It! A Dictionary of the Forbidden.* London: Athlone Press.

Thomas, Mark. 2003. "The Blaine That Nobody Noticed: Observations on Hunger Strikes." *New Statesman,* December 8.

Toups, Melanie L., and William R. Holmes. 2002. "Effectiveness of Abstinence-Based Sex Education Curricula: A Review." *Counseling and Values* 46 (3): 237–40.

Traas, Wendy. 2000. "'Born-Again' and 'Coming Out': Narrative Structures of Turning Points and Defining Moments." Unpublished manuscript, Department of Sociology, Rutgers University. New Brunswick, NJ.

Trimpey, Jack. 1992. *The Small Book: A Revolutionary Alternative for Overcoming Alcohol and Drug Dependence.* New York: Dell.

———. 1996. *Rational Recovery: The New Cure for Substance Addiction.* New York: Pocket Books.

Trubetzkoy, Nikolaj. 1975. *Letters and Notes,* ed. Roman Jakobson. The Hague: Mouton.

Trudgill, Eric. 1976. *Madonnas and Magdalens.* New York: Holmes and Meier.

Turner, Bryan S. 1982a. "The Government of the Body: Medical Regimens and the Rationalization of Diet." *British Journal of Sociology* 33 (2): 254–69.

———. 1982b. "The Discourse of Diet." *Theory, Culture, and Society* 1:23–32.

———. 1996. *The Body and Society: Explorations in Social Theory,* 2nd ed. Thousand Oaks, CA: Sage Publications.

Vance, Carol. 1989. "Social Construction Theory: Problems in the History of Sexuality." In *Which Homosexuality?* ed. Dennis Altman, 13–34. London: GMP Publishers.

Vandereycken, Walter, and Ron van Deth. 1990. *From Fasting Saints to Anorexic Girls: The History of Self-Starvation.* New York: New York University Press.

Van Gennep, Arnold. 1960. *The Rites of Passage.* Chicago: University of Chicago Press.

Vinitzky-Seroussi, Vered. 1998. *After Pomp and Circumstance: High School Reunion as an Autobiographical Occasion.* Chicago: University of Chicago Press.

Waters, Mary C. 1990. *Ethnic Options: Choosing Identities in America.* Berkeley: University of California Press.

Weber, Max. 1994. *The Protestant Ethic and the Spirit of Capitalism.* New York: Routledge.

Webster, Hutton. 1942. *Taboo: A Sociological Study.* Stanford, CA: Stanford University Press.

Welton, Donn. 2000. *The Other Husserl: The Horizons of Transcendental Phenomenology.* Bloomington: Indiana University Press.

Whorf, Benjamin L. 1956. "Science and Linguistics." In *Language, Thought, and Reality,* ed. John B. Carroll, 207–19. Cambridge, MA: MIT Press.

Williams, Donna Marie. 1999. *The Sexy Woman's Guide to Using Abstinence for Recharging Your Spirit, Discovering Your Passions, and Achieving Greater Intimacy in Your Next Relationship*. New York: Simon and Schuster.

Zerubavel, Eviatar. 1981. *Hidden Rhythms: Schedules and Calendars in Social Life*. Berkeley: University of California Press.

———. 1991. *The Fine Line: Making Distinctions in Everyday Life*. Chicago: University of Chicago Press.

———. 1997. *Social Mindscapes: An Invitation to Cognitive Sociology*. Cambridge, MA: Harvard University Press.

———. 1998. "Language and Memory: 'Pre-Columbian' America and the Social Logic of Periodization." *Social Research* 65:315–30.

———. 2003. *Time Maps: Collective Memory and the Social Shape of Time*. Chicago: University of Chicago Press.

Zussman, Robert. 2000. "Autobiographical Occasions: Introduction to the Special Issue." *Qualitative Sociology* 23:5–8.

INDEX

Abbott, Andrew, 87
abstainers: four categories of, 84–85; multiple, 112, 147, 151; nevers, 89–91; new, 80–81; quitters, 91–93; responses to not-doing, 164–66; time-outers, 93–94; waiters, 87–89
abstinence: as acting, not lacking, 72–75; approaches to studying, 11–13; as a "boo word," 8; breaks from, 138–43; "characteristic," as frame of, 149–51; "choice" of, 173–75; conjoint, 15, 98–99, 101; contingent, 15, 37, 98–99, 101; as a crusade, 51, 54–58; cyclical, 94–98; defined, 2; entertainment frame, 41–44, 61; entrances to, 112; external definitions of, 153–54; external reactions to, 159, 160–64; food, 28, 52–54 (*see also* fasting); "for your (our) own good" frame, 50–61; gains meaning from the expectation of doing, 20–21; gains meaning under specific historical conditions, 21–22; as a generic category, 2, 13, 183–84; as a high-control, low-cost identity option, 15, 173–74; "hot topics" of, 11, 28; "how-to" of, 12–13; and identity, 175–81; instrumental uses, 12; integrity, 42; and language, 20, 25–33; and location, 23–25; luxury component of, 60, 174–75; and morality, 9–11, 12, 50–61, 62, 196n15; move from voluntary to involuntary, 97–98; narratives, 85–87; "normal," 97; as not-doing, 6; pathways to, 82–101;

perceived duration of, 84–85; physical health frame, 69; as a point, 108–9; for profit and entertainment, 41–44; protest frame, 44–50; psychological focus on, 67–69; and purity, 75–80; recurrent, 94–98; religious frame, 37–41, 62; as a set point, 15, 131; as shift from involuntary not-doing to voluntary not-doing, 93; sociomental perceptions of, 19–20; symbolic functions, 12; vs. taboo, 203n6; temporal location, 20–23; thresholds, 107–8; "unacceptable," 165; verbal performances of, 16, 157–71; view of as a lack, 67; view of as a panic response, 67–68; work of, 74–75; as a zone, 15, 16, 110–12, 121, 124, 202n8
abstinence entrepreneurs, 10, 14
abstinence-only programs, 10–11, 179
abstinence strategies, shifting, 146–56
Adam Ant, 72
addiction: disease model of, 135; fences, 133; recovery programs, 12
adolescence, theorists of, 58, 199n16
advertising, 123
akatharsia (impurity or uncleanness), 39
alcohol abstinence, 12, 24, 58–61, 113
Alcoholics Anonymous, 12, 58, 115, 135, 178, 183, 197n25, 198n17
ambiguous performatives, 169–70, 171
American Idol (TV show), 202n1
"anonymous" groups, 58, 68, 92
anorexia nervosa, 118, 199n17, 204n1
(conc.)